MEDITATIONS ON FRANTZ FANON'S WRETCHED OF THE EARTH

New Afrikan Revolutionary Writings

by James Yaki Sayles

MEDITATIONS ON FRANTZ FANON'S WRETCHED OF THE EARTH

New Afrikan Revolutionary Writings

by James Yaki Sayles

Spear and Shield Publications &
Kersplebedeb Publishing and Distribution

Meditations on Frantz Fanon's Wretched of the Earth:
New Afrikan Revolutionary Writings
by James Yaki Sayles

ISBN 978-1-989701-01-0
Published in 2010 by Kersplebedeb and Spear and Shield Publications
Copyright © Spear and Shield Publications

For inquiries about reproduction rights or other questions about use of the writing in this book, please contact:

>Spear & Shield Publications
>1321 N. Milwaukee Ave #441
>Chicago, IL 60642
>USA

To order copies of the book, contact:

>Kersplebedeb
>CP 63560, CCCP Van Horne
>Montreal, Quebec
>Canada
>H3W 3H8
>www.kersplebedeb.com
>www.leftwingbooks.net

Our thanks to Kevin "Rashid" Johnson, Minister of Defense of the New Afrikan Black Panther Party–Prison Chapter, for the use of his artwork, which appears on pages 152, 172, 185, 211, 240, 289, 318 and 340, and in the montage on page 49.

Contents

Preface *by Hondo T.*	1
An Introduction to the Words of James Yaki Sayles	3
War for the Cities	43
Free the RNA-11: Prisoners of War	59
On Transforming the Colonial and "Criminal" Mentality	63
Scenes From *The Battle of Algiers*	87
Raids on Chicago Public Housing	95
From One Generation to the Next!	101
Martin Luther King Jr. On Extremism, Capitalism and Imperialism	106
Malcolm X: Model of Personal Transformation	111
Reflections on Victor Serge's "What Everyone Should Know About (State) Repression"	119
Stop! You Must Read This First	**137**
Meditations on Frantz Fanon's The Wretched of the Earth	141
Part One: By Way of Introduction	143
Part Two: Concerning "Violence" and *the Development of New People*	183
Part Three: On The De-construction of "Race"	241

Part Four: On the "Restoration of Nationhood,"
            the Constitution of Revolutionary
            (Nationalist) Consciousness,
            and the Socialist/Humanist Objective
	341

Preface

Was trying to make sense of the world as a baby nationalist when i met Yaki. He helped me digest Marx & Lenin, fed me Mao & Cabral, and shook me out of the doldrums of narrow, cultural nationalism. i grew up on the southside of chicago. My parents came from the hard-working west virginia hills, and raised me with a decent moral compass & an eye toward a college education. As i learned more of what it meant to be a Black man in America, my outrage at injustice & oppression grew. i remember the murder of fred hampton and the terror in my mother's eyes and voice when i expressed this outrage and a desire to become active in the struggle for liberation. i was too young to be a Panther, but i was inspired by their example. i loved to read, and always found non-fiction and political science compelling.

It was in this context that i met Yaki. His writing intrigued me, and i was drawn to his analysis. Naturally, i jumped at the chance to meet him. i travelled more than 100 miles to dixon, illinois (the hometown of ronald reagan!) to visit with him at a state prison. The visiting room was usually less than half full, but on some weekends or holidays, our visits would be cut short due to overcrowding. Mostly, We could sit for hours & talk about any and every thing.

The first time We sat down together, We had to feel each other out, having only corresponded up to that point. He was clean cut, with a neatly trimmed mustache. He kept his hair cut short, but not bald. He had an easy smile and a knowing demeanor, often seeming bemused when We discussed the movement or different comrads. He would ask probing questions about different aspects of the work, and when he wasn't satisfied with an answer, he was sure to ask more detailed questions. If he thought an answer was totally useless, he would simply say "why not"? i hated leaving him there, and he jokingly suggested that i take his place. He got a kick out of my stammer as i demurred.

Just like his writing, Yaki worked very hard on precision. It was very important for him to say exactly what he meant. You could see the mental process at work, and it was a joy to watch. He also worked very hard to encourage one to think for oneself. In fact, he felt that We should be working with people to help them learn *how to think* instead of telling them *what to think*. This difference in methodology was a great source of frustration for him as he watched others attempt to agitate, educate & organize.

This collection is important because Yaki put his prodigious intellect and drive to work in the study of the descendants of enslaved Afrikans (**New Afrikans**), and our current social, economic and political reality. Because he was a "bottom of the pile negro" (thank you, Malcolm), he wrote to and for the oppressed masses, who often have no representative amongst our so-called "leaders." He concentrated on developing theory for the voiceless in their struggle against neo-colonialism and settler-imperialism. Yaki helped me understand this contradiction: the united states of amerikkka is a prisonhouse of nations, where nations become like classes. Even in the age of Obama, though the analysis begs for some finetuning, there's more truth & clarity in his journals than can be found in the vast majority of stuff which passes for "radical" analysis of amerikkka today.

Re-Build!
Hondo T.

An Introduction to the Words of James Yaki Sayles

James Yaki Sayles was one of the most important revolutionaries here in the generation following Malcolm X and George Jackson. Who were worldwide icons, like Frantz Fanon, the revolutionary activist and writer of the great book, *The Wretched of the Earth*. But, unlike them, Yaki was an obscure figure, and is still

aka **Owusu Yaki Yakubu, Atiba Shanna, etc.**

largely unknown. Not by accident, but by his own design. We will explain.

In *Meditations on Frantz Fanon*, we meet a student of Fanon's guiding us into rediscovering his thought. Fanon was one of the most influential revolutionary theorists of the anti-colonial rebellion, writing for the oppressed. In sharp contrast, today almost all of the books and articles on his work are by the careerist professors that Fanon so wisely distrusted. Those whom Fanon called the "wily intellectuals." This book is not. Yaki was one of those rebels for whom Fanon wrote his *Wretched of the Earth* in the first place. One of those stateless youths who followed Fanon and other liberating voices into taking up the political violence that the white colonialist had tried to reserve for himself.

Like the revs that he most considered his teachers—Malcolm X and George Jackson—Yaki grew up poor and found his maturity in prison, the place that Malcolm called *"the Black man's university."* A child of Chicago's South Side streets, Yaki always just thought of himself as a blood, "just another nigger doing a bit" (to borrow the laconic words of one of the Pontiac state prison revolt defendants). And it was in the prison movement that he found his place in the battlefield. Although he made revolutionary theory his work, his life was rooted in a time of urban guerrillas and the armed struggle. Which makes his writing much more difficult to read, but with a warning of danger and commitment that is so often missing in these neo-colonized times between the storms.

In the Nation, prison has always been part of the larger community. New Afrikan imprisonment is perversely "normal" because of the highly *abnormal* relationship of *colonialism*. Yaki always liked to remind people that for hundreds of years, in the 1600s, 1700s and the first half of the 1800s, white settlers had almost no state prisons or federal prisons for New Afrikan people. They didn't need them, because We already lived and labored and died in the permanent prisons of the "beautiful" white plantations. As Yaki wrote about himself, using Malcolm's words: *"In the society to which I was exposed as a black youth here in America, for me to wind up in prison was really just about inevitable."*

The mood of revolt back then was touching everyone's lives in sudden unexpected changes. It felt like making your point with dice, only much bigger. Two examples out of so many of what we mean: Throughout the Sixties, Yaki's hometown was rocked by children's revolts, the great citywide school boycotts. Starting in 1963 and 1964, hundreds of thousands of students emptied the public schools demanding an end to institutional racism. Especially demanding the firing of the klanish school superintendent, Ben Willis. In October 1963, 225,000 students followed the leadership of New Afrikan high school students in the first walk-out. Spreading to New York City, some 400,000 children walked out of their schools. By 1968, the mass boycotts were being coordinated by a nationwide youth organization, the Afro-American Students Association, with high school branches (often using the name, "The New Breed") not only in Chicago and New York, but

Cleveland, St. Louis, Detroit, Los Angeles, and other cities. In Chicago, the A.S.A. headquarters were in the Uhuru Center on the South Side, where nationalist martial arts classes and revolutionary politics were taught. Citywide teenage strategy meetings were held in rooms hung with large posters not only of Malcolm X, but of Ho Chi Minh and Che Guevara (while hostile police crowded the street outside).

One by one, New Afrikan GIs and sailors and airmen were bringing the war back home from the other front: the distant invasions and military outposts of the worldwide U.S. empire. In Vietnam, the Black Revolution had brought the U.S. invasion to a standstill by the early 1970s. Drafted as cannon fodder for a war that was hardly ours, *"Using the nigger to kill the gook"* became a bitter GI saying about U.S. government policy back then. Black GIs and Marines were not ten percent or even a third, but often 70% or 80% of the line rifle companies that were actually pushed into the jungles to make bloody contact with the Vietnamese fighters.

Their nationalist disaffection swept the ranks, and reached the brink of mutiny. Units became disfunctional. Or, rather, protesting soldiers reorganized the military life around them into a different function. In camps, New Afrikan GIs set up separate areas, with their own tent cities where whites were not allowed. Some

refused to salute officers except with the Black Power raised fist salute. Soul music played very loudly at all hours, as GIs in their own non-regulation afros smoked up and talked politics. Soul music at top volume, in fact, became a recognized cultural dividing line, marking 'villes under our control. One night in Danang, for instance, two white army majors coming back from drinking at the officers club heard loud soul music coming from a Black barracks. They barged in and ordered the offending music turned off, and after the brothers refused the two majors yanked the plug out of the player themselves. In the ensuing disagreement, somehow the two clueless settler officers were M-16ed out of this life. (Private Alfred "Brother Slim" Flint was later convicted and sentenced to 30 years.)

Fragging obnoxious officers (the trusty old grenade tossed under the tent edge late at night, right under the sleeping officer's cot) became common enough that some white officers changed their tents every night in "musical beds." One U.S. army brigade in 'Nam experienced 45 fraggings and other assassination attempts on

white officers in eleven months. Black soldiers were nowhere close to being pacifists or being anything but tough in defending themselves in firefights, but other than that bare survival minimum they sabotaged the U.S. war effort at every turn; as many white GIs were doing, too. (Not that a Custeristic war planned by the country-club brass at the Pentagon needed much sabotage.) In 1971, GIs at Long Binh celebrated the Rev. Martin Luther King Jr.'s birthday with a large march around the base, headed by our nationalist black, green and red liberation flag, with the GIs chanting *"Free Angela Davis, Free Angela Davis"* (the famous Black Panther Party woman fugitive from Los Angeles). It wasn't because of civilian anti-war sentiment alone, that President Nixon's regime was forced to give up and pull U.S. ground forces out of Southeast Asia. Never again would the Pentagon make the mistake of having New Afrikan soldiers dominate the composition of U.S. combat units.

The Freedom movement of the 1960s grew in the prisons just as much as in colleges, churches, and housing projects. The prison poet Etheridge Knight described the kind of change coming down, with some young prisoners who had organized a sit-down strike over racism at their reformatory then being transferred to a higher-security Indiana State Prison:

> *The morning of August 5, 1968, began like all other mornings in prison: dismally. A thick fog, rising out of nearby Lake Michigan during the night, had crept over the walls and permeated the prison… And we had settled into our usual routine when the news of the arrival of "some young brothers from downstate"*

rumbled through the prison like an earthquake, shaking us out of our lethargy. Within minutes a crowd of onlookers lined the street leading to the admissions building.

Through the back gate in the south wall the young ones came. Chained and manacled like a coffle of slaves, they hobbled along in their leg irons. They wore their hair long, flaring out from their heads, and tikis and other charms hung around their necks. And as the line hobbled along, the young men would raise their manacled hands in the Black Power sign as they smiled or shouted to some recognized onlooker…

At noon the mess hall buzzed with conversations about the new arrivals. And despite the fears and anxieties expressed by some of the older black convicts in regard to the militant posture of the young blacks, there was a general air of pride among the black population—an almost imperceptible lifting of the shoulders. (in the months to come, the beneficial effect of the young blacks on the older ones was to be proved: knifings and fist-fights among "brothers" decreased; the boxing program, once a main sports interest, went out of existence; interest in things "black" increased to such a degree that a history book, such as Lerone Bennett's Before the Mayflower, *was worth ten cartons of cigarettes— prison currency; and even though the guards tried to break them up, gangs were formed to protect the more timid young blacks from some of the old convicts who wanted to make "girls" out of them.)*

Such political awakenings were taking place in most prisons, whether on a large or small scale. The 1970 Manifesto of striking prisoners at famous Folsom prison in California was typical in denouncing "THE FASCIST CONCENTRATION CAMPS OF MODERN AMERICA." In September 1971, the spreading prison struggle crashed right onto the nightly television news, when part of New York's maximum-security Attica state prison was violently taken over by a primarily Black uprising. Earlier there, back in that July of 1971, N.Y. state prison commissioner Russell

Oswald had received a detailed, signed petition from five prisoner representatives of the Attica Liberation Faction, demanding an end to "brutal, dehumanized" conditions. Commissioner Oswald, worried about the threat of revolt, corresponded with the prisoners but refused in the end to do anything. He vaguely promised future reforms in a taped loudspeaker broadcast to the entire prison.

Then, on August 21, 1971, George Jackson and two other New Afrikan prisoners were killed (along with three guards) in a puzzling gunfight *inside* California's maximum-security San Quentin prison. Prison authorities said that Jackson had attempted to escape, using a large 9mm automatic pistol somehow smuggled in by his lawyer (later acquitted of the charges). The government said that this gun was then carried back out of the visiting area through a physical search, on top of Jackson's head, hidden under a wig. This was a scenario thought ludicrously improbable by Black prisoners, to whom George Jackson was a hero. (If you try balancing a large military pistol on your head and then put an afro wig on top of that, you'll immediately see what they meant.) Kept inside California's prisons for life since he was fifteen years of age for unsuccessfully trying to rob a grocery store, Jackson's radical understanding of amerikkka had helped make his autobiography a best-selling book around the world. And exposed the bitter life struggles of the Black underclass in a way even Malcolm's earlier-generation autobiography hadn't.

Across the country there were demonstrations and meetings among prisoners. The next day, August 22nd, back in New York at Attica, 800 prisoners filed into the mess hall at breakfast and sat silently, each wearing some black article of clothing (if only a black shoelace tied around one arm) in a defiant memorial to their fallen comrade and brother.

When, on September 9, 1971, a spontaneous tussle at Attica between a prisoner hiding from punishment and a few guards chasing him touched off an exploding, running battle for control over first common rooms and then entire buildings, the prisoners emerged controlling part of Attica. They also held some fifty guards hostage (the prison then was 54% Black, 9% Puerto Rican, with all the guards being white settlers except for one Puerto Rican token). In their Five Demands addressed not to commissioner Oswald but "To the people of America," the Attica rebels stated: **"WE are MEN! We are not beasts and do not intend to be beaten or driven as such."** It was a declaration that made history.

On September 13th, after five days of a heavily-armed seige, the surrounding state troopers and guards started massed gunfire into the yard, and retook the prison at the order of N.Y. governor Nelson Rockefeller. But only after 32 prisoners and 11 guard hostages had been shot down and killed by the forces of "law & order." They fired thousands of rounds of rifle, handgun and shotgun fire into men defended for the most part only by public opinion. Many

Attica's aftermath: after the massed shooting and the retaking of the yard, the recaptured inmates were made to lie down in the mud and strip naked. They were then assembled in files with hands on heads in the yard, prior to being made to run the gauntlet one by one, and returned to their cells.

of the dead could have been saved, but were denied blood transfusions or any medical care at all for hours by the victors. Severely wounded just bled out lying there on the ground. One doctor who later was admitted to the yard remembers being told by a guard: "Why do it? They're not people, they're animals."

The prison movement, which except for those rare moments of spontaneous breakthrough was usually a very small minority of the most aware and self-disciplined prisoners, nevertheless took on great cultural and political significance in the 1960s–1970s: It brought into the light of day a standard in which human rights are not conditional; respect and humane living conditions and freedom from fear are basic rights even for the damned. It exposed the enduring illegality of being New Afrikan, and the contradiction between the neo-colonial surface "equality" of amerikkka and the real separate societies of oppressor and oppressed. While there have always been occasional prison "riots," what was different with the prison movement was its politically conscious dimension of being one stream in the greater river of the liberation struggle.

When Malcolm X said that "prison is the Black man's university," he meant it in a much larger way than simply studying books in a cell. Yaki as a person was forged and hammered and honed down by lifelong imprisonment, which was the unforgiving workshop in which he made his character and abilities. It was where as an adult he spent 33 years, almost his entire adult life. Just to give the reader some mental picture: Yaki was a man of average height, slim but not slender, wiry; the afro he had when young became short, close-cut hair with grey in it when he was older. For a long time you might see him in his favorite, worn light gray sweatshirt and a pair of plain cotton pants. Or a blue workshirt or other plain button-down shirt with long sleeves. Prison isn't Saks Fifth Avenue, and living his life without Western consumerism became normal and then a conscious political choice for him.

Even after finally getting out, Yaki never did concede that meals should be a treat or anything special. "It's just fuel to me," he'd always say, looking irritated. Like a number of other state prisoners who had some commissary, Yaki avoided the regular mess hall food. "The food in here will kill you," he'd say quite seriously. Instead, he picked at the over-cooked institutional vegetables but mostly relied on high-protein food like packaged tunafish and peanut butter bought from commissary and eaten in his cell. Self-discipline in every area of life became his style.

Back when Yaki had gotten out of juvenile prison and started a new life at age twenty-one, he joined an intense time of nationalist activity. He had been into poetry, and managed to become a salesman for a cultural nationalist publisher. He tried to learn from talking to more accomplished writers who were around then, such as the famous poet Gwendolyn Brooks. In his plans, Yaki had looked forward to making the rounds of churches, schools, and social clubs, talking about the new ideas of liberation and tipping people to the latest young author. To his surprise, instead he was ordered to concentrate on visits to white bookstores and getting them to place orders. Forget about selling to ordinary people. Yaki said that it was his first lesson about "Black capitalism."

On his own time, in 1969 Yaki started a small revolutionary

nationalist magazine, called *The Juggernaut*. In the first issue Yaki warned others who were taking the revolutionary path: "Our job is to bring about change. It is not to face reality but to change it. And this cannot be done by attending meetings once or twice a week, reading a few books or writing a few poems, praying, or waiting to see what someone else is going to do. We must work every day of the year, twenty-four hours a day. And every day must be a day of preparation and rehearsal. We must keep the goal always in mind." In a rough poem written in Malcolm's memory back then, young Yaki said that he remembered "my despair, my worthlessness" as a man-child lost inside Babylon's steel cages, but after being healed by Malcolm's words, "it's faded!"

During those brief three years outside in the burning 1960s, Yaki was being drawn into primitive rebellion. Like millions of other people around the world. Primitive rebellion is the most basic or preliminary stage of armed struggle. Euro-capitalism slants the word "primitive" to disrespect Others, misusing it to imply "backward" or "ignorant." In reality, "primitive" simply refers to the earliest stage of things, the starting. As in the prehistoric cave paintings of primitive art, which are nevertheless among the world's great art treasures. The 1950s Kenya Land and Freedom Army, which the West knows under the British label "Mau Mau," is one of the best examples of this primitive rebellion. Seeing that there were millions of Afrikans and only tens of thousands of British settlers in Kenya, those early freedom fighters thought that an each-one-kill-one strategy would easily

> **Malcolm X Says Mau Mau Needed**
>
> NEW YORK —(P)— Malcolm X, black nationalist leader, told about 400 followers in a Harlem ballroom last night:
> "We need lots of Mau Mau here. The Mau Mau were the greatest people in Africa, the greatest freedom fighters in Africa," he said.
> The Mau Mau was a secret terrorist society formed to drive Europeans out of Kenya.
> Malcolm X said there is a need for a Mau Mau in this country when one of his audience asked if he thought "there is anything" to the idea of a black Mau Mau in the United States. Malcolm did not elaborate.
> He said later that he will leave Thursday from Kennedy Airport on a three-week tour of African countries. He refused to disclose his itinerary.
> Malcolm X also told the Harlem audience he endorses the proposal of the Brooklyn chapter of the Congress of Racial Equality to halt traffic to the opening of the World's Fair April 22 by stalling cars on main highways to the exhibition.
> "I believe any strategy used by any group to bring the spotlight of the world on the problems of the 22 million black people here is right," he said.

work. If each Kikuyu warrior would only go out and kill at least one nearby white settler, then the whole colonial occupation would collapse from the losses, the shock and chaos. Unfortunately, revolutionary armed struggle against a militarized capitalism turned out to be much more complex and difficult than that.

Just jumping out and killing white people may seem like an understandable angry fantasy, but not something that you'd want to throw your life away doing, then or now. But for Yaki and those bloods stepping into that unknown, it signified something important—the awareness that an undeclared state of war existed. Whatever anyone personally wanted. Once, H. Rap Brown was stopped by a journalist as he was boarding an airliner, and asked what the Civil Rights struggle in the South had been like. "It was a war, man," he answered. "It was a war."

It wasn't just the world-echoing assassinations of Malcolm X and the Rev. Martin Luther King, Jr. Or the daily harassment and arrests of local leaders and organizers. Many New Afrikan people were "disappeared" by the Klan and police in the South—in one early 1960s case, a ten year-old boy was "disappeared" in Mississippi after daring to wear a voter registration t-shirt. It was also the gigantic urban uprisings from 1962 on, in which millions of people took over the streets and entire neighborhoods, threw rocks and bottles at police and firemen, sniped with rifles, smashed open stores and redistributed the goods, and torched buildings and entire blocks. In reply, the occupying police and National Guard everywhere made New Afrikan neighborhoods into free fire zones as though it were Vietnam. In Washington, D.C., National Urban League Assistant Director Horace Morris was about to drive off from a family visit, only to witness police drive up and just shoot down both his younger brother and his 73 year-old father standing at their door. In Detroit, at night during the curfew, a young man lit a match for his cigarette near his living room window. A settler National Guardsman standing at his jeep-mounted .50

caliber machine gun swung around and hosed the apartment with its deadly heavy fire, instantly killing a young girl and tearing off the arm of her aunt. "It was a war, man. It was a war."

The nonviolent Civil Rights movement of the 1960s didn't advertise it, but it was quietly armed to the teeth itself. It had to be. Driveby shootings and assassinations by Klan and police "nightriders" were a normal hazard of life then & there. In reaction, self-defense militias such as the Deacons for Defense, which spread from Baton Rouge, Louisiana, took up the battle for survival of New Afrikan communities with rifles and shotguns. A good example was the small, Mississippi River town of Cairo, Illinois, which was one of the hardest fought local battles. White Citizens Council "nightriders" with police assistance did drivebys shooting up Black homes and the housing projects every night, month after month, for years. Not only did a local defense militia have to be formed by Rev. Koen and other church leaders, but on the weekends a loose alliance of Chicago gang youth (started by communist teenagers in the Black Disciples gang) would arm up and drive downstate to take part in the fighting. A grim battle fought without any headlines, as remote from the suburban shopping mall and Wall Street as if it were in Chechnya. However covered over with political cosmetics, amerikkka was in a low-intensity war of assassinations and militias, of extra-legal police actions and vigilantes, of gangs and handfuls of guerrillas back then.

This was a time when killing whites was something openly talked about again, in a way that it hadn't been since the days of Nat Turner & the slave revolts. The respected writer Amiri Baraka was winning awards for his off-Broadway plays in which "innocent" whites were confronted and even killed. His poetry demanded:

> *We want poems*
> *Like fists beating niggers out of Jocks…*
> *We want "poems that kill."*

Which is one reason that George Jackson's x-ray vision of capitalism, his defiant guerrilla warfare politics, resonated with so many oppressed youth. Even in chains, publicly forseeing his own assassination in prison, he still hurled his defiance: *"I'm going to charge reparations in blood... war without terms."* Small groups and individuals had begun to do just that. It was just natural. And it wasn't just Mark Essex sniping so lethally from a rooftop in downtown New Orleans. Some in the group De Mau Mau, which liberal journalists later described as a loose network of forty to fifty New Afrikan 'Nam veterans, carried out random executions in 1972. White settlers in the suburban Chicago and Boston areas were targeted. The Cook County states attorney warned his public of a "nationwide conspiracy to kill whites," while the Chicago newspapers ran hysterical headlines like **"MURDER GANG**

De Mau Mau mystery
Kill whites... a conspiracy?

By FRANCIS WARD
Los Angeles Times News Service

CHICAGO — The name De Mau Mau has suddenly burst upon Chicagoans with much the same chilling impact that it had on white settlers in Kenya from 1952-60 when the original Mau Mau movement was waging war against British colonial rule.

Nine blacks identified by police as belonging to the organization have been charged with nine murders that date back to May, all but one of which occurred in the Chicago area.

Cook County Sheriff Richard J. Elrod, announcing the arrest of the initial suspects last week, said police believe there are about 150 De Mau Mau members in the Chicago area and "it is possible De Mau Mau is a nationwide organization" with a membership that could mount into the thousands.

Chicago newspapers have quoted police sources as saying De Mau Mau is a national conspiracy of 3,000 to 4,000 militant blacks (many of them Vietnam veterans) whose intent is to kill whites. About a tenth of them live in Chicago, according to these sources.

Black community sources, such as Dr. Charles G. Hurst, president of Malcolm X College in Chicago, vigorously denied these allegations, and painted a much different picture of De Mau Mau. Other sources, some returning veterans, say they now or once belonged to the organization, but asked not to be identified.

However, some basic conclusions emerge from these sources:

De Mau Mau originated among black servicemen in South Vietnam, probably in the late 1960s, as a sort of fraternity of fellowship that blacks thought they needed in face of rising hostility and alienation between black and white servicemen.

—It was never a formal structured organization with stated goals or hierarchy, but rather a name taken by blacks who found themselves in frequent social contact. The most frequent symbol was a black arm band made of plaited cord.

—De Mau Mau members seldom met in formal meetings, but most often would gather on the basketball court, in mess halls, bars, or even in the field. Discussions most often centered on race relations in the military and at home.

—There was never a stated purpose to kill or harm whites, although bitterness among black GIs was strong in Vietnam, and has been heightened among veterans by frustrations stemming from lack of job opportunities.

—At least four suspects in the Chicago area killings — Reuben Taylor, 22; Nathaniel Burse, 23; Michael Clark, 21, and Edward Moran, 23, all of Chicago — are veterans, although only Taylor served in Vietnam.

3,000 STRONG" and "DE MAU MAU TAKING OVER FROM PANTHERS." Separate from that, but in that same city and in the same year of 1972, Yaki and a friend were convicted of taking part in other killings. It was during a period when Illinois' death penalty had been knocked down by the higher courts, so the judge sentenced Yaki instead to 200 years in prison.

The prisons that Yaki re-entered back then mirrored the grassroots politics of the larger community, in that they were nationalist not integrationist. Remember that by the early 1960s the membership of the original Nation of Islam, led by the Honorable Elijah Muhammad and Malcolm X, was usually estimated at over 200,000. Making it by far the largest Black political organization. Inside the prisons, on the Left the largest progressive groupings were the nationalist religious sects, most notably the NOI itself and later, on the East Coast, the Nation of Gods and Earths (aka Five Percenters). There were independent political survival organizations like the Black Guerrilla Family in California, and small conscious collectives with members from old civil rights groups, the Black Panther Party, Black Liberation Army, Provisional Government of the Republic of New Afrika, etc. all scattered in various prisons. When Yaki re-entered the Illinois prisons he joined young but experienced fighters such as Lance Bell from the Black Panther Party and Don Taylor from De Mau Mau, both in the Pontiac Prisoners Organization, and Abdul from the B.P.P. in the Stateville Prisoners Organization.

(On the nationalistic Right politically within the prisons, were the large youth gangs with their "colonial & criminal mentality" and belief in lumpen capitalism. Typically, the gangs might conflict on a lower level with the guards and prison administration, but at the same time had extensive illicit business and political arrangements with the higher ups. This only made partially visible the complex political terrain usually hidden beneath the surface of the colony.)

To understand Yaki's politics, you first have to understand that revolutionary nationalism was at its intense core. In this, Yaki was a direct heir of Malcolm X. Revolutionary nationalism recognizes that We, having been developed historically as a colony, in reality comprise a separate nation of our own; a people who have the right of self-determination and who are sovereign unto ourselves. Although the u.s. empire likes to encourage the myth that its "America Inc." is somehow immortal and permanently fixed in shape, like all nations it has been deliberately changed many times. And will inevitably be changed again whether anyone likes it or not.

Within the continental euro-settler empire, We have always been an oppressed internal colony—as Yaki liked to say: *"The Black Nation exists, objectively and subjectively, but it is not yet independent."* A *Newsweek* magazine survey in 1969 found that 27% of Northern Black youth under 30 "would like a separate Black nation," while 50% supported the urban "riots," and 68% approved of "the idea of Black Power." The government's own U.S. National Advisory Commission on Civil Disorders did surveys which discovered that the typical "rioter" had: "great pride in his race... He is extremely hostile to whites... He is almost equally hostile toward middle-class Negroes. He is substantially better informed about politics than Negroes who were not involved in the riots."

Yaki always pointed out that there is no question of New Afrikan people escaping the acceptance of one nationalism or another. In fact, the ever-changing debate over what name people here should use, to Yaki only reflected the inescapable inner search for nationhood:

> *It's generally understood that "integration" is a rejection of "nationalism," but it's only the rejection of one nationalism, and the acceptance of another. When we refer to people as "integrationists" We're saying that they embrace the ideology of the "dominant society," (i.e., "white nationalism" or "American nationalism" or*

capitalism or imperialism), while rejecting the ideology of, say, "black nationalism" (i.e., anti-capitalism and socialism).

We tend to be unmindful of the fact that "nationalism" is about ideology and politics, not color. When We refer to people as "nationalists," We're saying that they have, or are shaping, an ideology and a particular set of social relations…

The context and process of our "name debates" on these shores had their effective point of origin at the on-set of the oppressive relationship—the moment that We were captured, sold, placed into pens and dungeons and aboard ships bound West. The context and process evolved as We set foot on these shores. All of this constituted an assault upon our freedom, our history and humanity, and upon our identity.

(Do you recall the scene in the movie Roots—We're inside the slave ship and the brother says: Talk to the Sister or Brother next to you. Learn their language; teach them your language. We must become one people!)

We didn't land on these shores with a collective identity as "slaves," "negroes," "blacks"—not even as "Africans." We arrived here as, say, Wolof, Ibo, or Fula. However, We had already begun to change, to develop an identity as a new people.

We initially called ourselves "Africans," but underneath it all We knew (then, better than most of us know now), that We were "New" Africans—a new people, forged through our collective oppression, by an emerging capitalism and a unique form of settler-colonialism…

We became "Africans," but soon, some among us wanted to be other than what we were—"negro," "colored," "American"—anything but "African" or New Afrikan. These some no longer wanted to identify with the majority of the people and our interests; they no longer wanted to maintain a united opposition to the oppressive social order… Instead, these some opted for *"inclusion" and "equality" as defined by the oppressor! These some were the embryonic "native elite" among us, and on these shores— the emerging pseudo-bourgeoisie and petty-bourgeoisie, whose successors were among those who, in the late 1980s, called for a new term by which to identify us, by way of renegotiating the terms of rule previously agreed to by them and their colonial masters…*

The 1830s, 40s and 50s weren't the first, nor the last periods during which We waged class struggle under cover of debates over what to call ourselves. Most people over 30 years of age will recall the debate in the 1960s over "negro" and "black," while people under 30 may best recall the debate in the late 1980s over "black" and "African-American."

Few of us, however, understand these debates as forms of class struggle among the people, which also mark changes in the development and structural form of our collective oppression.

Yaki and his comrads took up the name "New Afrikan" after a convention of nationalists on March 29, 1968, named their Nation in a Declaration of Independence. That convention of 500

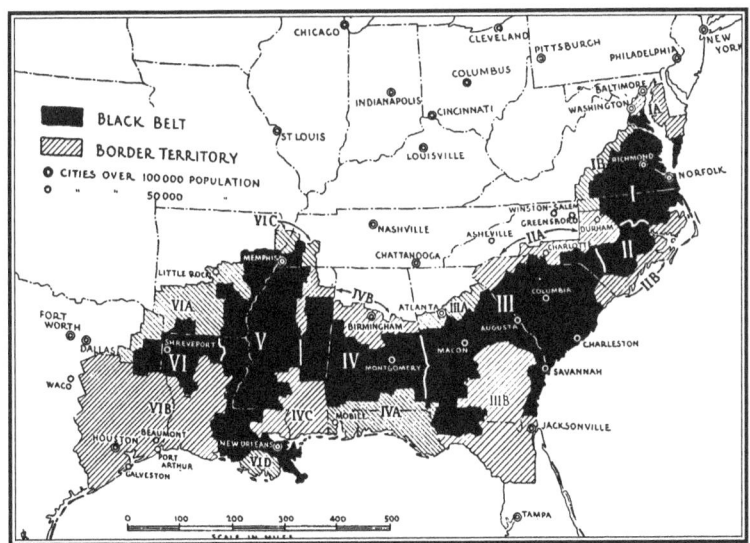

BLACK BELT AND BORDER TERRITORY

Black nationalists gathering in Detroit formed the Provisional Government of the Republic of New Afrika (PG-RNA). With the active support of tens of thousands in many different cities. A five-state national territory was imaginatively claimed out of the historic "Black Belt" of fifty New Afrikan-majority counties, that had stretched in a contiguous arc up from the Louisiana Delta all the way to the Atlantic Ocean for much of the past several centuries. This not only reflected the traditional roots in the rural South that We had created with our labor, but an always present sense of separate territory. It isn't an accident that—to use just one example—in the former Harold Ickes public housing project on Chicago's South Side, which had a number of large apartment buildings (together with its own illicit fried chicken shop and illegal DVD-music store and other informal apartment businesses), residents called their housing complex "the Land." In revolutionary nationalist understanding, our national territory is always called "the Land," and this phrase is a constant presence behind Yaki's teaching.

While this pioneering attempt at New Afrikan self-government didn't fully survive the violent police repressions and the neo-colonial offensives that followed (Yaki was later briefly Minister of Information for the PG-RNA), the subversive name "New Afrikan" is still heard. The great hip hop artist Tupac Shakur, himself the son of Black Panthers and PG-RNA militants, and the famous Los Angeles youth gang writer Sanyika Shakur (a rad of Yaki's and the author of the best-selling autobiography, *Monster*) are among those who have kept the name alive. It's a hardcore thing now.

The 1960s revolutionary nationalism was different from our globe's familiar old zombie capitalistic nationalism in two important respects: this revolutionary nationalism was fundamentally *internationalist*, and involved not the separating of some old society or narrow-minded ethnic group but liberation through the making of a "new people." Being part of making a new, non-exploitative world. Both ideas were central to Yaki's politics.

This internationalism was common to both his main teachers. It was Malcolm, after all, who used to declare dramatically to his brothers and sisters: "*The Black Revolution is sweeping Africa! The Black Revolution is sweeping Asia! The Black Revolution is sweeping Latin America!*" So to "X," "Black" didn't mean simply race or skin color in the shallow amerikkkan sense. To "X" it stood for the whole world of the oppressed. Even more, Yaki followed George Jackson in insisting that revolutionaries here have to develop themselves up to the level of other anti-colonial revolutionaries worldwide. That internationalism also means admitting that so many people here in Babylon are confused politically, and can learn much from thinkers and fighters in other countries and times.

George (when Yaki and his generation just said "George," you knew that they meant George Jackson) had a special place as a model to Yaki. Because George had spent part of his childhood and his entire adult life in amerikkka's gulag, and was largely self-taught as a revolutionary just as Yaki was. George, like "X," refused to let people hold pity parties for themselves. He ruthlessly criticized people on all levels for deceiving themselves so often and for not reaching up to the advances of world liberation struggles.

The clearest example of this was after the Illinois Black Panther Party's young leader Fred Hampton was assassinated by a Chicago Police death squad. Killed in a predawn attack on the Panthers' communal house & headquarters on December 4, 1969. (Hampton, who was shot in his bed, was killed on the spot, as was Mark Clark, while four other Panthers were seriously wounded in the surprise attack.) There was a storm of community anger about the police tactics, which hardly even bothered hiding the fact that the police death squad was not about doing "arrests" but planned assassination. But George without hesitation went against the liberal tide, and placed the spotlight squarely on the confusions of Black activists and revolutionaries:

> ...It should never be easy for them to destroy us. If you start with Malcolm X and count ALL of the brothers who have died or been captured since, you will find that not even one of them was really PREPARED for a fight. No imagination or fighting style was evident in any one of the incidents. But each of them died professing to know the nature of our enemies. It should never be easy for them. Edward V. Hanrahan, Illinois State Attorney General, sent fifteen pigs to raid the Panther headquarters and murder Hampton and Clark. Do you have any idea what would have happened to those fifteen pigs if they had run into as many Viet Cong as there were Panthers in that building? The VC are all little people with less general education than we have. The argument that they have been doing it longer has no validity at all, because they were doing it just as well when they started as they are now. It's very contradictory for a man to teach about the murder in corporate capitalism, to isolate and expose the murderers behind it, to instruct that these madmen are completely without stops, are licentious—totally depraved—and then not make adequate preparations to defend himself from the madman's attack.

It should go without saying that George personally fought pigs in the most difficult of environments. No excuses. Yaki filed that lesson away, too, and referred to it often. *"If you have George,"* Yaki would say thinking about Jackson's two books, *"that's all you'll ever need."*

Like Jackson and Malcolm X—for that matter, like the Rev. Martin Luther King Jr., Amiri Baraka, Kwame Toure, and many other New Afrikan leaders and activists—Yaki was an anti-capitalist and a socialist. He usually called his politics "scientific socialism" or communalism. He didn't call himself a "Marxist" since the whole idea of Europeans owning or having naming-rights to communalism as an idea was just messed-up to him. He took his global economics from people like the revolutionary intellectual Samir Amin. And his ideas about how to do revolution from comrades like Amilcar Cabral, the brilliant founder of the Guinea-Bisseau revolution in Afrika, Ho of Vietnam, and many others. Yaki tried to learn from the whole revolutionary world, and strongly taught that viewpoint to others.

It didn't take long after you met Yaki to realize that he was not just smart, but unusually smart. Freaky smart. Smarter even than his writings seem. This is hard to describe, but it was like walking at night and then coming under a streetlight. In that diffuse cone of light, all of a sudden you can clearly see yourself and others by you, even read a newspaper you couldn't a few steps before. Being around Yaki was like walking under that steetlight in the darkness. He had gone through terrible events, losses that can break you at an age when most young men are thinking about sharp clothing and romance. As a young Ho Chi Minh once wrote in a prison poem that Yaki liked: "Calamity has hardened my mind / And turned it into steel."

What you met was someone who was seriously disciplined. Something revs always talk about but so few of us really are. Disciplined not in any macho stiffness, but mentally, in personal development. He did have one strange habit: he seriously worked at never lying to his brothers and sisters. How impossible is that, if you really think about it? Which meant that political discussion with him had a different rhythm to it—many times a topic or a question would be met with only silence. When he thought that what he did believe was too offensive to you or too undigested to be useful. But what he did say was what he believed to be true, popular or not. He worked at being calm, which with his anger and razor sense of the costs of human weakness was sometimes hard. One afternoon, as we were talking about some well-known political prisoner who was loudly proclaiming to the world his total innocence, Yaki looked around the crowded visiting room and said with a straight face: "Oh, yeah, we're all innocent in here."

Yaki soon became a leading activist in the small prison collectives in his state. First in the Stateville Prisoners Organization, which quickly grew into the New Afrikan Prisoners Organization (N.A.P.O.). There were groups in Stateville, Pontiac, and Menard prisons, as well as individual members in other prisons outside Illinois and rads on the street. Yaki also became an influence in less public organizations.

One thing he never became was well-known. There were definite reasons for this. In part, because Yaki was a very private person who rarely talked about his inner life or childhood, and who never wanted to write about his own past to a curious public (in fact, he turned down a potential major book contract for just such an autobiography). Becoming a radical celbrity was not anywhere in his plans.

Yaki was also unknown because of the role he chose for himself. Much of his writings were not for the public, or even the community as a whole. Most of them were cadre teachings. Typically, Yaki wrote and spoke as a teacher for those already New Afrikan revolutionaries who were cadre. Those who had accepted the responsibility of being organizers and local teachers themselves. Although he was often repeating or underscoring basic political lessons, sometimes these were almost technical discussions. Craft discussions. In the same way that young Five-percenters proudly talk about, "i can do the math," "i know the numbers." And as such his words weren't meant to be entertaining, and rads often complained of finding them as hard to read as some textbook. Far from easy reading. But it's like, if you wanted to be able to design the flow of water through a hydoelectric plant or do brain surgery on an infant, at the very start you'd be cracking the books late into the night and studying for all you were worth. Yaki didn't think that trying to transform society was any easier.

If you were Yaki's chosen audience, that meant he expected that you were reading carefully, hour after hour, dictionary by your side, just as he had to. Taking notes, rereading often, thinking about what every sentence means. It is your work to do this. In this book, incidentally, are a variety of kinds of writing from Yaki, some more difficult and some easier to get into.

And as a revolutionary, Yaki felt no need to put himself out on front street. Remember that by this time, Huey Newton's Black Panther Party for Self-Defense had been crushed in blood, with over thirty Panthers killed, a thousand in the prisons from California to Maryland, and many other Panthers as fugitives and exiles. Even the poet Amiri Baraka's hopeful community cultural project in Harlem, his Black Arts school, had been drowned in blood. By police infiltrations and convenient anonymous murders. It was open hunting season on New Afrikan radicals, and Yaki was moved to write and work politically under many different names. Often doing things but not taking any public credit for it. Again, nothing new there. Ho Chi Minh of Vietnam, for example, worked so carefully at effacing himself that by the start of the Vietnam War, U.S. intelligence agencies and scholars weren't sure even what his "real" name had been (not "Ho Chi Minh").

It was through his revolutionary writings that Yaki has primarily been known. Professor Theresa Perry of Marquette University assembled her landmark book, *Teaching Malcolm X*, a collection of essays for educators teaching students about "X," in 1996. She asked Yaki to contribute his article on "The Meaning of Malcolm X for Imprisoned Africans in the U.S." for this university book. His essay has been often reprinted. Yaki also contributed the Introduction to a new edition of *Can't Jail the Spirit*, the widely circulated collection of biographies of leftist political prisoners in the U.S.A.

But it wasn't just his pen that was at work. Yaki also played an active role in a number of prison and community struggles,

although seldom leaving his name attached to them. In 1977–78, the New Afrikan Prisoners Organization helped the legal defense—and mobilized public support "on the bricks"—for the Stateville Four, after two guards had been attacked. The phonied-up murder and aggravated assault charges against the four prisoners just blew away in the wind after this sudden resistance. Injustice is so routine in the kamps that men really woke up when a serious State attack like that was beaten off. Of course, it being the pigs, Amin Akbaar, Wadud, Kenyatta, and Ha-Shim just became the targets of extra-legal vengeance by the prison administration. All four were given back-dated administrative tickets for possessing weapons (in essence, the same bogus, no-evidence charges that the State had to drop criminal prosecution on). They lost "good time" and were transfered for a time to isolation cells in other prisons. Still, it was a relative victory, for sure.

That was like the storm warning for a much larger, much more complex prison struggle soon to come: the 1978–81 Pontiac Prison revolt and its subsequent trials. Pontiac was the second-oldest prison in the Illinois system, having been constructed shortly after the end of the Civil War, with cell houses and buildings tacked on as needed throughout the years. It was both a maximum-security kamp and a medium-security one, holding some 2,000 men who were mostly from the Chicago area. On July 22, 1978, at around 9:45 AM, as some hundreds of prisoners were filing from the rec yard back to a cell house, a small band of prisoners suddenly attacked the few guards. Within minutes, a lieutenant and two other male guards were dead, two male guards were down but alive, with seriously stab wounds, and a woman guard was assaulted. Much of the cell house was seized by suddenly loosed prisoners. To retake that part of the prison that afternoon, the State police and guards fired canister after canister of CS gas into the building. Prisoners who were running around and prisoners who had been already locked in their cells alike were gassed. Fires were set, it was general chaos.

The State had the bodies of the three slain guards and an upset white community (the prison is a major institution locally, one of the two largest employers in Livingston County). But they had no idea of why it had happened or who had done it. What was typical, the government didn't even care, really. Just so long as they could "make an example" and assemble enough New Afrikan victims for a mass lynching. An impressive sacrifice to terrorize and to show that they were firmly in charge. Just like at the infamous Abu Ghraib and Guantanamo prisons, the U.S. empire didn't care who was innocent or guilty just so long as they had enough colonial subjects in chains to vent their fear and anger on.

In this case, the government claimed that a fictional grand conspiracy existed in which all the Black gangs in the prison had banded together to plan and carry out the attack together, although there was no evidence against anyone (desperate prosecutors finally spent many tens of thousands of dollars freeing and bribing a few prisoners who promised to testify the State's way, although most ended up not doing it). What followed was much more significant than the outbreak itself. Forty-eight prisoners were indicted (except for several Latinos, all were Black), of whom thirty-one ended up being tried. Some were tried downstate in various towns, primarily Bloomington, for "lesser charges" such as arson, mob action, aggravated assault, or burglary. But seventeen prisoners were charged with capital murder, and after defense motions they were divided into several trial groups and the first mass trial set in Chicago.

This was one of the larger mass death penalty cases in U.S. history since the old Slave Rebellions. And, as usual, the defendants were primarily poor New Afrikans. But other than that, nothing at all about this was usual. It wasn't anything like "Perry Mason" or "CSI" on television. Not even like anyone's idea of what criminal trials were like. Whoever spun that saying about, "We don't always get to choose our battles in life," hit this one right on the head. The Pontiac Rebellion murder trial was like an attempted mass lynching, but like one held in the middle of a three-ring circus.

Yaki played an important leadership role, in which he led activists to adopt innovative tactics and strategy. Sometimes people hearing about this assume the stereotypical, capitalistic concept of what that might mean: of someone like Yaki sitting in his cell, sending off little kites "do this" and "do that" to followers, like a Godfather scenario. Far from the reality.

First off, since the State was putting on trial key members from all the Black youth gangs inside Pontiac, there was no lack of decision-makers and leaders, good or bad. The dominant gang in Pontiac were the Gangster Disciples, whose brilliant leader, Larry Hoover, was a major target of the prosecution and among the first group of defendants up for trial. You should know that Hoover was to the development of U.S. youth gangs as Thomas Edison was to electricity, and every question involving this trial and his gang's future was being seriously thought out by them. Then you had an aggressive crowd of many attorneys, especially the radical lawyers from the

Peoples Law Office (who had successfully represented Fred Hampton's family and other Panthers in long, bitter legal battles against the U.S. government and Chicago police) and Chokwe Lumumba of the PG-RNA. For that matter, other veteran New Afrikan activists became seriously involved, too. Like Don T. of the Pontiac prison collective. (Lawyers visiting potential witnesses and remaining defendants imprisoned there would often call Don T. and other revolutionaries out to the visiting room, too, so that they could talk to the young prisoners about the political nature of this fight.) So there was not only leadership, but so much of it that at times there was almost a cacophony of many strong voices.

Nevertheless, Yaki's leadership was plain to insiders by the battle's end. What he had done was to shape a radical overall strategy, in ways both large and small. Yaki set the political line of identifying the battle as a continuation of White Amerikkka's war on the New Afrikan community as a whole. It was about genocide. It wasn't really about the death of those guards as individuals, it wasn't about gangs, and it certainly wasn't about "crime." These gang members were being set

up for death row in the same way that so many Black men had been arrested & convicted almost at random, whenever a white settler had been touched and the ruling class wanted to strike terror into colonized minds.

Meanwhile, the white public at large knew nothing about this. Aided by the instant white-out of television news and the daily newspapers, the prosecutors and politicians pounded home their white lie that the defendants had no chance of escaping conviction. Really, the biggest lie was that the police and prosecutors had any real idea of who had done it. They literally didn't have a clue (the prison wasn't even searched for weapons or other evidence until October 2nd, over two months later—it was less like "CSI" and more like "Three Stooges"). Since the government's plan was the tried and true All-American strategy of just whipping up more and more racism as their lethal weapon. The defendants were pictured in the State's propaganda as not only Black criminals, but Black *gang* criminals, and even worse, Black gang criminals who were *conspiring* together against white people. The lowest of the low, the worst of the worst. The government led the docile white public into the assumption that any Black youth gang members had to be guilty of anything and everything, so long as it was evil.

So the public got a big shock in 1981, when the jury came back in the first of the mass murder trials and found the defendants innocent on all charges. All the murder prosecutions had to be dropped. Politicians and police and media were stunned and outraged. All along, many prisoners had talked about how a tiny, not-too-bright crew had tried to vault over all the established gangs by pulling a stunningly stupid attack, which immediately got way out of hand. But why listen to New Afrikan men who were officially "the scum of the earth"?

In Yaki's strategy, educating and organizing against genocide in the community was the main thrust. Support from white liberals was good, but wouldn't be a priority. Almost immediately, outside

THE FUSE

No. 9   Aug. 1979 / 14-ADM

NEW AFRIKAN PRISONER ORGANIZATION

UPDATE ON THE PONTIAC 31

The 17 Pontiac Brothers charged with murder and facing the death penalty were transferred to the Cook County Jail in Chicago on Aug. 1, 1979, where their trials will be held.

All 31 Pontiac Brothers urged their attorneys and supporters to fight to have all the trials held in Chicago. But the colonial state has divided the Brothers in an attempt to weaken the effectiveness of their in-court battles and the strength of their families and supporters.

Fighting to have all the trials in Chicago was based on the reality that a *"fair trial"* is totally impossible anywhere in amerikkka for black people, but that in Chicago, with its large black population, the Brothers would have a better chance of obtaining a *"jury of their peers"*, the assistance of trusted counsel and of an organized black community. But, this is possible only if the appropriate trial strategy is employed, and if the black community can be rallied behind the slogan of *"Free The Pontiac Brothers--Put the Colonial State on Trial"*.

*   *   *   *   *   *

'Il. Gov. James Thompson' is, in reality, a Colonial Administrator......

*   *   *   *   *   *

Pre-trial motions for the 17 are scheduled to be filed in September, and the state is trying to rush it through before the support for the Brothers builds on a national and international scale.

continued

New Afrikan Prisoners Organization (N.A.P.O.) members and supporters began a coalition of concerned organizations. A very vocal demonstration of several hundred protesters drove down from Chicago and chanted loudly outside the Pontiac gates. Although far from the big city and media attention, N.A.P.O. understood that the major media would be whiting out their grassroots struggle anyway. But the Pontiac prisoners would be encouraged by the show of support, and word would spread through them and their families into the larger community.

In an innovative move, Yaki scrapped the usual way that defense committees were set up. Instead of a single committee or coalition, which usually ends up being dominated by white left groups with their own agendas and feuds, N.A.P.O. pushed to have two separate committees, coordinating but different: A New Afrikan committee built around the mothers and families and friends of the defendants, did low-key but important work educating people around them at the grassroots level: church presentations and meetings in the housing projects, pressuring lower-level Black politicians to take stands, even passing around literature on the special buses which take women down to the prisons for visits.

While the white support committee, built around a few fulltime organizers who had themselves been organized and politicized by Yaki himself, concentrated on both coalition activity with other progressive causes and working closely as the intelligence system for the legal defense. With their initial disadvantage of having no legal case (seldom just by itself a barrier to shipping New Afrikans to death row), the prosecution was further shot down in jury selection. Unable to bar all New Afrikan jury candidates as they wanted, the prosecutors never noticed that one woman juror lived right around the corner from where the Black Panther free health clinic had been. While another had gone to school in the town of Maywood with Fred Hampton's family. Just like in guerrilla warfare, we know the terrain but the enemy does not. While white potential jurors who would automatically vote for convicting New Afrikan men were identified (so that they could be eliminated as jurors) by N.A.P.O. supporters working as investigators in their neighborhoods. It was a full court press.

The separation was a controversial move, as it tossed aside the usual show of "interracial unity" for the substance of specific functions and grassroots political work. While N.A.P.O. worked with the most political of the attorneys to push the courtroom focus onto government misconduct and genocide. Putting the State on trial, not the defendants. The resulting victory—especially after some pivotal New Afrikan jurors joined the celebrating familes of the defendants in the court—was happy proof of an effective campaign. One of the largest mass lynching attempts in many years had been smashed down—and smashed down hard! The score in this battle? New Afrika 17, pigs 0. Yaki had proven that his way radical, guerrilla approach was perfectly practical for the oppressed.

By the late 1990s, though, the situation had changed substantially for Yaki. For the kamps everywhere in the U.S. were shifting, more filled with "knuckleheads" caught up in the macho drug selling and auto-homicide way of life. Young men who had been increasingly drugwashed and brainwashed by neo-colonialism. Obediently taught that their goal should be killing off themselves and people just like them as quickly as possible. Also, the Black Revolution that had lifted and carried him along from the 1960s on, had finally turned and was ebbing rapidly at generational change time. Many of his closest prison movement rads had gotten out and scattered or had died.

Even his ability to do his political teaching by pen was affected. When Yaki started out in prison, he had amassed a real library of political and history books, together with magazines and files of documents and correspondence. And he spent hours and hours studying and writing. This gradually became more and more choked off by prison authorities. As he put it: "Inside it only grows worse, not better. Because they keep changing wardens, and every warden has to prove that they've made some change or new shit they can point to. Which is only more restrictions."

By the start of the 21st century, he was limited to one thin cardboard case, only a few inches high, which had to hold any books, magazines, newspapers, notebooks, files, letters, blank paper, pencil and pens he had in his cell. And he had to work mandatory eight-hour shifts every day at the usual makework prison jobs (such as counting out and counting in the checkers pieces in the day room), which cut down on his intellectual hours. All this led him to decide to center himself on one major project which only required two books, a reappraisal and explanation of Frantz Fanon's great revolutionary writing, *Wretched of the Earth*.

Winning his release in 2004, after 33 years, was an incredible thing for Yaki and his comrads. Anytime afterwards that he was complaining about a bad day, he'd often be quick to add: "But it's a lot better than being in Dixon!" And he was adjusting to a world that had changed so much since he had gone inside. After walking through a Target one afternoon, he said: "It was disorienting to me. i've never been in a store this large!" (In his generation and place, it was commonplace for youth to have no experience with "American" things like department stores or sit-down restaurants other than fast food.)

Then, in the late Fall of 2007, he became ill, coughing a lot. Soon, it was discovered that Yaki had terminal lung cancer, and he passed across the river of life and death on March 28, 2008. Still young at almost 60. It was a blow from an unexpected direction, a loss that is too much to measure right now. At his memorial, rads came from all over the country to show their respect and talk about how much he had done for us all.

This came as, politically, Yaki was quietly trying to start things all over again. He had played an active role in the Free Zolo campaign committee, to get the Indiana nationalist prisoner and artist, Zolo Azania, off of death row (with a fierce legal defense, Zolo did indeed get his death penalty overturned, and won a real release date, as well.) Together with outside rads and supporters, Yaki had already helped found the Committee To Free C-Number Prisoners, which has grown into a regular and active presence in Chicago's New Afrikan community. Once outside, Yaki became the group's coordinator. C-Number prisoners in Illinois were sentenced for major crimes during a strange interim stage in the early 1970s, before the full transition to new sentencing laws were made (Yaki was a C-Number prisoner himself). The major characteristic is that they do not earn "good time" or "day for a day" to reduce their sentences; instead, C-Number prisoners must serve their full sentences unless they are granted release by the parole board. It has become something of a settler political patronage scheme. Former police and other law enforcement officials and ex-prosecutors who are politically connected get paid for being on the board. Coming

to occasional meetings, in which they grudgingly release a few prisoners every year just to keep their racket going. Yaki strongly believed in keeping the heat turned up under them!

As he was insisting with characteristic bluntness, right now *"there is no revolutionary movement at all."* He was frustrated and more than ready to build all over again. While, as he confessed, still learning this new world of the 21st century. Yaki was preparing to move to a new stage, to focus revolutionary thought on the more subtle but even more violent new type of neo-colonialism that had changed the rules of the game. That's why he thought it was so important to do a re-take of Frantz Fanon's *Wretched of the Earth*, which had first started to deal with this neo-colonialism much more clearly. Yaki was still dead-set on anti-capitalism, still a socialist and still a warrior for the Nation.

The main writing in this book is his Meditations on Frantz Fanon's book, *Wretched of the Earth*. Some comrades reading his early drafts of this were upset. They thought that Yaki would give them some easier read than *Wretched* itself. A simplified version. Maybe some summary, or some condensed version of the high points. Yaki could have done that. He didn't want to. Teaching himself wasn't easy. He worked hard for what he knew, and respected the understanding of that work as much as the goal itself. So what Yaki wrote was a guide to help us more seriously study Fanon. Put more effort into it. Dig even deeper into what Fanon was really saying. Which is the opposite of trying to breeze through it, hopefully hitting the exciting points, which is all too often our normal approach to study. So Yaki was telling us to become more serious people, to change ourselves so that we could change the world around us. That's the start of what he left us.

But first, we begin with a selection of some of Yaki's most important earlier writings. This is only a small sample, since his work in different publications probably totals many hundreds of pages. The first of these is an article, **War for the Cities**, serialized in three issues of the mimeographed prison magazine, *The Fuse*, between January and April 1978 (this magazine grew out of the newsletter, *Stateville Raps*, and was published by the New Afrikan Prisoner Organization in Chicago). "War for the Cities" was significant because it put on the table, in plain language, the u.s. empire's sweeping plan to empty out the great Black inner city communities. To end the threat of Black Revolution by breaking up, marginalizing and imprisoning our populations. What Yaki urged everyone to mobilize against when it was still early enough to block. This article was also important because it was where Yaki started to "make it plain" about the hidden reality of Black Genocide, a subject that he would never let go of as long as he had breath to speak.

Then there is a short but important article, **Free the RNA-11: Prisoners of War**, which first appeared in the January-February 1978 issue of *The Fuse*. It reports on a now little-known struggle in the Deep South, which turned critical in 1970–1971. When a campaign of violent police repression began in Jackson, Mississippi and Louisiana against the pioneering attempts of the Black nationalist Provisional Government of the Republic of New Afrika (PG-RNA) to organize a mass vote among Black citizens on democratically setting up a country of their own. Local and federal white officials made no secret of the fact that the main crime was holding Black liberation views, and that they were determined to remove every Black person there with such views by peaceful or violent means. (Ironically, a generation later in Jackson, Mississippi, Chowke Lumumba, a leader of the PG-RNA, has been elected to the City Council.)

Transforming the Colonial and "Criminal" Mentality is one of the most deeply probing works of theory/practice of the Sixties Black Revolution. Exploring the nature of our widespread youth rebellion through crime, Yaki uses several scenes from the famous film "Battle of Algiers" to show the relationship between young criminal rebellion and the deeper change of liberation. First written in 1977 and published by the Stateville Prisoners Organization in *Notes from a New Afrikan P.O.W. Journal, Book One*. It was revised and added to in 1981, and it is Yaki's latter version that is printed here.

This is followed by both **Scenes From THE BATTLE OF ALGIERS**, which pins the lessons of "Colonial and 'Criminal' Mentality" down by revisiting parts of the film's script, and **RAIDS ON CHICAGO PUBLIC HOUSING**. This is a leaflet that had been distributed in the Chicago Projects, together with Yaki's added commentary about the campaign of police raids and prison-like restrictions on Black residents. All these writings were reprinted in CROSSROAD newsletter, published by Spear & Shield Publications in April 1989.

Three articles close this first section of the book: **From One Generation To The Next!**, about the rich continuity of the New Afrikan culture of communality & struggle (published in 1980); **Malcolm X: Model of Personal Transformation**, about prisoners using Malcolm's lessons to change their own lives (published in CROSSROAD Spring 2001); and **Reflections on Victor Serge's "What Everyone Should Know About (State) Repression,"** a guide on thinking about security against police surveillance. This last article was published as a part of Spear & Shield's pamphlet, *So That We Don't Fool Ourselves—Again*.

Few had the opportunity to work with Yaki, but in these writings his revolutionary politics still burn and help light the difficult path ahead for all of us.

the editors

War for the Cities

PART ONE

Chicago's Afrikan (black), Puerto Rican and poor white communities are showing much concern over the plans now in progress to remove them from the inner city into outlying areas. Throughout amerikkka the populations of major cities are increasingly poor, and the majority of the poor are Afrikans.

These growing populations have the potential to acquire and use great power. Those who rule amerikkka know instinctively that the cities are politically, economically, and militarily too valuable to them to be allowed to fall under the control of the Afrikan and other oppressed nations.

We intend to devote more space in future issues of the FUSE to this and other essential areas of struggle taking place outside the walls. What we would like to do here is make several points about Afrikan inner city removal.

We think these points have clear connections to the reasons for there being such large numbers of young Afrikan men and women in illinois and other U.S. prisons. We also think that a better understanding of these and other points will help bring the struggles outside closer to the struggles inside.

We'll start with what should be some of the most evident, easily understood and accepted points. The first of these is that Afrikan inner city removal is a nationwide strategic objective of those who rule amerikkka. This objective is made necessary in large part by the deepening economic crisis, and the threat of political/social revolution.

The wealth and high standard of living the U.S. prides itself on is based on its history of trickery and robbery. The U.S. is wealthy because it takes the wealth of others, depriving most of the world from using their resources for their own development. When the people in Afrika, Asia, and South America begin to change this state of things, it is reflected in the U.S. by an "energy crisis" and in many other forms.

Also, when amerikkka has less to steal from other countries it has less booty to distribute inside its own borders, jobs grow scarce. So-called affirmative action in employment and school admissions is challenged. School lunch and daycare programs are cut-back or halted. Poor women are denied federal funds for abortions and larger numbers of Afrikan and other oppressed nation women are "intensively encouraged" to adopt birth control and become sterilized. Prison populations increase. And increasing attention is focused on the cities in ways too numerous to list and analyze here. The next point is that the plans now being carried out to achieve Afrikan inner city removal are not "new," and certainly not in Chicago. Neither are such plans the only ones being carried out or experimented with to contain and/or manipulate U.S. third world/oppressed nation populations.

The plans being effected now were first formulated 10–20 years ago. People are able to make long range, strategic plans when they have, or at least understand, power. Power is not acquired or maintained by being "issue oriented," unclear on who and where you are, or by mistaking enemies for friends.

The need to not mistake enemies for friends is especially great for us. Part of the reason for our being "issue oriented" is that we don't yet see the need to assume responsibility in the development of the strategies affecting our lives. Those who rule develop strategy.

Those who are mis-governed and oppressed merely respond to the oppressive issues and conditions as they arise, and as the suffering triggers our awareness.

We leave the strategy to others because we do not yet think of ourselves as able and worthy of self-government. We still think of the oppressor as the "rightful," only-capable-authority under which our lives can continue.

Until we begin to see those who rule amerikkka as ADVERSARIES, we will always be the objects of inner city removal—which is simply one of the forms of amerikkka's unique brand of fascist administration and genocide.

Point three is that the oppressed are not simply being pushed from the inner city to roam and settle wherever we may please. Just as it's being decided where we will move FROM, it's also being decided where we'll be allowed to re-locate.

In raising this point many things come to mind. The most immediate is simply the fact that there is no "free choice," no "equal opportunity" for the oppressed in amerikkka to participate in the "democratic process" of city planning.

What also comes to mind are visions of south african-type "bantustans"... of the Soweto-type "suburbs" which surround the white city that Afrikans are allowed to enter only to work and only if they have their pass books. Point four is that all of the above helps us to see more clearly exactly why our communities have been allowed to deteriorate, why there are increasing cases of arson, why the schools our children attend don't offer them the "quality education" which would allow them to acquire the skills and confidence required of peoples who have the need and desire to govern themselves.

Our communities are filled with abandoned buildings because it's part of the plan to remove the Afrikan and other oppressed peoples from the inner city. Our schools lack qualified teachers in sufficient number, are in poor physical condition, and lack books and other essential equipment because it's part of the plan to re-locate us and to keep us ignorant, unskilled, and dependent upon those who rule amerikkka.

Point five is that we are likely to see more "low income housing" going up in suburbs like Arlington Heights. Truly designed with the oppressed in mind.

This low income housing will likely include innovations which are now being tested in U.S. prisons and in areas such as Cabrini-Green. City, state and federal money has been spent liberally over the past several years on "pilot projects" such as that now operating in Cabrini-Green Housing Project.

The streets and buildings surrounding the housing area have been altered to fit police and military "emergency" needs. The design of the buildings are altered to give only one way of exit and entrance. So-called "convenience shops" for laundry, dry cleaning, food shopping and other essential services have been placed in the buildings so that movement outside of them is reduced. Offices are installed for the welfare agent and the security officers. All occupants are issued identity cards to be shown upon entering or leaving the building. The occupants of each apartment are listed in a central register. Electric cameras and other surveillance equipment is installed, allegedly to "provide resident security against crime and criminals."

But cameras operate 24 hours a day. They don't turn themselves on automatically by the scent or sound of a "criminal." The cameras watch EVERY BODY, all the time. Just like they do here in Stateville and other prisons in amerikkka.

Everything described above as part of the "pilot projects" being carried out in Afrikan and other oppressed communities in the U.S., were first pilot projects in the prisons—usually those with the largest number of Afrikan and other oppressed nation prisoners.

The sixth and last point deserves more space than we're able to give it. That is that, clear and important connections can be drawn between the plan to remove the oppressed from the inner city, and the presence of such a large number of non-white youth in illinois and other amerikkkan prisons. In essence, the prisons are filled with Afrikan youth because of the danger they did and do present to the rulers of the U.S. In the 60s and early 70s, Afrikan people's fight for self-determination was at a high point, and Afrikan youth were playing important roles in many areas of struggle. In the schools, at the job site, on picket lines and demonstrations, and on the street, Afrikan youth were daily becoming a greater threat to the oppressive power. One area where this threat was most clear was among Afrikan youth organizations, where their revolutionary and nationalist potential was evident through their actions in the community.

Afrikan youth were united, disciplined, concerned about Afrikan people, and committed to changing our condition. They provided leadership and had the respect and love of the people. They were in many cases providing some of the best examples and love of the people. They were in many cases providing some of the best examples of community/self-government. During this period it was expedient for Jesse Jackson to have his picture taken sitting at the feet of Jeff Fort, and for other Afrikan youth leaders to be invited to the white house.

Once the revolutionary and nationalist potential was clearly recognized by the enemy, drugs poured into the community. Afrikan youth organizations became the targets of the f.b.i.'s COINTELPRO program—a program designed to prevent Afrikan unity, to stifle revolutionary nationalist development, to crush the movement for self-determination among Afrikan people.

The enemy media began to create a climate of fear in the Afrikan community by distorting "crime" figures and occurances. They made all Afrikan youth, especially Afrikan youth organizations, appear as "criminals" and the enemies of Afrikan people and our progress.

And because the enemy made Afrikan youth appear as the

enemies of Afrikan advancement along the road to self-determination, Afrikan people felt relieved rather than alarmed when Brothers were given long sentences and placed in prison.

Those who rule Chicago and the rest of amerikkka were truly relieved after they separated Afrikan people in this way. They considered the imprisonment of Afrikan youth a sufficient means of bringing to an ebb the rising tide of Afrikan resistance—time enough at least for them to regroup, rethink, devise and employ other tactics and strategy, and to strengthen their flanks.

But as Afrikan youth entered amerikkka's prisons in larger numbers, the prisons became a front of battle. The development of awareness and commitment, the formulation of revolutionary and nationalist consciousness, and the fight for Afrikan self-determination did not end when the prison gates closed.

Afrikan men and women in prison know why we are here, and what we must do. We know that our ties to our people are unbreakable, and our determination cannot be shaken. The prisons are incubators. We study and struggle daily, and grow strong from the repression, concrete and steel. The walls can't contain our minds nor our bodies. We're bringing the prison and the community closer together.

Those who rule must tremble at the thought of the purpose of our imprisonment being nullified.

The commune. The central citywide revolutionary culture. But who will build the commune that will guide the people into a significant challenge to property rights? Carving out a commune in the central city will involve claiming certain rights as our own – out front. Rights that have not been respected to now. Property rights. It will involve building a political, social and economic infrastructure, capable of filling the vacuum that has been left by the establishment ruling class and pushing the occupying forces of the enemy culture from our midst.

The _revolutionary_ is outlawed ... Revolution is illegal. It's against the law. It's prohibited. It will not be allowed. It is clear that the revolutionary is a lawless man. The outlaw _and_ the lumpen will make the revolution. The people, the workers, will adopt it. This must be the new order of things, after the fact of the modern industrial fascist state.

You will find no class or category more aware, more embittered, desperate or dedicated to the ultimate remedy – revolution. The most dedicated, the best of our kind – you'll find then in the Folsoms, San Quentins and Soledads.

George Jackson

Build To Win!

PART TWO: A GENOCIDAL WAR

The war for the cities is part of a larger war; it is not an end in itself. The larger war involves Afrikans (Blacks), other oppressed nations (Native Nations ["Indians"], Chicanos, Mexicans, Puerto Ricans), and the masses of the amerikkkan imperialist state. All oppressed people inside U.S. borders are pitted against those who rule amerikkka in a war to determine the future of the cities.

The war for the cities is a small example—a reflection—of the larger war. One way to define this larger war in easily understood terms is to define it as genocidal.

WHAT IS GENOCIDE?

Most of us use the word "genocide" incorrectly, because we don't apply it broadly enough. We think of genocide only in realtion to Hitler, Jews, and gas ovens. When Afrikans in amerikkka think of genocide, all we see are millions of some <u>other</u> people being killed "all at once"—in some place besides amerikkka. In the past.

Some Afrikans may think of genocide in relation to Native Nation people, but even here, <u>we tend to associate the victims of genocide with someone other than ourselves.</u>

And even those Afrikans who think of genocide in relation to Afrikan people in amerikkka merely point to the period of chattel slavery. Or only to those areas where Afrikan lives are taken by the lynch mob, or by the police bullet. Or in the area of sterilization.

We must see that whenever we speak of our oppression and exploitation—in any form—we're speaking of the genocide being practiced against us. The very word "genocide," which was first used by Rafael Temhin, means the physical, political, social, cultural, biological, economic, religious, and moral oppression of a people.

Article II of the Convention on the Prevention and Punishment of the Crime of Genocide, adopted by the United Nations General Assembly on December 9, 1948, states in part that "genocide" means ANY of the following acts, committed with even the

INTENT to destroy—in whole or in part—a national, ethnical, racial or religious group, as such:

a. Killing members of the group;
b. Causing serious bodily or mental harm to members of the group;
c. Deliberately inflicting on the group conditions of life calculated to bring about its physical destruction in whole or in part;
d. Imposing measures intended to prevent births within the group.

New York's Day of Black Outrage, 1988

When looked at from this perspective, we see that genocide occurs when any member of the group is killed. When one of our Brothers or Sisters is shot by city police, or when one of our Sisters or Brothers is shot or beaten to death by a prison guard. Either case is an actual instance of genocide—against the entire group: An Afrikan killed on 47th St. or an Afrikan killed inside Stateville is an Afrikan Killed; it's genocide being committed against all Afrikan people. The Genocide is nothing but the oppression of the nation—in many forms thru which our national oppression was initiated and is maintained.

Any form of serious bodily or mental harm inflicted upon any one Afrikan is an instance of genocide against the nation. No matter where this takes place—in the cities or in the prisons—it's genocide against us all. Brothers and Sisters in prisons are forced into behavior modification programs and institutions, and are made to undergo behavior modifying surgery, and filled with behavior modifying drugs. At the same time, our Brothers and Sisters, our Children, are forced into similar programs and institutions outside the walls (in the cities), and are made to undergo surgery. Our children are filled with behavior modifying drugs in the enemy controlled schools.

This behavior modification, all forms of serious bodily or mental injury inflicted upon any single Afrikan individual, is a means of maintaining our collective political oppression. The physical brutality which maims us, the psychological injuries which numb us, push us towards forms of escaping reality, and which drive us in increasing numbers to suicide—all these are symptoms of our economic oppression, our social and cultural oppression. And it's <u>genocide</u>.

Our every condition of life is a manifestation of the genocide being practiced against us. The "mis-education" of our children, the bad housing and food, short life expectancy, unemployment, lack of adequate medical facilities in our communities, the instability of our families, high mortality rates for our mothers and infants—all these and more constitute <u>genocide</u>.

Whenever Afrikans in amenikkka talk of changing the conditions under which we now live, we're talking about ending genocide. If we talk about a "push for excellence" in education, we better understand that we're talking about bringing an end to the genocidal treatment of our children in the enemy-controlled schools.

The conditions of life experienced by our people in the cities are genocidal conditions. The conditions of life experienced in the war for the cities, as we are forced to re-locate our communities, are aimed at maintaining our political, economic, social and cultural oppression. So when we talk about freedom and national liberation, we're talking about ending genocide. When we talk about independence, truth, and justice, we're talking about ending genocide. And whenever we talk about ending genocide—in any of its forms—we're talking about self-determination for our people, about self-government, about Black state power.

Genocide: 1) can be committed with the <u>intent</u> to destroy a group—the intent need not be fully realized before the group can be legitimately recognized as the target of genocidal practices; 2) genocide can be practiced against a <u>group</u> if the intent is to destroy that group "in whole or in part." In other words, genocide can be committed against a single individual belonging to the group; 3) genocide can occur without the actual killing of members of the group. Genocide can exist where "serious bodily or mental harm" is inflicted on members of the group, and environmental conditions of life are such that the physical destruction of the group is threatened, and where any one or more forms of such oppression exist to prevent the group's progressive, self-determined development.

Genocide is a conscious, systematic policy practiced upon Afrikans (Blacks) by those who rule amerikkka, and it is carried out on all levels by both public and private political, economic, and socio-cultural institutions.

In one form or another, genocide has been practiced against us for more than 300 years. It began with the aggressive european invasion of Afrika; it progressed with the euro-amerikkkan slave trade, during which millions of Afrikans died during the "middle passage." All the deaths of Afrikans on slave ships, at the hands of village raiders and kidnappers, plantation owners, masked night riders, and city police, were acts of genocide.

The plantation alone didn't undermine our culture and destroy our families. Amerikkka destroyed our culture, ripped our families apart, and took away our freedom and independence as self-governing people.

Amerikkka is still the enemy, and today it uses its prisons as genocidal weapons. Amerikkkan prisons are instruments used to practice political, economic, and social <u>oppression</u> of Afrikan people. Prisons are used to practice genocide, to practice physical and mental destruction of the group, and as one of the instruments used to prevent the group's successful struggle for liberation.

Amerikkkan prisons <u>are</u> koncentration kamps. The entire U.S. "criminal justice system" is used as an arm of the government to repress and destroy the national liberation struggle.

PART THREE

The war for the cities of amerikkka should be looked upon as a "means to an end," and not as an "end" itself.

The cities are the "nerve centers" for the amerikkkan nation, and act in ways similar to the nerves and blood vessels of the human body. The cities pump life into the nation; many cities are combined to form nations/states.

In modern societies, the city is the center of trade, commerce, and industry. The life-blood of a nation passes thru the cities similar to the way blood passes thru the heart.

The modern city is the center of communication, culture—the brain and its nerves sending messages and impulses to the other parts of the body, making it possible for the body to move, breathe, feed itself, find shelter, and protect itself from harmful, negative elements.

Those who rule amerikkka are locked in battle with us, in a war for the cities. This war will decide amerikkka's fate—and our own. Amerikkka seeks to maintain control of the cities so that it can maintain its life. We seek control of the cities to use them in making a new life for ourselves. Amerikkka wants to remain a nation, and we want to build a nation. Amerikkka wants to suppress the new life, the creativity and independence which stirs within us. We intend to destroy the U.S. as a nation which oppresses and exploits others, because this is the only way we can survive the present, and grow beyond survival to develop new ways of life.

> *The question I've asked myself over the years runs this way: Who has done most of the dying? Most of the work? Most of the time in prison (on Max Row)? Who is the hindmost in every aspect of social, political and economic life? Who has the least short-term interest—or no interest at all—in the survival of the present state? In this condition, how could we believe in the possibility of a new generation of enlightened fascists who would dismantle the bases of their hierarchy?*

Just how many Amerikans are willing to accept the physical destruction of some parts of their fatherland so that the rest of the land and the world might survive in good health? How can the black industrial worker be induced to carry out a valid worker's revolutionary policy? What and who will guide him? The commune! The central city-wide revolutionary culture. But who will build the commune that will guide people into a significant challenge to property rights? Carving out a commune in the central city will involve claiming certain rights as our own—out front. Rights that have not been respected to now. Property rights. It will involve building a political, social and economic infrastructure, capable of filling the vacuum that has been left by the establishment ruling class and pushing the occupying forces of the enemy culture from our midst. The implementation of this new social, political and economic program will feed and comfort all the people on at least a subsistence level, and force the "owners" of the enemy bourgeois culture either to tie their whole fortunes to the communes and the people or to leave the land, the tools and the market behind. If he will not leave voluntarily, we will expel him—we will use the shotgun and anti-tank rocket launcher.
Comrade/Brother George Jackson, *Blood In My Eye*

We begin with the fact that there is a "vacuum" which has been created by the absence of "goods and services" in our communities. This "vacuum" serves to weaken our areas, and to weaken us as peoples/nations, to lessen our powers of resistance.

Those who rule amerikkka have deliberately gone about the business of making us dependent upon its "boards of education," its "kourts of Just-Us," its welfare agencies, city housing authorities, etc. Amerikkka has broken the sense of community that used to abound in our neighborhoods, and in this way makes people feel isolated from each other, and dependent upon the state to solve all problems and satisfy all needs, and to define all wants.

People on the block used to stick together. The neighborhood was a big, "extended family." The children were the responsibility of the community, and all members of the community were responsible to and for each other.

Young black brothers and sisters should ask older bloods what our 'hoods were like in the 30s, 40s, 50s and even early 60s. We need to check our history, and give special attention to the "Northern Migrations," when we started moving to the southern cities, the northern cities, in the years following "emancipation," the first two decades of this century, the 1920s, 1930s and 1940s. The more "urbanized" and "amerikkkanized" black people became, the more we abandoned each other, and the more shaky our family/social structure became. We came to depend less and less on each other, and to depend more and more on the oppressive state. Therefore, the first phase of our war for the cities must involve recreating a sense of community.

If black/non-white/poor people are to survive and have a future in amerikkka, we must become responsible to and for each other. We must have mutual respect, and we must come to depend on ourselves/each other, and break our dependence upon the enemy.

We must accept the fact that those who rule amerikkka are neither willing nor capable of satisfying our needs. It is not in their interest to have us employed, fed, clothed, properly housed, educated, and healthy.

Build To Win!!

first published in *The Fuse* #6 (Jan/Feb. 1978), #7 (March 1978) and #8 (April 1978).

THE BLACK MISSISSIPPIAN

JUSTICE 1916 ?   JUSTICE 1971 ?

Violence and injustice against Black people in Mississippi is a long established pattern. If We do not die at the hands of racist whites, We become victims of a white racist system of justice. Untold hundreds of our sisters and brothers have rotted in Mississippi's prisons. They were robbed of the opportunity to lead productive and useful lives.

How can We forget Medgar Evers, Emmett Till, Vernon Dahmer, Jo Etha Collier, Andrew Goodman, Michael Schwerner, James Chaney, Phillip Gibbs, James Earl Green and Ben Brown.

The governor of Mississippi, a few weeks ago approved sentence suspension for Charles Wilson one of the convicted murderers in the fire bomb death of Vernon Dahmer, so he can operate his business. Others convicted for same murder have had a number of sentence suspensions in the past year.

Yet, Gibbs and Green were murdered in the Jackson State College massacre and no criminal charges have been brought against their murderers.

The injustice of the Mississippi court system continues today in the prosecution of eleven citizens of the Republic of New Africa (RNA), four of whom were not even in the vicinity when Jackson police and the F.B.I. made their sneak, pre-dawn attack on the Government Center of the RNA on August 18, 1971.

Although they were defending themselves against a sneak attack by gunfire and tear gas, RNA citizens have been charged with murder, conspiracy and treason. Our Brother Hekima Ana has already been sentenced to life imprisonment in Parchman Penitentiary on weak, conflicting testimony from the police themselves.

Mississippi justice is oppressing the RNA -11 just as it oppresses <u>all Black People</u> regardless of their personal beliefs or philosophies.

On July 17, 1972, Offagga Quaduss goes on trial for murder at the Hinds County Courthouse. <u>Your support for our Black Brother is needed.</u>

Free the RNA-11: Prisoners of War

On March 31, 1968, 500 Black Nationalists from throughout the U.S. met in Detroit and issued a DECLARATION OF INDEPENDENCE FOR THE BLACK NATION. The subjugated Black Nation—the New Afrikan Nation—in north amerikkka dates back to the anti-black colonial laws of the 1660s. The first LAND under new Afrikan governments was in the Mississippi Valley and the South Carolina-Georgia Sea Islands during and just after the amerikkkan civil war.

Milton Henry, right, in 1969, as vice president of the Republic of New Afrika, with Mabel Williams, center, wife of the RNA's first president Robert Williams. On the left is Queen Mother Moore of Harlem.

The 1968 Detroit Convention (1) named the nation the Republic of New Afrika; (2) designated the Five States of the Deep South (Louisiana, Mississippi, Alabama, Georgia and South Carolina), as the subjugated "National Territory," and (3) created basic law and a formal, provisional government, with officials elected in Convention under a mandate to "Free The Land!"

As with all nations, RNA citizens are born into it: all blacks, descendants of slaves, born in north amerikkka are citizens of the Black Nation, the Republic of New Afrika. Blacks may choose to give up their New Afrikan citizenship, or they may choose to have dual RNA-U.S.A. citizenship. But New Afrikan citizenship is a right of birth. And the right of choice in this matter lies at the heart of the Independence straggle.

In 1970, Brother Imari Obadele—elected Second President in conventions—moved the center of the struggle to the Deep South, seeking to organize an open plebiscite—a popular vote—on the question of RNA vs. U.S.A. citizenship and on the right of the Black Nation, the RNA, to sovereignty over the Kush District, the 20,000 square miles of Black counties and parishes lying 350 miles along the Mississippi River from Memphis to New Orleans. Six weeks after the RNA Provisional Government held a successful reparations convention at Mt. Calvary Baptist Church in Jackson, Mississippi, the police and the f.b.i. attacked. Jackson's white mayor, Russell Davis, was quoted in the press as saying the attack occurred after white officials had "explored all legal means for driving the RNA out."

At 6:30 on the morning of August 18, 1971, a force of heavily armed Jackson policemen and f.b.i. agents surrounded the official residence of President Imari Obadele of the Provisional Government of the Republic of New Afrika. Inside were seven persons: 15-year old Karim, who lived there, and Offogga, and Njeri Quduss, pregnant, and Brother Chuma, 19, who also lived there, and three visitors: Vice President Hekima Ana of Milwaukee and his wife

Tamu Sana, recently returned from the University of Ghana, and Addis Ababa of Detroit. The Three had arrived less than 48 hours earlier. Tanu and Hekima were starting their vacation and on their way to Georgia. They occupied Brother Imari's bedroom, the windows of which, like the windows of Brother Offogga's and Njeri's bedroom, looked out onto the spacious backyard.

Brother Imari, a young woman, and two young men—somehow unknown to the usually vigilant f.b.i.—were spending the night at the new RNA office, some blocks away. Nevertheless a smaller force of police and f.b.i. agents also surrounded this building.

At the residence, following a pre-determined plan, the police and agents—supposedly seeking a fugitive who was not there—gave the sleeping occupants 90 seconds to come out and then opened fire into the back bedroom windows with lethal rockets carrying gas charges. In the general firing that followed, a police lieutenant was killed and a policeman and an f.b.i. agent were wounded.

At the new RNA office Brother Imari walked out of the office and challenged the policemen and agents as they moved in; all four here were arrested, as were the seven at the house, who suffered no injuries in the heavy firing and gassing at the house but were beaten and trussed afterwards. All eleven were originally charged with murder and lodged at Parchman Prison Farm. Nine were also indicted by the U.S. for conspiracy to assault federal officers and for having assaulted than.

In 1972, in three separate trials for murder, held in racially charged atmospheres, Vice President Hekima was sentenced to life; Offogga Quduss was sentenced to life; Karim Njabafudi was sentenced to life; and Addis Ababa received two ten-year terms.

The three people at the office with Imari were released by habeas corpus action after two months. Sister Njeri was released after three months because she was pregnant. Sister Tamu was released after ten months; Brother Chuma, after 14 months, and Imari after 20 months.

But the month after Imari's release on $25,000 federal bond, the U.S. federal government moved to take the nine whom they had indicted to trial. Seven were found guilty of everything charged, by a racist jury in Biloxi, Mississippi—the home of trial judge, Walter L. Nixon, who had moved the trial there (the site with the least Blacks in the Division) over the objections of defense attorneys. The one elderly Black man on the jury was obviously terrorized by the other jurors. The convictions were appealed and argued before a three-judge Fifth Circuit panel in New Orleans on October 16, 1974. On March 19, 1976, the Fifth Circuit freed Tamu but confirmed all the life sentences. The Mississippi Supreme Court has confirmed all the life sentences and the U.S. supreme court has already refused to review them. The U.S. supreme court has also refused to hear the appeals of the federal convictions.

The struggle of the RNA PRISONERS OF WAR is our struggle. They—like ourselves—are being moved on by the U.S. government in an attempt to keep the Nation subjugated.

first published in the January-February 1978 issue of *The Fuse*.

On Transforming the Colonial and "Criminal" Mentality

Revolutions are fought to get control of land, to remove the absentee landlord and gain control of the land and the institutions that flow from that land. The black man has been in a very low condition because he has had no control whatsoever over any land. He has been a beggar economically, a beggar politically, a beggar socially, a beggar even when it comes to trying to get some education. The past type of mentality that was developed in this colonial system among our people, today is being overcome. And as the young ones come up, they know what they want (land!). And as they listen to your beautiful preaching about democracy and all those other flowery words, they know what they're supposed to have (land!).

So you have a people today who not only know what they want, but also know what they are supposed to have. **And they themselves are creating another generation** *that is coming up that not only will know what it wants and know what it should have but also will be ready and willing to do whatever is necessary to see that what they should have materializes immediately.*

El Hajj Malik El Shabazz (Malcolm X),
"The Black Revolution," from *Malcolm X Speaks*

During a conversation with a Comrade, the movie *Battle of Algiers* was mentioned, within the context of using that film as a way of making a comment on the present and probable direction that many prisoners are taking and that many more will take, in the escalating class and national liberation struggles inside U.S. borders.

An apology is made in advance, should We make errors in our recollection of events taking place in the film, or the order of their appearance.

In the opening scene, or, in one of the early scenes, the setting is a prison, and the principal character was, We believe, portrayed as Ali Aponte.

Ali Aponte was an Algerian who had entered the prison as a "common criminal," or a "bandit"—and was then in the process of being politicized, and of politically educating himself. He was being approached by a revolutionary—a Prisoner of War—who had noticed Ali's strong sense of nationalism and his revolutionary *potential*; thus, his *potential* of becoming a Revolutionary Nationalist, rather than his remaining a bandit, a criminal, or a "lumpen" with nationalist *sentiments*, an *emotional commitment to nationalism*.

We know this already sounds familiar to many: "I've been in rebellion all my life. Just didn't know it." (Comrade-Brother George Jackson.) And, "For a young New Afrikan ('black') growing up in the ghetto, the first rebellion is always crime."

A clear distinction must be drawn between "rebellion" and "revolution," because unless this is done, We become confused in our thought and our actions. Arriving at clarity on this and other issues is a necessary aspect of transforming the criminal, and the colonial, mentality.

We can rebel against something, without necessarily "rebelling" or *making revolution* for something. A rebellion is generally an "attack" upon those who rule—but it is an "attack" which is spontaneous, short-lived, and without the purpose of replacing those who rule.

Rebellions bring into question the *methods* of those who rule, but stop short of actually calling into question their very right to rule, without calling into question the entire authority and the foundation upon which that authority or "legitimacy" rests.

We rebel as a means of exposing intolerable conditions and treatment, but We seek to have someone other than ourselves change these conditions, and to change the *treatment*, rather than to assume responsibility ourselves for our whole lives. A rebellion essentially wants to "end bad housing," have "full employment" and "end police brutality and change prison conditions," etc.—to *reform* the system, and leave the power to make these reforms in the hands of the massa.

A revolution, on the other hand, seeks not merely to reform the system, but to completely overthrow it, and to place the power for overthrowing it, and the power for running the new system that is established, in the hands of the revolutionary masses. Thus the slogan, "All Power To The People!"

It is hard to go beyond rebellion to revolution in this kountry because of the widespread belief that revolutions can be made as simply and instantly as one makes coffee. Therefore the tendency is to engage in acts of adventurism or confrontation which the rebels believe will bring down the system quickly. It is always much easier for the oppressed to undertake an adventuristic act on impulse than to undertake a protracted revolutionary struggle. A protracted revolutionary struggle requires that the oppressed masses acquire what they never start out with—confidence in their ability to win a revolution. Without that confidence, the tendency of many militants is toward martyrdom, in the hope that their death may at least become an inspiration to others…

Revolutionary thinking begins with a series of illuminations. It is not just plodding along according to a list of axioms. Nor is it leaping from peak to peak…

…A revolution… initiates a new plateau, a new threshold… but it is still situated on the continuous line between past and future. It is the result of both long preparation and a profoundly new, a profoundly original beginning. Without a long period of maturing, no profound change can take place. But every profound change is at the same time a sharp break with the past…

What is the relation between wants and thoughts? Between wants and needs? Between masses and revolutionists? Masses have wants which are not necessarily related to human needs. Revolutionists must have thoughts about human needs. They cannot just rely on the spontaneous outbursts of the masses over their wants. A revolutionist must absorb and internalize the lives, the passions, and the aspirations of great revolutionary leaders and not just

those of the masses. It is true that revolutionary leadership can only come from persons in close contact with the masses in movement and with a profound conviction of the impossibility of profound change in (a new) society without the accelerated struggle of the masses. But leaders cannot get their thoughts only from the movement of the masses.

A revolution begins with those who are revolutionary, exploring and enriching their notion of a "new man/woman" and projecting the notion of this "new man/woman" into which each of us can transform ourselves.

The first transformation begins with those who recognize and are ready to assume the responsibility for reflecting on our experiences and the experiences of other revolutionary men and women. Thus the first transformation can begin with our own re-thinking. That is why We believe it is so crucial that before We undertake to project the perspectives for (New Afrikan) revolution, We review what previous revolutions of our epoch have meant in the evolution of man/womankind. As We study these revolutions, the first thing We shall learn is that all the great revolutionists have projected a concept of revolution to the masses. They did not just depend on the masses or the movement of their day for their idea of what should be done. They evaluated the state of the world and their own society. They internalized the most advanced ideas about human development which had been arrived at on a world scale. They projected a vision of what a revolution would mean in their own society. They analyzed the different social forces within their country carefully to ascertain which forces could be mobilized to realize this vision. They carried on ideological struggle against those who were not ready to give leadership to the masses or who were trying to lead them in the wrong direction. Only then did they try to lead their own masses...

The failure to make a similar distinction between a *rebellion* and *revolution* is what prevents many bloods from recognizing, and then making, the transformation from Captive Colonials to Political Prisoners, and prevents those outside the walls from making the transformation from colonial subjects to conscious citizens and active cadres.

It prevents us from consciously and systematically "bringing up a new generation" who know the difference between New Afrikan reform and rebellion, and New Afrikan revolution. It prevents us from consciously and systematically creating New Afrikan *revolutionary* leadership, to lead a *revolutionary* movement, as opposed to new forms of "civil rights" struggles under bourgeois leadership, for bourgeois ends.

It prevents us from making a class analysis of the forces inside our own neo-colonized nation, so that We can carefully ascertain exactly which forces can be mobilized to realize the vision of a New Afrikan revolution.

More of Comrade-Brother George Jackson's words are familiar to us: "Prisons are not institutionalized on such a massive scale by the people. Most people realize that crime is simply the result of a grossly disproportionate distribution of wealth and privilege, a reflection of the present state of property relations…." And, "We must educate the people in the real causes of economic crimes. They must be made to realize that even crimes of passion are the psychosocial effects of an economic order that was decadent a hundred years ago. All crime can be traced to objective socio-economic conditions—socially productive or counter-productive activity. In all cases, it is determined by the economic system, the method of economic organization…"

Many prisoners, and many people outside the walls—many Political Prisoners and even some POW's—have, We believe, not taken the interpretation of the above words far enough. We feel this way because many Comrades have based many of their beliefs and positions on the "inherent" revolutionary capacity of "lumpen" on their understanding of the above-quoted statements. We tend to overlook the fact that Comrade George was making a broad analysis, describing objective factors and presenting a general ideological perspective. The grossly disproportionate distribution of wealth and privilege, and the "crime" that results from it, does not automatically make us revolutionaries.

The real causes of crime are not necessarily—not of themselves—the causes of commitments to revolutionary struggle. Objective economic conditions, the method of economic organization, are not of themselves factors which inspire and/or cement conscious activity in revolutionary nationalist People's War.

Comrade George described the *objective* set of conditions—the economic *basis* of "crime"—and he recognized that he had been *objectively* in "rebellion" all his life. But he also said "Just didn't know it." He wasn't aware of his acts as being forms of rebellion. He wasn't *conscious* of himself as a "victim of social injustice." And, he wasn't *consciously* directing his actions toward the destruction of the enemy.

> *I met Marx, Lenin, Trotsky, Engels, and Mao...* **and they redeemed me.** *For the first four years, I studied nothing but economics and military ideas. I met the black guerrillas, George "Big Jake" Lewis, and James Carr, W. C. Nolen, Bill Christmas, Tony Gibson and many others.* **We attempted to transform the black criminal mentality into a black revolutionary mentality.**

And Comrades asked, in the past, "What is the difference between these mentalities?" primarily because it was hard to see the difference, and it had been assumed that there was no difference between the "lumpen" and the "outlaw" or the revolutionary.

Some bloods simply want the "lumpen" to be the outlaw, the revolutionary, and some say that this is what "George said." George said that the revolutionary was a lawless man, because revolution is illegal in amerikkka. Thus, the revolutionary, the "outlaw" and "the lumpen" would make the revolution... Some bloods read revolutionary actuality into the potentiality alluded to by George in his analysis of the economic basis of crime. This is also related to the "learning by rote" of Marxism-Leninism, and to the overemphasis of the "economics of Marxism" and failure to grasp the significance of the "conscious element."

> *The materialist doctrine that men are the products of circumstances and education, that changed men are therefore the products of other circumstances and of a different education, forgets that circumstances are in fact changed by men and that the educator himself must be educated.* (Marx)

> *Marxist philosophy holds that the most important problem does not lie in understanding laws of the objective world and thus being able to explain it, but in applying the knowledge of these laws actively to change the world... Only social practice can be the criterion of truth.* (Mao)

In order for us to know Ali Aponte today as an Algerian *revolutionary*, he had to become politicized, consciously joining with the Algerian F.L.N., and point his guns at the enemies of the Algerian people.

The employment of the skills he acquired and sharpened as a "bandit" continued to "violate the law" of the colonial state—but the difference was fundamental.

Aponte's previous violations of the colonialist state's law were violations of an individual, for personal gain. But more important, they were seen even by him at that stage as true "violations of law" because the "law" and *the state* that it upheld were still recognized by Aponte as being legitimate. He *was* a "criminal" because he still saw himself as a "criminal" within the definition and the practice of colonialist oppression. This is an aspect of the "criminal" and the colonial mentality: continued recognition and acceptance of the legitimacy of colonial rule; to continue to feel that the colonial state has a right to rule over the colonized.

> For every system of state and law, and the capitalist system above all, exists in the last analysis because its survival, and the validity of its statutes, are simply accepted (by the colonized)... The **isolated** violation of those statutes does not represent any particular danger to the state **as long as such infringements figure in the general consciousness merely as isolated cases**. Dostoyevsky has noted in his Siberian reminiscences how every criminal feels himself to be guilty (without necessarily feeling any remorse). He understands with perfect clarity that he has broken laws that are no less valid for him than for everyone else. And these laws retain their validity even when personal motives or the force of circumstances have induced him to violate them.
>
> George Lukacs, "Legality and Illegality,"
> *History and Class Consciousness: Studies In Marxist Dialectics*

When We break this down more, We see that key phrases are those pointing to the *isolated* violations of the oppressive state's law—isolated violations because they do not represent a danger to the oppressive state. And they do not represent a danger to the oppressive state because they continue to "figure in the general consciousness merely as isolated cases." Now, "general consciousness" represents both the general consciousness of individuals, who have not yet come to recognize the oppressive state as illegitimate, and it represents the general consciousness of the masses of the oppressed. Because We continue to regard the massas as a legitimate, rightful authority, We continue to feel that the laws it imposes upon us are laws "that are no less valid for us than for anyone else." This is why We can feel guilty, without feeling remorse—the lack of remorse stemming from the "bad conditions" We know to exist, which becomes the reformist-oriented "rebellious tendency." As long as We continue to see the oppressive state as legitimate ruler, even the circumstances and personal motives which push us toward "crime" continue to be isolated cases, presenting no danger to the foundations of the oppressive state, and offering no benefits toward the struggle for independence and socialism.

This "criminal/colonial" mentality was similarly described by Comrade-Sister Assata Shakur: "I am sad when I see what happens to women who lose their strength. They see themselves as bad children who expect to be punished because they have not, in some way, conformed to the conduct required of 'good children' in the opinion of prison guards. Therefore, when they are 'punished' they feel absolution has been dealt and they are again in the 'good graces' of the guards. Approval has been given by the enemy, *but the enemy is no longer recognized as an enemy.* The enemy becomes the maternal figure patterning their lives. It's like a plantation in prison. You can see the need for a revolution. Clearly…"

Before Comrade George met Marx and the black guerrillas, *his* mentality was best characterized as "criminal." It was only after he was "redeemed" that he was able to see himself as a victim of social injustice; that he was able to know that his past "criminal" acts had been an embryonic form of rebellion, had constituted a *tendency* and *potential* for undermining the oppressive state's "authority," its prestige, the "legitimacy" of its law, and to overthrow it.

> *The prestige of power as the subjective effect of a past deed or reputation, real or fancied, then has a very definite life process. The prestige of the capitalist class inside the U.S. reached its maturity with the close of the 1860–1864 civil war. Since that time there have been no serious threats to their power; their excesses have taken on a certain legitimacy through long usage.*
>
> *Prestige bars any serious attack on power. Do people attack a thing they consider with awe, with a sense of its legitimacy?*

> *In the process of things, the prestige of power emerges roughly in that period when power does not have to exercise its underlying basis—violence. Having proved and established itself, it drifts, secure from any serious challenge. Its automatic defense-attack instincts remain alert; small threats are either ignored away, laughed away, or in the cases that may build into something dangerous, slapped away. To the masters of capital, the most dreadful omen of all is revolutionary scientific socialism. The gravedigger evokes fear response. Prestige wanes if the first attacks on its power base find it wanting. Prestige dies when it cannot prevent further attacks upon itself.*
> Comrade-Brother George Jackson

To kill the prestige of the oppressive state, is, first of all, to kill the image of its legitimacy in the minds of the people. To transform the criminal mentality, and the colonial mentality, into a revolutionary mentality, is to destroy within the minds of the people the sense of awe in which they hold the oppressive state.

For Comrade George to become first the Political Prisoner, and then a Prisoner of War, he had to move beyond the mere understanding of the objective economic law and its relationship to "crime"; he had to begin *applying* his knowledge of revolutionary activity aimed toward changing the world, toward changing these objective economic laws and eradicating their effect upon the people. We know George today as a revolutionary because he educated himself and then went on to change existing circumstances.

If We were to leave the objective analysis/understanding of the economic basis of "crime" and proceed no further, We end up legitimizing the dope pushers in our communities, the pimps and other backward, reactionary elements who engage in such activity because of the circumstances caused by the present economic order. We can't continue to say "the devil made me do it." If We don't move beyond an explanation of objective socio-economic conditions, and consequently don't move beyond the acceptance of "criminal" activity on the part of "lumpen" as somehow honorable and inherently revolutionary, simply because they reflect the present state of property relations, what We will end up doing is condoning those relations in practice if not in words. We will end up accepting the ideology behind those relations as well.

> *Revolution within a modern industrial capitalist society can only mean the overthrow of all existing property relations and the destruction of all institutions that* **directly** *or* **indirectly** *support the existing property relations. It must include the total suppression of all* **classes** *and* **individuals** *who endorse the present state of property relations or* **who stand to gain from it.** *Anything less than this is reform.*
>
> Comrade George

And this applies not only to those who rule, to the monopoly capitalist, the world-runners. It applies to "lumpen" as well:

> *Actually, for those who are not incorporated into the system, for whatever reasons, (capitalist) society provides its own alternative—organized crime. In the ghetto this alternative is legitimized by the fact that so many people are forced to engage in at least petty illegal activity in order to secure a living income. The pervasiveness of the lucrative numbers racket and dope peddling rings further enhances organized criminality in the eyes of ghetto youth. Social scientists have observed that the role of criminal is one model to which such youth can reasonably aspire. It provides a realistic "career objective," certainly more realistic than hoping to become a diplomat or a corporation executive. Consequently, many ghetto youths turn to illegal activity—car thievery, pimping, prostitution, housebreaking, gambling, dope pushing, etc.—as a way of earning an income. Those who don't turn to crime still come into contact with and are affected by the mystique of organized crime, a mystique which is widespread in the ghetto. This mystique asserts that it is possible to spit in the face of the major legal and*

moral imperatives of (amerikkkan capitalist) society and still be a financial success and achieve power and influence.

To the extent that the Panthers were successful in penetrating the hard core of the ghetto and recruiting black youth, it would seem that they would be forced to confront the social implications of organized crime and its meaning for black liberation. They were well equipped to do this, since many of their own activists and leaders—such as Cleaver—were ex-criminals. Cleaver did attempt to present such an analysis shortly before he disappeared from public view… but he did not take his analysis far enough and consequently his conclusions only served to confuse the matter further.

Numerous sociological studies have shown that in many respects organized crime is only the reverse side of amerikkkan business. It provides desirable—though proscribed—goods and services, which are not available to the public through "normal" business channels.

And, although there is much public ranting against crime, organized crime—and it must be organized to succeed as a business—enjoys a certain degree of immunity from prosecution due to the collusion of police and public officials. Moreover, organized crime constantly seeks—as would any good corporation—to expand and even legitimize its own power, **but it has no serious motive to revamp the present social structure because it is that structure, with all its inherent flaws and contradictions, which provides a climate in which organized crime can flourish.** *Hence, it comes as no surprise that in at least one major riot (in Baltimore) police recruited local criminals to help quell the rebellion. The criminals gladly collaborated with the cops because heavy looting during the riot had seriously depressed prices for stolen goods and otherwise disrupted the illegal business operations upon which the criminals depended for their livelihood.*

Cleaver in his analysis, however, misread the social function of organized crime. In speeches and articles, he voiced approval of such underworld notables as Al Capone and Machine Gun Kelly on the grounds that their criminal activities were instrumental in building the present power of ethnic groups such as the Italians and the Irish. He concluded that beneath the public facade there is a history of intense struggle for ethnic group power in the urban centers of amerikkka, and that organized criminal activity has played an important part in advancing the status of various groups. But Cleaver failed to note that organized crime has sought to advance itself **totally within the framework of the established society.** *It seeks more power for itself, and as a side effect it may bring more money into the hands of this or that ethnic group,* **but organized crime is far from being a revolutionary force.** *On the contrary,* **its social function is to provide an informally sanctioned outlet** *for impulses that officially are outlawed (like revolution). It thereby acts to* **uphold and preserve** *the present social order.*

Cleaver's analysis, to the extent that it reflected Panther thinking, revealed the organization's uncertainty about its objectives. This problem stemmed from an inadequate analysis of the manifold ways in which the amerikkkan social structure absorbs and neutralizes dissent...

Robert L. Allen, *Black Awakening in Capitalist America*

There is a scene/sequence in *Battle of Algiers* where Ali Aponte, the ex-criminal, the revolutionary nationalist and member of the F.L.N., confronts "lumpen"/criminal elements who are "surviving the best way they know how"—under the existing circumstances. Ali makes this confrontation in accordance with the F.L.N. view that a weak and disorganized, demoralized and diseased people cannot successfully attack and defeat the enemy.

The pimps, dope pushers and otherwise backward elements were asked, warned, encouraged to find other means of "survival"— means which would be more in tune with the needs and direction of the people, and the national liberation struggle. The backward elements refused, resisted the transformation of their mentalities, and thus placed themselves squarely in the path of the nation's progress. Ali Aponte responded to this refusal, to this blocking of progress and national salvation, with a short burst from his Thompson.

What We've said about the need for conscious awareness and conscious activity, in order for there to be a transformation of the "criminal" and colonial mentalities, into revolutionary mentality, also applies to the definition of Political Prisoners and Prisoners of War.

We think that Howard Moore's definition of Political Prisoners, as quoted by Comrade-Brother George Jackson in *Blood In My Eye*, is insufficient:

> *All black people, wherever they are, whatever their crimes, even crimes against other blacks, are political prisoners because the system has dealt with them differently than with whites. Whitey gets the benefit of every law, every loophole, and the benefit of being judged by his peers—other white people. Black people don't get the benefit of any such jury trial by peers. Such a trial is almost a cinch to result in the conviction of a black person, and it's a conscious political decision that blacks don't have those benefits...*

This definition is cool for helping to explain the colonial relationship that blacks have to amerikkka—as a people. But it fails to lay out the true, proper, and *necessary* criteria for Political Prisoners: *Practice* is that criteria. On the bottom line, Political Prisoners are revolutionaries; they are conscious and active servants of the people. Political Prisoners direct their energies toward the enemies of the people—they do not commit "crimes" against the people.

We say that Moore's definition—and any similar definition—is insufficient because it simply defines the situation of New Afrikan ("black") people vis-a-vis the oppressive state. The definition says that all New Afrikan people—the whole New Afrikan nation—have a particular political relationship to amerikkka which is clearly separate and distinct from the political relationship that white people share with their government and its institutions. But this definition is insufficient from the perspective of a theory put forth by the nation, with the aim of building consciousness and providing a guide in the successful execution of a struggle for national liberation. In developing and spreading such a theory, it becomes necessary to analyze "the different social forces within (the nation) carefully, to ascertain which forces can be mobilized to realize the vision of a New Society."

In *Book Two* of the *Journal*, the following position was put forth in regard to Captive Colonials, Political Prisoners, and Prisoners of War:

> *Moving to define Afrikan Political Prisoners and Prisoners of War must also be within the context of national liberation revolution. Remembering that We're in the process of freeing and* **Building** *a nation.*
>
> *The first and major problem We run into is the present tendency to view* **all** *Afrikan prisoners as Political Prisoners. There are reasons why many or most of us say that* **all** *Afrikans (in prison) are PP's or POW's. Some folks start from the fact of our kidnapping and enslavement more than three centuries ago, and the continuous struggle to break de chains. Some folks deal with the fact of "objective socio-economic conditions," and trace the "cause of all crime" to this source. By this means, to say that "political-economic" circumstances make all those who become a "victim" of them, automatic Political Prisoners and/or Prisoners of War. Still others point to the enemy "criminal justice system," which deals with Afrikans in ways different from whites.*

The point is that all these definitions simply point out the objective colonial relationship.

The objective existence of Afrikan peoples' enslavement over three centuries ago don't alone make for **national liberation***. The objective conditions of the socio-economics of our neo-colonial status don't alone make for* **building** *a nation. The objective reality of a "criminal justice system" which operates throughout the empire, and touches neo-colonial subjects as well as the oppressed inside the mother kountry, but treats the oppressor nation nationals differently from those of the oppressed nation, don't alone make for the independence and socialist development of New Afrika.*

What We got to see more clearly is that, while all colonial subjects are "the same," vis-a-vis the oppressor, one of the requirements for genuine and successful national liberation revolution is the making of an analysis of the oppressed nation's social structure. The conditions that **all** *Afrikans in amerikkka experience are essentially and objectively colonial. But this doesn't mean that all Afrikan people have the same revolutionary capacity or inclination.*

When We define **all** *Afrikan prisoners as Political Prisoners and/or POW's, We* **aren't** *really defining "Political Prisoners"—We're simply defining Afrikan prisoners* **as colonial subjects—captured** *colonial subjects.*

*Plain and simply: our objective status as colonial subjects gives the political content to our entire lives, our overall condition and experiences. Yeah, all Afrikans are POW's and PP's, whether inside or outside of prison—***if** *We simply deal from our status as a neo-colonized nation. But in dealing in this way, We* **only** *see ourselves as opposed to the oppressor, and the implications of this view are that We only perceive a re-form of the oppressor's system, so that We'll be treated "the same" and with "equality" with the oppressor and the masses in the oppressor nation. Such a view is not revolutionary, and runs counter to other ideo-theoretical and* *political lines rooted in a colonial perspective, and aim toward independence and state power—the building of a nation, based on class analysis of the colonized people.*

If We continue to see nothing but *"all* Afrikans are POWs and PP's," We'll end up struggling *against* imperialism, but not necessarily *for* national liberation. Saying that *all* Afrikans are "political prisoners" is, if the truth be told, an essentially idealist and bourgeois nationalist position. It would allow stool-pigeons and all kinds of backward and reactionary elements to claim the status of Political Prisoners and even of POW's, simply by pointing out that they are in amerikkka against their will, had their culture destroyed, etc. Such a position actually liquidates the politics behind the status of Political Prisoners and Prisoners of War, thus, in the same process, liquidating the politics behind the struggle for national liberation.

All New Afrikans in amerikkka are members of an oppressed nation, which in itself is "political," and lends automatic political meaning to the conditions suffered by us all, whether in prison or out. But the recognition of the political significance that our colonial status has, does not define revolutionary nationalist consciousness or practice.

Recognizing objective colonial status is the point of departure, but We won't begin the journey of nation building without an analysis of our own internal, neo-colonial, social structure. Just as We see the need for class analysis to take place outside the walls, the same analysis must take place for those inside the kamps.

Thus We say that in making our analysis of the nation, and in focusing particularly on those of us inside the kamps, We see three sectors: the Captured Colonials, the Political Prisoner, and the Prisoner of War.

The Captured Colonials are the mass, general prison populations which Afrikans comprise. The simple status of a 20th century slave gives political character and significance to us all. But it doesn't determine whether that political character and significance will be good or bad—for the nation and the struggle.

The New Afrikan nation in amerikkka was formed because of and during the battles with europeans in which We lost our independence.

During our enslavement the many nations and tribes from the Continent shared one history, developed essentially one consciousness, acquired objectively one destiny—all as a result of the suffering We all experienced as a dominated *New*... Afrikan nation.

> ...*But so far as the struggle is concerned, it must be realized that it is not the degree of suffering and hardship involved as such that matters: even extreme suffering in itself does not necessarily produce the* prise de conscience *required for the national liberation struggle.*
>
> Amilcar Cabral, Revolution in Guinea

While the "criminal" acts of all Afrikans are the results of our general economic, political and social relationships to the oppressive, imperialist state, there is no automatic, unquestionable revolutionary nationalist capacity and consciousness.

If We say that "crime" is a "reflection of the present state of property relations," then We must also say that for us, these relations are those between a dominated nation and its oppressor and exploiter. The method of economic organization which governs our lives is an *imperialist, a neo-colonialist* method. Altho this colonial system is structured so as to force many of us to take what We need in order to survive, and altho there are conscious political decisions made by the oppressor, once We find ourselves in the grips of his "criminal justice system," it must also be seen that a *conscious political decision* must also be made on the part of the colonial subject before his acts can have a *subjective, functional political meaning within the context of the national liberation struggle*.

Put another way: if the "criminal" acts of Afrikans are the results of a "grossly disproportionate distribution of wealth and privilege," which stems from our status as a dominated, neo-colonized nation, then the only way to prevent crime among us is to make a conscious decision to liberate the nation and establish among ourselves a more equitable distribution of wealth and privilege.

Thus, We see Captured Colonials.

For us, the Political Prisoner is one who has made and who acts on a conscious political decision to change the present state of property relations. Altho the Political Prisoner and the Prisoner of War levels of thought and practice sometimes overlap, We use the element of organized revolutionary violence to distinguish between them—organized revolutionary violence of a distinct military type.

Political Prisoners are those arrested, framed, and otherwise imprisoned because of relatively peaceful political activity against the oppressive conditions of the people. Political Prisoners are also those Captured Colonials inside the walls who have adopted a "revolutionary mentality" and become politically active. Activity on the part of PP's behind the walls results in denial of release, punitive transfers, harassment and brutality, long periods of isolation, close censorship of mail and visits, behavior modification attempts, and even assassination at the hands of prison administrators, who sometimes employ reactionary prisoners to do their jobs for them.

We regard as Prisoners of War those Afrikans who have been imprisoned as a result of their having taken up arms or otherwise engaged in acts of organized revolutionary violence in its military form, against the U.S. imperialist state. The act of expropriation, acts of sabotage, intelligence and counter-intelligence activities, and support activities when directly linked to acts of military organized violence and/or organized groups which are part of the "armed front." Also, those activities of an overt or covert nature which are linked to the actions of armed people's defense units—those New

Afrikans involved in such activities and imprisoned because of them, are considered as Prisoners of War.

We also regard as Prisoners of War those Captured Colonials and Political Prisoners who consciously commit acts of military organized revolutionary violence while behind the walls, as well as those who join or form organizations which are or will become part of the organized "armed front" and/or part of the armed people's defense units of the "mass front."

"Prestige bars any serious attack on power. Do people attack a thing they consider with awe, with a sense of its legitimacy?"

While destroying the legitimacy of the enemy, We must establish our own! The allegiance of the people must pass from the enemy state to the New Afrikan.

Ali Aponte's "military" activity was political activity—was inspired by, complemented, and was guided by the politics of the F.L.N., was guided by the new revolutionary nationalist theory and practice of the emerging Algerian People's State.

Ali could make no *serious* attack on the power of the colonialist state until its prestige had been destroyed. And this destruction of the colonialist state's prestige and its substitution by the prestige, the legitimacy, of the people's state—this does not take place all at once, but is a process; it builds in stages. Decreeing that dope pushers must find other means of survival is a part of the process. Enforcing the decree is part of the process. Satisfying the needs of the people, involving the people in the actual control of their own lives, moving with the people in seizing and using and further developing control of the productive forces and means of production is the process in its essence.

Ali Aponte's elimination of pimps and dope pushers was the fulfillment of a "state function." When Ali abandoned his "criminal mentality" and became a conscious revolutionary cadre, he became one of the most responsible members of the revolutionary people's state.

Ali Aponte, ex-bandit, aspiring revolutionary, was formally politicized in prison, made a general commitment to the people, a particular commitment to the F.L.N.—both of which had to first base themselves on a commitment to himself.

We come to a scene in the film where We see Ali after his release from prison, about to carry out an order, using his "skills" for the first time in the conscious commission of a revolutionary, rather than a "criminal"/personal, act.

In brief, Ali has been told to walk in a certain place, at a certain time, where he'll be met by a Sister carrying a piece inside a basket. He's to approach the Sister, take the piece, and approach a dog from behind and render a bit of criticism. Then he's to return the piece to the Sister's basket, and then space.

But, rather than follow these instructions, Ali takes the piece and jumps in front of the dog, waving the piece and running off at the mouth. When Ali's lungs are tired and his ego satisfied, he pulls the trigger only to learn that the piece is empty.

Ali had been tested—a test which revealed more than it was designed to.

There are many factors involved in the process of successful revolutionary struggle, a successful party or organization. Only two of these factors are discipline and security. Discipline and security are concerns of parties and organizations, but parties and organizations are composed of individuals. What happens to each individual in the party or organization happens to the entire body, and vice versa. When Ali went back and screamed on comrades for giving him an empty piece, it was pointed out to him that the issue was not the empty piece, but Ali's failure to follow orders. This failure to follow orders endangered Ali, the Sister, and in effect, endangered the entire organization.

Of course, in a general sense, any failure to follow instructions demonstrates a lack of one or a combination of several things. In this case, We think Ali demonstrated that his commitment to himself, the people, and the organization was, at that point in time, still primarily emotional. When he jumped in front of the dog, he did so because he wanted to be seen. For him, at that point, his commitments were based heavily on the fact that the colonialists wouldn't "see him as a man, as a human being," and he wanted to be heard, to be recognized—*by the oppressor!* As slaves, colonial subjects, We tend not to feel worthy unless the oppressor in some way acknowledges our existence. When Ali jumped in front of the dog, he demonstrated that emotionalism in commitments is one of the major hindrances in the development of the degree of sophistication We need for success. He demonstrated that, at that point, the struggle for him was not yet a struggle for power, a struggle for self-government, and for seizure of property.

Tests of the kind mentioned here, as well as other kinds, will continue to be necessary. An understanding of, and a practice of discipline and adequate security are things that more attention should have been devoted to before Ali was released from prison. More attention should have been devoted to ridding Ali of his emotional commitments and related lingerings of a colonial mentality.

We see this in Algeria, but most of us see it better in places like Guinea-Bissau, Angola, and Zimbabwe: Cadre are sent to training schools. PAIGC cadre spent years in their school in Conakry before they returned and began their work with the people. In other countries where national liberation struggles were and are taking place, the leading bodies in these struggles had schools established inside and outside the country where ideological and military training took place. ZANU cadre were so trained in Tanzania; our cadres are being and will be trained in places like Stateville, Trenton, San Quentin, Attica and Angola, La.; our cadres are in what We must consciously recognize as training schools in Bedford Hills, Jackson, Terre Haute, Dwight, Atlanta and Alderson and all other prisons and jails in amerikkka.

As Comrade-Brother Sundiata Acoli has reminded us: "The jails (and prisons) are the Universities of the Revolutionaries and the finishing schools of the Black Liberation Army. Come, Brothers and Sisters, and meet Assata Shakur. She is holding seminars in 'Getting Down,' 'Taming the Paper Tiger,' and 'The Selected Works of Zayd Malik Shakur.' So Brothers and Sisters, do not fear jail (and prison). Many of you will go anyway—ignorance will be your crime. Others will come—awareness their only crime." (Sundiata Acoli, "From the Bowels of the Beast: A Message," from *Break De Chains*)

The prisons and our communities must establish "cadre training centers." There must be planned, systematic programs to meet us when We arrive behind the walls. "Seminars" are part of a well thought out, concretized curriculum. Organized.

"The 'Prison Movement,' the August 7th Movement, and all similar efforts educate the people in the *illegitimacy* of the establishment power and *hint* at the ultimate goal of revolutionary consciousness at every level of struggle. The goal is always the same: the creation of an infrastructure capable of fielding a people's army." From one generation to the next,

Build To Win The War!
For Independence and Socialism!
All Power To The People!

first published in
Notes from a New Afrikan P.O.W. Journal, Book 7, 1981.

Scenes From
THE BATTLE OF ALGIERS

SCENE 17

Terrace. Kader's House. Outside. Night.

It is a starry night and there are few lights visible in the windows of the Casbah. In the background, there is the triumphant neon of the European city, the sea, the ships at anchor, the shining beams of a lighthouse. Kader turns around gracefully, and goes to sit on the wall of the terrace.

KADER: You could have been a spy. We had to put you to the test.

Ali looks at him sullenly.

ALI: With an unloaded pistol?

KADER: I'll explain.

Kader is a few years older than Ali, but not so tall. He is slender with a slight yet sturdy bone structure. The shape of his face is triangular, aristocratic, his lips thin, his eyes burning with hatred, but at the same time, cunning. He continues to speak in a calm tone which has an ironic touch to it.

KADER: Let's suppose you were a spy. In prison, when the F.L.N. contacts you, you pretend to support the revolution, and then the French help you to escape…

ALI: Sure. By shooting at me.

KADER: Even that could be a trick. You escape, then show up at the address which the brothers in prison gave to you, and so you are able to contact me…

ALI: I don't even know your name yet…

KADER: My name is Kader, Ali… Saari Kader… In other words, in order to join the organization, you had to undergo a test. I could have told you to murder the barman, but he's an Algerian… and the police would let you kill him, even though he is one of theirs. By obeying such an order, you still could have been a double agent. And that's why I told you to kill the French policeman: because the French wouldn't have let you do it. If you were with the police you wouldn't have done it.

Ali has followed Kader's logic a bit laboriously, and he is fascinated by it. But not everything is clear yet.

ALI: But I haven't shot him.

KADER (smiling): You weren't able to. But what's important is that you tried.

ALI: What's important for me is that you let me risk my life for nothing.

KADER: C'mon… you're exaggerating. The orders were to shoot him in the back.

ALI: I don't do that kind of thing.

KADER: Then don't complain.

ALI: You still haven't told me why you didn't let me kill him.

KADER: Because we aren't ready yet for the French. Before attacking, We must have safe places from which to depart and find refuge. Of course, there is the Casbah. But even the Casbah isn't safe yet. There are too many drunks, pushers, whores, addicts, spies… people who talk too much… people who are ready to sell themselves, undecided people. We must either convince them or eliminate them. We must think of ourselves first. We must clean out the Casbah first. Only then will we be able to deal with the French. Do you understand, Ali?

Ali doesn't answer.

Kader has come down from the wall and looks toward the Casbah.

Ali too looks toward the Casbah, immersed in the night.

ALI: And how many are We?

KADER: Not enough.

SCENE 18
Areas Of Casbah Underworld.
Outside/Inside. Day.
March 1956.

A warm spring wind, large white clouds. At the western edge of the Casbah, from the Upper to Lower Casbah, the street of the Algerian underworld descends to the brothel quarter.

SPEAKER: "National Liberation Front, bulletin number 24. Brothers of the Casbah! The colonial administration is responsible not only for our people's great misery, but also for the degrading vices of many of our brothers who have forgotten their own dignity…"

Shady bars of gamblers and opium smokers, shops filled with tourist trinkets, merchants, fences, pimps, children with adult faces, ghastly old women, and young girls, whores standing in the doorways of their houses. The girls having their faces uncovered have put scarves on their heads, knotted at the nape.

SPEAKER: "Corruption and brutality have always been the most dangerous weapons of colonialism. The National Liberation Front calls all the people to struggle for their own physical and moral redemption—indispensable conditions for the reconquest of independence. Therefore beginning today, the clandestine authority of the F.L.N. prohibits the following activities: gambling; the sale and usage of all types of drugs; the sale and usage of alcoholic beverages; prostitution and its solicitation. "Transgressors will be punished. Habitual transgressors will be punished by death."

SCENE 24

Brothel. Inside. Day.

Ali has entered a brothel. It is morning and there are few clients. The whores are Algerian and European. Some of them are pretty.

The madam is an Algerian, dressed in European clothes. She is about forty, heavily made up. When she spots Ali, she interrupts her usual professional chant. She seems curious, yet glad.

MADAM (shouting): Ali la Pointe!

She stops herself, already sorry for having spoken so quickly and imprudently. Ali doesn't answer her, but approaches with a steady and serious glance.

MADAM (changing tone): Haven't seen you around for some time. I thought you were still in prison.

Ali leans against the counter, never once taking his eyes off her.

ALI: Is Hacene le Bonois here?

MADAM: No. He left early this morning. You know how it is with the boss…

ALI: I want to see him. If he shows up, tell him that I'm around.

Ali moves away from the counter and turns. He leaves without a word. The woman tries to understand what has happened, and follows him with a worried glance.

SCENE 25

Small Street. Hacene. Outside.
Day.

HACENE: Ali, my son… Where have you been hiding?

Ali turns suddenly, then pulls back so that his back is against the wall of the alley.

ALI (in sharp voice): Don't move!

Then he glances at the others.

ALI: Hands still.

The others are three young Algerians, Hacene's bodyguards. Hacene le Bonois is tall with short legs out of proportion with his enormous chest. He is somewhat corpulent. He has a wide face, a cheerful and self-confident expression. His clothing is a strange combination of Algerian and European which does not, however, appear ridiculous, but imposing. At Ali's remark, his expression changes, becomes amazed and baffled. But at the same time, his eyes give away the brain's attempt to find an explanation and a solution.

HACENE (astonished): You know I never carry weapons…

Ali keeps his arms and hands hidden under his djellabah.

ALI: I know.

Hacene laughs warmly, and stretches out his hands which are enormous, thick and rough.

HACENE: You afraid of these…?

ALI: Don't move, Hacene.

HACENE: Why are you afraid? We've always been friends. One might even say that I brought you up… Isn't it true, Ali?

ALI: It's true.

HACENE: What's happened to you?

ALI: The F.L.N. has condemned you to death.

Hacene is stunned. He speaks aloud his thoughts in a soft voice.

HACENE: Ah, so it's come to this…

Then he bursts into loud laughter, and seems to turn to the three guards at his back.

HACENE: I'm dying of laughter! Ha… ha… ha…

Ali doesn't speak. He continues to stare at Hacene. Hacene suddenly stops laughing. His tone of voice changes, becomes brusque and hurried.

HACENE: How much are they paying you?

ALI: They're not paying me anything. They've already warned you twice; this is the last warning. Decide.

HACENE: What... What must I decide?

ALI: You've got to change occupations, Hacene. Right away!

Hacene makes a gesture as if to emphasize what he is going to say.

HACENE (with irony): Okay, you convince me.

Then suddenly, unexpectedly, he lets out a ... shrill scream, like fencers who before plunging their swords, try to frighten their adversaries.

Simultaneously, he hurls himself forward, head lowered and arms outstretched. Ali steps aside and releases a blast of machine-gun fire. Hacene falls flat on his face. There is movement. Some passersby approach. The three boys try to escape.

ALI (shouting): Stop!

The barrel of the machine gun is visible through the opening in his djellabah. Ali's voice is quivering angrily:

ALI: Look at him well! Now nobody can do whatever he wants in the Casbah. Not even Hacene... least of all you three pieces of shit! Go away now... go away and spread the word... Go on!!

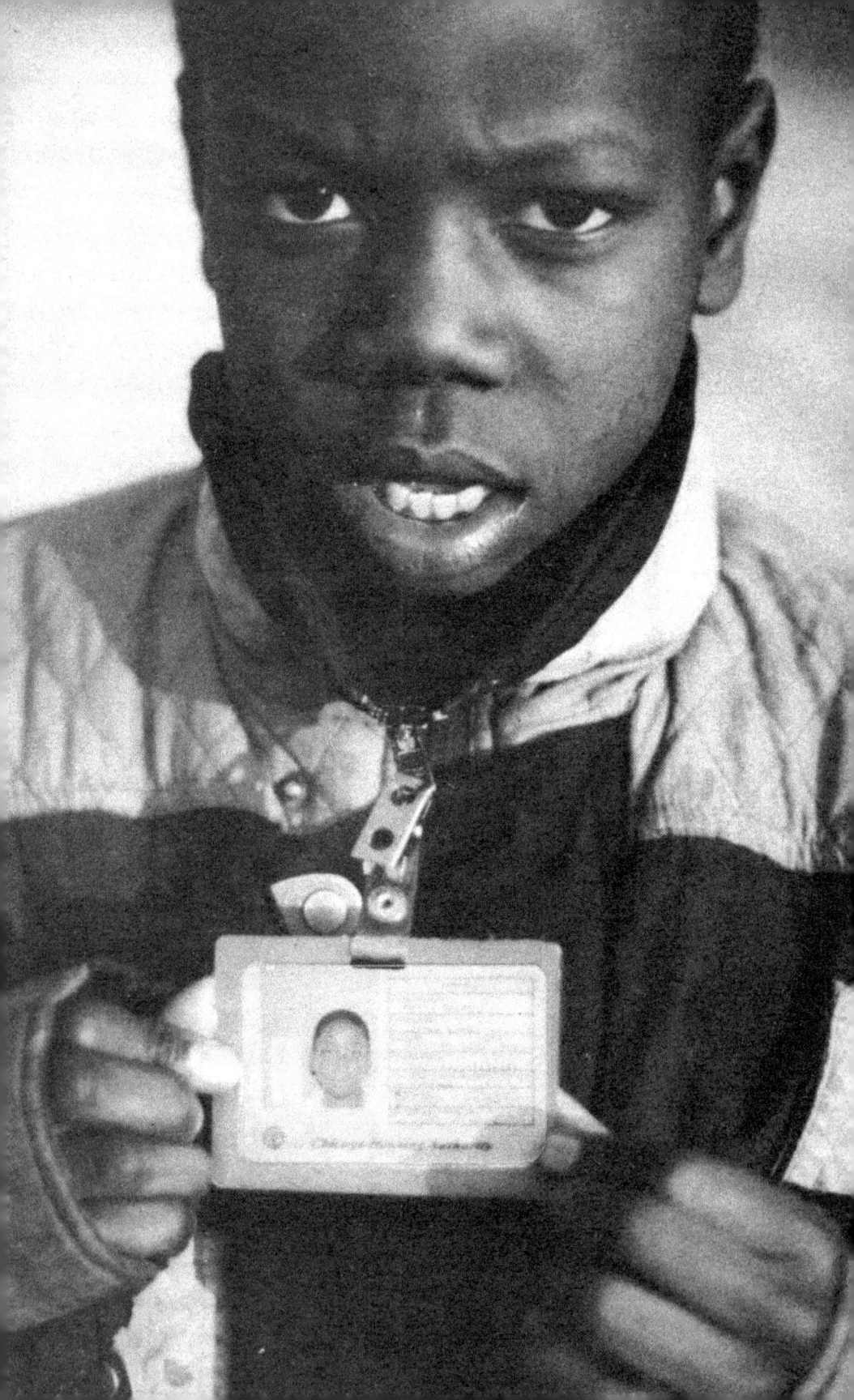

RAIDS ON CHICAGO PUBLIC HOUSING

The following "Fact Sheet" is taken from a leaflet distributed in Chicago neighborhoods in December, 1988. The commentary following the "Fact Sheet" was written by staff. The most recent raid upon the Chicago Housing projects took place on February 3, 1989, in Rockwell Gardens. *[Editors note: these words were written in 1989.]*

FACT SHEET

RAIDS ON CHA PUBLIC HOUSING BY CHICAGO HOUSING AUTHORITY/ CHICAGO POLICE DEPARTMENT

Since Sept. 20, the Chicago Housing Authority in conjunction with the Chicago Police Department has conducted raids on four buildings in three public housing projects. The alleged purpose of these raids is to uproot gangs and drugs from public housing, but this fact sheet will demonstrate that this crackdown has meant a massive violation of the rights of people in public housing. CHA head Vincent Lane has promised to raid up to 100 other buildings in public housing.

CHRONOLOGY OF THE RAIDS

- Rockwell Gardens, 2417 W. Adams, Sept. 20, 1988. Two CHA managers backed up by 60 police staged an assault that netted one arrest for possession of a weapon. About 100 of the 138 units in the building are occupied. A mass wedding of women whose live-in friends were not on the lease occurred after the raid. The CHA and other donors paid for limousines, tuxedos, brides' dresses, flowers, gifts, an overnight stay in a motel, etc.
- Prairie Courts Annex to the Harold Ickes Homes, 2822 S. Calumet, a 208-unit building, Dec. 2, 1988. Nineteen persons arrested, 13 on criminal charges of trespass (because they couldn't show identification proving that they lived in the apartments), six charged with gun and drug violations. Fourteen children picked up for truancy.
- Cabrini-Green, 1015–1017 N. Larabee, a 10-story building with 140 units, 41% vacant, raided on Dec. 6. Massive show of force is assembled of 150 CHA personnel and cops. All seven arrests are for criminal trespassing.
- Cabrini-Green, 500 W. Oak St., Dec. 8. Of the 200 or so apartments in the 19-story building, about half are vacant. Seventy-five cops raid the building. Seven people are arrested, including a CHA janitor charged with theft for illegally renting out a vacant apartment for $50 per month. Six people are charged with criminal trespass.

BASIC MODUS OPERANDI

- CHA and Chicago police surround and seal off the building, generally between 9 and 10 AM. Armed cops, sometimes with dogs, are posted on all floors to prevent anyone from escaping from the building.
- A door-to-door warrantless search of all apartments follows. The nature of the searches varies from a walk-through to rifling through cabinets and drawers and closets. For apartments where people are asleep, don't answer the door or are not home, pass keys are used to gain access. Some residents' reports of forced entry need further confirmation.
- Anyone who cannot show proper identification to prove they are on the lease is forced to leave, including boyfriends, relatives and friends. Starting with the raid on Prairie Courts, charges of criminal trespass were brought against these people.
- Residents are taken to a makeshift headquarters where they are photographed and issued ID cards. Every child seven years of age and older must carry ID to gain entry to the building. At Rockwell Gardens, all residents were also subjected without explanation to a retina scan which records the blood vessels in the eye. This high-tech form of identification is said to be more accurate than fingerprints.
- Entrances to all locked down buildings have been secured with steel gates where armed security guards control access.
- A 9:00 PM curfew was initially imposed at Rockwell; after an outcry it was changed to midnight to 9:00 AM. Midnight curfews have been imposed at all locked down buildings. No visitors, friends, relatives, or boyfriends can stay past midnight and no residents will be admitted to their own apartment after midnight.
- All visitors must sign in and out and show ID at the security desk. Tenants must come downstairs to the security desk to

admit their visitor. At Rockwell one man told the *Chicago Tribune* that security guards came and ejected him from his girlfriend's apartment when he had not left the building by midnight.

- A 72-hour (3 day) ban on all visitors was imposed at Prairie Courts and Cabrini-Green buildings.
- Vincent Lane has said that background checks will be conducted on all tenants in the locked down buildings. Anyone who has a criminal record or complaints of "anti-social behavior" on file with the CHA may be evicted.
- Lane has promised to institute surprise "housekeeping inspections." Anyone who does not meet the CHA's standards can be evicted.

There are many things that We can say about the CHA raids. However, We are conscious New Afrikans and, despite being behind the walls of prisons, We continue an active involvement in the struggle to liberate the nation and to build a socialist society. Therefore, no matter what We say about the raids, We always return to basic questions concerning our movement's need and ability to become the legitimate representative of Afrikan people who, consciously or not, require realization of these same goals.

Obviously, the Chicago Housing Authority is not the legitimate representative of the Afrikans living in the raided buildings. One question then, for us, concerns the means that our movement must use in order to truly serve the interests of Afrikans throughout Chicago and elsewhere.

One of the means that We use involves our manner of study and preparation, and another involves the way We carry on dialogue with other prisoners who may return to the communities outside the walls and become consciously active. When We study, We learn facts and We ask questions about those facts. For example, if it was a fact that the Algerian F.L.N. issued a communique such as that on page 31 of this issue[*], how did it acquire its image of legitimacy among the Algerian masses?

To find only parts of the answer, We'd have to look beyond the F.L.N. itself. We'd have to learn something about the prior <u>years</u> of practice, the years of educating and serving the people on the part of those organizations that formed the F.L.N.. Before there was an F.L.N. for the people to know, they knew only those organizations that had served the separate and varied interests of particular classes, groups and strata of the people. The F.L.N. represented a unity that had not previously existed—a unity not merely of the represented organizations, but through those organizations a unity of the Algerian people that had not previously existed. But before such unity comes much work.

Our own movement needs ever greater unity; it will be the result of the work We put into creating it. And, the creativity must manifest itself above all in the cadres who work with/among/for the people... in the "Casbah."

We also impress upon ourselves that being a cadre, or a "freedom fighter," involves much more than being able to pull off expropriations or to challenge the colonialist state's "first line of defense."

For our part, one of the things We say is: If the NAIM is really on its job, most or all potential cadres will not be given the chance to perform armed actions until they've proven themselves on the toughest battlefield there is: the "mass front."

---

[*] Editors: By "page 31 of this issue" Yaki is refering to that part of the film script for *The Battle of Algiers* which is printed here on pages 89–90, in which the clandestine liberation front issues a bulletin on gambling, brothels, and other such activities.

Bloods shouldn't be allowed to "pick up the gun" until they've proven how well they can organize a service that will, say, pick up the elderly from their homes, take them to cash their checks, to see the doctor, or to attend a meeting on some issue facing them and the rest of the community. You won't be trusted with the task of gathering or using intelligence for the movement until you win the trust of the people in the neighborhood. Performing such services and winning the trust of the people in such ways, are necessary if the NAIM is to come to be the authority upon which the masses seek out to help solve daily problems. It makes little sense to shout "Free The Land!" if We can't "free" a few square blocks or square miles in cities, towns or counties where New Afrikan and other oppressed peoples are a majority of the population.

Re-Build!

this text was published in CROSSROAD in April 1989.

> **To describe a revolution one doesn't have to describe armed actions. These are inevitable, but what defines and decides any revolution is the social struggles of the masses supported by armed action.**
>
> **Frantz Fanon, *A Dying Colonialism***

From One Generation to the Next!

Ours is a struggle with continuity, unbroken except occasionally in our own minds. We have, and must continue to struggle from one generation to the next; evolving in time and space, a people in motion, regaining independence and making history.

Ours is a mass struggle, a people's struggle, a struggle involving the participation of the young and the old, the female and the male.

Ours is the struggle of an entire people, a whole nation oppressed and moving toward a new way of life on a planet made mad by greed and fear.

Our struggle involves our elders, the refugees who were forced to abandon the National Territory, head north and northwest, during the "migrations."

They were REFUGEES, those who "migrated" from the National Territory during the WWI and WWII years. Our elders were REFUGEES during the years of the "Black Codes" when they fled the National Territory.

The cities of amerikkka are full of New Afrikan refugees who entered them during the 30s, the 40s, escaping the klan and the southern prison. One step ahead of the hounds, a few minutes

ahead of the lynch mob is how many New Afrikans came north. Refugees, from the National Territory.

New Afrikans now living in Peoria, Brooklyn, Oakland and Des Moines, were born in Clarksdale, Mississippi, and Greensboro, North Carolina. Twelve-year-old bloods boarded trains in New Orleans, Mobile and Atlanta, loaded with stained brown paper bags of cold chicken, cardboard suitcases, and dreams of big cities where work was available and where white folks weren't so mean.

New Afrikan women who cooked in big pots for white folks in Charleston, came to New York and Chicago only to cook in "greasy spoons" or in the quiet kitchens of more white folks, for the same few dollars a week and all the left-overs they could carry.

> *What of our Past? What of our History? What of our Future?*
>
> *i can imagine the pain and the strength of my great great grandmothers who were slaves and my great great grandmothers who were Cherokee Indians trapped on reservations. i remembered my great grandmother who walked everywhere rather than sit in the back of the bus. i think about North Carolina and my home town and i remember the women of my grandmother's generation: strong, fierce women who could stop you with a look out the corners of their eyes. Women who walked with majesty; who could wring a chicken's neck and scale a fish. Who could pick Cotton, plant a garden and sew without a pattern. Women who boiled clothes white in big black cauldrons and who hummed work songs and lullabys. Women who visited the elderly, made soup for the sick and shortnin bread for the babies.*
>
> *Women who delivered babies, searched for healing roots and brewed medicines. Women who darned sox and chopped wood and lay bricks. Women who could swim rivers and shoot the head off a snake. Women who took passionate responsibility for their children and for their neighbor's children too.*
>
> *The women in my grandmother's generation made giving an art form.*

"Here, gal, take this pot of collards to Sister Sue"; "Take this bag of pecans to school for the teacher"; "Stay here while i go tend Mister Johnson's leg." Every child in the neighborhood ate in their kitchens. They called each other "Sister" because of feeling rather than as the result of a movement. They supported each other through the lean times, sharing the little they had.

The women of my grandmother's generation in my home town trained their daughters for womanhood. They taught them to give respect and to demand respect. They taught their daughters how to churn butter; how to use elbow grease. They taught their daughters to respect the strength of their bodies, to lift boulders and how to kill a hog; what to do for colic, how to break a fever and how to make a poultice, patchwork quilts, plait hair and how to hum and sing. They taught their daughters to take care, to take charge, and to take responsibility. They would not tolerate a "lazy heifer" or a "gal with her head in the clouds." Their daughters had to learn how to get their lessons, how to survive, how to be strong. The women of my grandmother's generation were the glue that held family and the community together. They were the backbone of the church. And of the school. They regarded outside institutions with dislike and distrust. They were determined that their children should survive and they were committed to a better future.

From "Women In Prison: How We Are"
by Comrade-Sister Assata Shakur,
printed in Black Scholar, April 1978

We became refugees from the National Territory; We came with dreams and We wanted "to forget the past," to forget the oppression and terror, to forget the snarls of rednecks and the strange fruit of poplar trees. Far too many of us forgot that the struggle goes on, from one generation to the next. We forgot that We were simply refugees, and not yet free.

The 40s, 50s and even the early 60s were years which saw New Afrikan faces rubbed with Royal Crown so they wouldn't be "ashy"; saw our heads plastered with Murry's, saw noses and lips as repulsive objects in the thin-shaped beauty standards of amerikkka.

These same years saw us move gradually farther from our first stops upon leaving the trains and buses; they saw the families that came north move farther "out south" and into dwellings just abandoned by whites; they saw us move further from each other and the strength which allowed us to survive and maintain the consciousness of ourselves as one people, struggling from one generation to the next, until We are free.

Being colonial subjects situated so near the seat of empire has blurred our vision. Slaves in "the richest country in the world"—while still slaves—are "better off" than slaves elsewhere. Amerikkka is the "big house" of the plantation it has made of a good part of the world. It is more difficult now than in the past, for us to feel acutely the chains that bind us—enough so that We begin again to pass on the history, to begin again to socialize the children and hand down the awareness that comes with being taught the survival/resistance techniques needed to overcome the obstacles to our independence presented by the settlers who rule.

From one generation to the next is how We must move, until the nation is sovereign.

Build To Win!
Free The Land!
February, 14 ADM

first published in Notes from a New Afrikan P.O.W. Journal, Book 3, 1980.

ON CAPITALISM

We are called upon to help the discouraged beggars in life's marketplace. But one day we must come to see that an edifice which produces beggars needs restructuring. It means that questions must be raised. You see, my friends, when you deal with this, you begin to ask the question, "Who owns the oil?" You begin to ask the question, "Who owns the iron ore?"

Martin Luther On Extremism, Imperialism

...The movement must address itself to the question of restructuring the whole of American society. There are forty million poor people here. And one day we must ask the question, "Why are there forty million poor people in America?" And when you begin to ask that question, you are raising questions about the economic system, about a broader distribution of wealth. When you ask that question, you begin to question the capitalistic economy.

King Jr.
Capitalism and

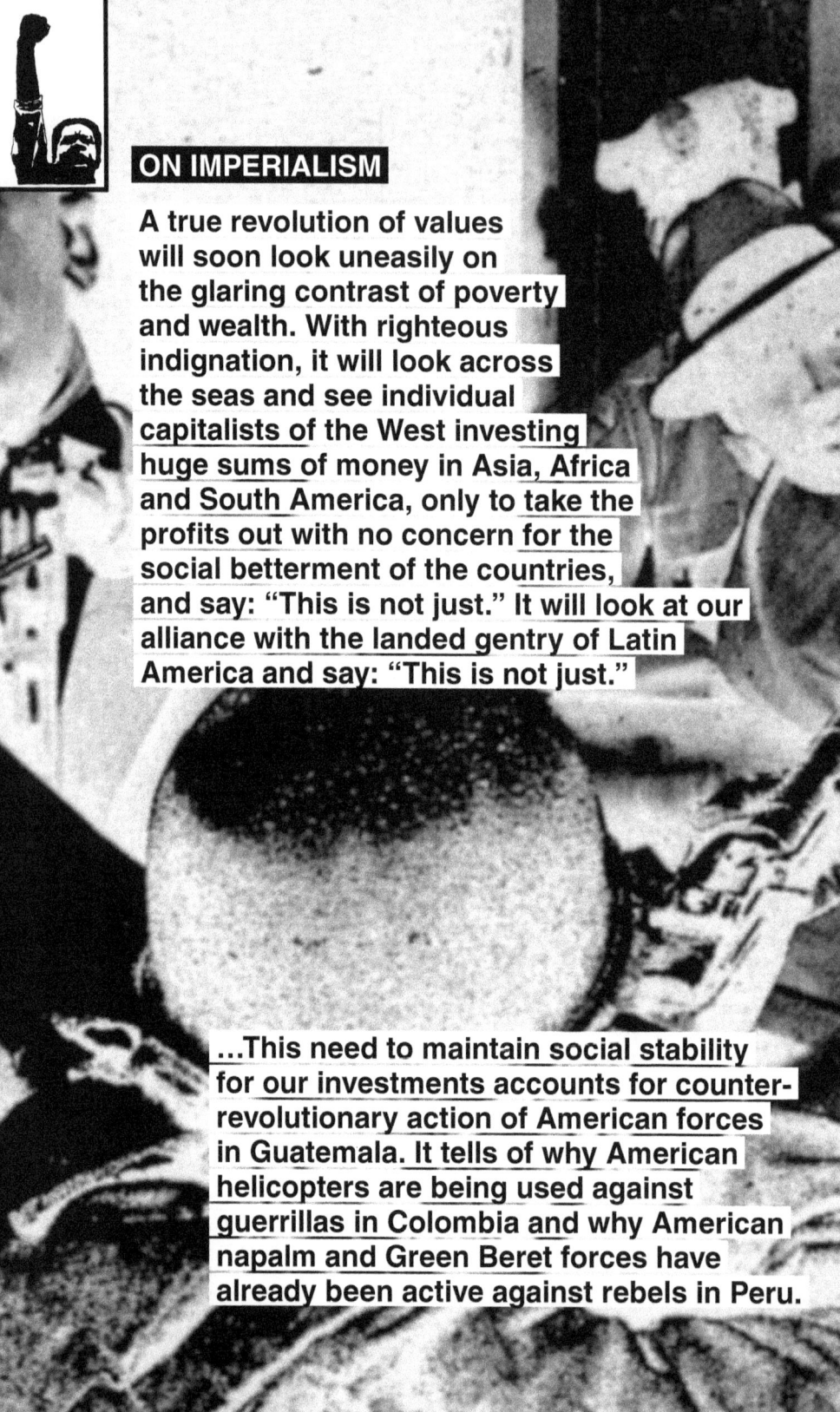

ON IMPERIALISM

A true revolution of values will soon look uneasily on the glaring contrast of poverty and wealth. With righteous indignation, it will look across the seas and see individual capitalists of the West investing huge sums of money in Asia, Africa and South America, only to take the profits out with no concern for the social betterment of the countries, and say: "This is not just." It will look at our alliance with the landed gentry of Latin America and say: "This is not just."

…This need to maintain social stability for our investments accounts for counter-revolutionary action of American forces in Guatemala. It tells of why American helicopters are being used against guerrillas in Colombia and why American napalm and Green Beret forces have already been active against rebels in Peru.

ON EXTREMISM

The question is not whether we will be extremists but what kind of extremists we will be. Will we be extremists for the preservation of injustice, or will we be extremists for the cause of justice?

Malcolm X: Model of Personal Transformation

Malcolm X often used the concept of prison as a metaphor to describe the situation of New Afrikan people. He implied that just as those in actual prisons are expected to "rehabilitate" themselves as a condition for their release, We must transform ourselves, as a people, as a condition for securing our freedom from oppression.

Malcolm's autobiography offers evidence of the pivotal role that prison played in his transformation (esp. chapters 10, 11, and 12), and provides guidance for imprisoned New Afrikans, who can begin a process of self-transformation similar to that undertaken by Malcolm. We have the added benefit of knowing the general outline of our identity, purpose, and direction.

Although in prison, We are not defined by this condition. We are New Afrikans (identity; nationality), citizens of an oppressed nation. Our purpose is to secure the independence of the nation, and socialist development is the direction.

The time spent in prison should be devoted to our self-transformation... to the further development of our identity, commitment to our purpose, and the pursuit of knowledge and skills needed to aid our people in the realization of the socialist development of our society.

II

While in prison, Malcolm began to think—in a systematic, critical way, about his past lifestyle, about the world and the society he lived in. He began to question the way things were, and he realized that change—in his life, and in the society—was both possible and necessary.

While in prison, Malcolm began to think—but only after he began to read. Prior to his imprisonment, Malcolm had been enclosed in the world of the hustler, the player, the pimp, the gangster—the parasite—and he couldn't imagine himself outside of that world. Reading exposed Malcolm to new worlds; it allowed him to see that there were alternatives to the lifestyle and values of the social parasite.

While in prison, Malcolm began to think, and to read—but only after he had been encouraged to do so by someone that he respected

and who had taken an unselfish interest in him. Malcolm was later motivated by a new sense of self-worth and identity and purpose, as his family introduced him to the religious and political philosophy of Islam, as taught by Elijah Muhammad, and practiced by the Nation of Islam.

Soon after leaving prison, Malcolm began to effect change upon the world—but he was able to do so because he had first changed himself, while in prison. Many imprisoned New Afrikans can follow his example, change themselves, become new men and women committed to acting upon the world to effect its radical transformation. As with Malcolm, such change would more likely occur if imprisoned New Afrikans are encouraged and assisted by individuals, groups, or a community seeking to make them part of a collective process of redemption and progressive social development.

III

When imprisoned New Afrikans read Malcolm's autobiography, We should reflect upon our own lives, as We can easily identify with Malcolm, and see similarities between his life and our own. In fact, Malcolm charges us to examine our lives when he says, "...*why am i as i am? To understand that of any person, his whole life, from birth, must be reviewed. All of our experiences fuse into our personality. Everything that ever happened to us is an ingredient.*"[1]

Critical review of one's own life is the first step in the process of personal transformation. It's also the hardest step to take, because it requires that one be brutally honest and unreserved in the examination and critique of one's fears and shortcomings.

Reading Malcolm can help us to understand how critical self-examination is done. What is there in Malcolm's life that's not in our own? Who was he, if not one of us? What does Malcolm mean to us if not that We, like him, can change? What does his prison experience mean to us if not that We, too, can use the prison as the environment within which We undergo our own metamorphosis? As Malcolm looked back on his life as a parasite, he acknowledged the degree to which it was a result of the bad choices he had made, due in part to "the wrong kinds of heroes, and the wrong kinds of influences." But those heroes and influences, those bad choices, should be examined within the context of the society that helped to produce them—We are all products of a unique form of colonial oppression.

IV

Most people enter prison thinking only of surviving the experience and returning to their previous way of life. They spend most of their time watching television, listening to music, playing sports or working jobs linked to the operation of the prison (e.g., kitchen or laundry or janitorial services). Educational programs in prison are designed so that only a few prisoners may participate. Rare are the self-motivated prisoners who decide to educate and transform themselves.

> *A prisoner has time that he can put to good use. I'd put prison second to college as the best place for a man to go if he needs to do some thinking. If he's <u>motivated</u>, in prison he can change his life.*[2]

> *I don't think anybody ever got more out of going to prison than I did. In fact, prison enabled me to study far more intensively than I would have if my life had gone differently and I had attended some college ... Where else but in prison could I have attacked my ignorance by being able to study intensely sometimes as much as fifteen hours a day?*[3]

When convicted in 1946, Malcolm was first sent to the prison in Charlestown, Massachusetts, where he initially wasted his time, engaging in aimless rebellion and drug use. He didn't begin to put time to good use until he was encouraged to do so by Bimbi, an older con who'd spent many years in many prisons—but he had not wasted his time. Bimbi was articulate and well-read, and he became a minister to Malcolm, who'd been drawn to Bimbi because *"he was the first man I had ever seen command total respect... with his words."*[4]

Bimbi reignited within Malcolm the passion for words and the acquisition of knowledge that he'd begun to lose in the 8th grade. He urged Malcolm to take advantage of the prison library, and to enroll in some of the correspondence courses allowed by the prison.

Malcolm admitted that at that point in his life, his working vocabulary may have been only two hundred words which, together with his penmanship, made it impossible for him to write a decent letter. He first took a correspondence course in English. He began to read from the prison library, saying later that:

> *I have often reflected upon the new vistas that reading opened to me. I knew right there in prison that reading had changed forever the course of my life. As I see it today, the ability to read awoke inside me some long dormant craving to be mentally alive.*[5]

However, it would take more time, and a different motivation, for Malcolm to develop the appreciation for reading just described. Initially, his reading was aimless, and he was motivated by little more than the desire to become a more literate hustler—he hadn't transformed that criminal/colonial mentality. It wasn't until Malcolm was transferred to another prison that he moved beyond his mere "book-reading motions":

> *Pretty soon, I would have quit even these motions, unless i had received the motivation that I did.*[6]

V

Malcolm was transferred to the Norfolk Prison Colony in Concord, Massachusetts, in 1948. There, he received a letter from his brother, Philbert, who said that he had joined the "Nation of Islam," and he urged Malcolm to "pray for deliverance." Malcolm wasn't ready to hear anything about religion. His attitude changed, however, after he received a letter from another of his brothers, Reginald.

Because Reginald knew how Malcolm's street hustler mind worked, his approach was more effective than Philbert's. Reginald told Malcolm to stop eating pork, to stop smoking cigarettes, and that he would show Malcolm how to get out of prison. Malcolm took the bait. What he initially regarded as probably a con to be worked on the prison authorities, turned out to be the next step in the process of his transformation:

> ...For the next years, I was the nearest thing to a hermit in the Norfolk Prison Colony. I never have been more busy in my life. I still marvel at how swiftly my previous life's thinking pattern slid away from me... It is as though someone else I knew of had lived by hustling and crime. I would be startled to catch myself thinking in a remote way of my earlier self as another person.[7]

It was at this point in his life that Malcolm began to read selectively and critically, and to develop intellectual discipline to complement his spiritual and moral development.

For New Afrikan women and men held in U.S. prisons, Malcolm stands as an example of the way in which We can free ourselves, even though behind prison walls.

Malcolm attained his freedom long before he was released from prison—when he began to read, to think, to question his old habits and values. If Malcolm had not used his time in prison to change his life, he would not have left us ideas and a life worthy of examination and emulation.

Moreover, if Malcolm had not changed his life while in prison, he would have returned to the life of the "criminal" and the oppressed colonial subject.

The parable of Job, which Elijah Muhammad used in introducing Malcolm to the Nation of Islam soon after Malcolm's release from prison, is instructive. Mr. Muhammad told the gathering that Malcolm had been strong while in prison.

Malcolm reports that he then said:

> *When God had bragged about how faithful Job was... the devil said only God's hedge around Job kept Job so faithful. "Remove that protective hedge," the devil told God, "and I will make Job curse you to your face." The devil could claim that, hedged in prison, I had just used Islam, Mr. Muhammad said. But the devil would say that now, out of prison, I would return to my drinking, smoking, dope, and life of crime.*[8]

We can go through the motions of changing our lives—while in prison, or otherwise—but the test of the truth comes when the prison doors are opened, or, when otherwise We're confronted with situations which test our characters.

Nevertheless—before We can remain faithful, We must first **become** faithful.

Malcolm's prison transformation can be a model for our own.

NOTES

(1) *The Autobiography of Malcolm X: As told to Alex Haley* (Ballantine Books, 1981). p. 173

(2) Ibid., 450–451

(3) Ibid., 207

(4) Ibid., 178

(5) Ibid., 206

(6) Ibid., 198

(7) Ibid., 196

(8) Ibid., 227

first published in CROSSROAD Spring 2001.

Reflections On Victor Serge's "What Everyone Should Know About (State) Repression"

Editors' Note: In the 1960s, as repression tightened, revolutionary groups needed an understanding of how to shield themselves from the f.b.i. and police. But there had been no tradition of such security knowledge either in the Civil Rights movement or the youth gangs. At that time, the New Left started passing around a translation of Victor Serge's little pamphlet, "What Everyone Should Know About State Repression." Serge had been a Russian revolutionary journalist and organizer, who had worked underground against the Czar's secret police and had a lot of first-hand experience. Yaki encouraged comrads to check Serge's booklet out; but since the russian had lived back a century ago, in a time when you could do things like jumping on a streetcar to evade surveillance, Yaki wanted to update and reinforce the basic lessons. To an active revolutionary, this understanding is like having a first-aid kit or emergency equipment. If you are reading this kind of literature you need to be prepared to fight the political police.

PART ONE: REFLECTIONS

1. Victor Serge quickly corrects a common misconception about repression. Most of us hold an image of imperialist repression formed by its spectacular, brutal and murderous results, i.e., the predawn raid by police, the invasion by military forces, or the bombings and lynchings by the state's paramilitary KKK-type garrison troops.

In other words, we view a **PART** of the repressive process as if it were the whole, because this part is the most visible and impacting aspect, and the aspect most portrayed by the imperialist media as well as the media of the colonized nation.

But, Serge points out that, at the center of what everyone should know about the repression of the bourgeois-imperialist state—what allows us to put the whole process into perspective—is, **THE IMMEDIATE AIM** of all repressive forces. That immediate aim is, "more **to know**, than to repress. **To know**, in order to repress at the appointed hour, to the exent desired—if not altogether." They can't repress what they don't know... about.

Therefore, the most immediate aim of revolutionary cadres and the revolutionary masses is, in this context, to allow the opposition to know as little as possible, about any thing, and any one.

We should understand that each time we perform the common act of opening our mouths and speaking, we're telling someone **SOMETHING** about ourselves which has the potential of becoming a weapon used against us by the state, should that information fall or be placed in their hands: the way we think; what we think about; our habits, likes and dislikes; what we've done, what we may do, and how we may do it, etc.

And, the body has a language of its own, too. That is, our

movements can tell the opposition things about us that they want **TO KNOW**, in order to be able to repress us. Thus, if they can't watch our movements, they'll be denied information that could be used to repress us and/or our people.

The enemy's attention to such things is part of their science of repression. Paying due attention to such things should be part of the science of revolutionary cadres, and of the science of the revolutionary masses. We must share revolutionary science even as we discipline ourselves to stand vigilant over **ALL** our words and actions.

2. While building the cadre and mass bases that must share revolutionary science and realize it in practical struggle, we must see that if the foundations that we build upon are shaky, then everything that comes to rest upon them will be shaky, too.

If we allow cracks to develop in the very foundation of the new movement, in the consciousness and practice of cadres and masses, then corrosion will be a characteristic element in and of the structures, and our consciousness will be flawed.

A major cause of cracks in foundations is undeveloped consciousness, incorrect political line, and unacknowledged or unrecognized liberalism and opportunism. These relate to the more apparent secondary causes, i.e., the "mistakes," complacency, and general failures to discipline our words and actions.

The discipline begins with experience, experiment, and the summation of these, which together form the core of the development of revolutionary science. In the words of one comrad, "To 'Heighten Discipline' means, first and foremost, that We heighten our grasp and practice of the ideology, line and strategy of the organization,

and of the Movement. To be 'under the discipline of,' or 'subject to the discipline of' any organization, but of the Army in particular, means that our comrades must heighten their efforts to understand our ideology, our political-military line, and our strategy; it means that We must accept these as our own; that We are therefore able to put them into practice, be responsible for them, and able to fight for them and defend them." (Shalimar B., "Against The Wind," NOTES FROM A NEW AFRIKAN P.O.W. JOURNAL, Book Six, 1980, p. 7)

3. The tasks ahead, and the conditions under which they must be performed demand that we not take anything for granted—least of all, our survival.

They know we're coming. In fact, they know far too much about those of us already here. And, unless we grasp this fact, in all its implications, we'll contaminate everything we touch, and expose everything we try to build.

We have to search for, and then apply, the consciousness, the skills and methods that will eliminate—or at least minimize—the disadvantages incurred especially over the past ten years, which have resulted in the further disruption of the revolutionary forces.

4. Serge also helps to place the image of the "professional" revolutionary into focus. It could be said that his entire book is about the most essential of those "special qualities" that enable the professional revolutionary (i.e., cadres), to carry on "the struggle against the political police"—the imperialist state's first line of **ARMED** defense.

This insight into the substantive composition of the (professional) revolutionary cadre, helps us keep in mind that:

A) The "political police" and other armed/intelligence forces of the state, are specialized defensive/offensive branches of the oppressive state, and to struggle against them is merely to engage the primary instruments of physical coercion and repression that the state has at its command. In other words, we must keep in mind that the **PRIMARY** struggle is against the state as a whole. In this way, we can avoid being diverted by the struggles against its parts. The enemy is the U.S. imperialist state, not merely the f.b.i., or the street cop that commits the most recent act of colonial terror.

Therefore, when we seek to raise consciousness about repression, we want to focus on the repression of the imperialist state, not merely the repression of the f.b.i. or the local police department.

B) The imperialist state also has other instruments of coercion and repression, which assume political, economic, and sociocultural forms, rather than physical/armed forms. Relative to the oppressed nation, **ALL** institutions directly or indirectly controlled by the imperialist state are repressive, perform counter-revolutionary functions, and are no less forces to be engaged in combat by revolutionary cadres and masses, than are the "political police."

C) The State's repressive apparatus is also "professional," and is organized on a scientific basis, with, as Serge says, "special attention to their character, education, training, recruitment, intelligence, service record; their knowledge of the programs, statutes, origins and methods of the revolutionary parties, and the histories of leading members…"

5. Hunters must be able to track, and to know the habits and feeding grounds of their prey. Intelligent prey, on the other hand, must know as much as possible about the hunter, which includes knowing what the hunter knows about the prey. If the hunter is tracking the prey, then the prey must learn to avoid leaving traces and trails. If the hunter pursues the prey based on knowledge of the prey's

habits and feeding patterns, then the prey must abandon those habits, avoid normal feeding areas, and maybe even change diets.

The opposition wants to know whatever possible—whatever we allow them to know. They wanna know who you know; where you go; when; how often; how long you stay; what you say and do while there...

Nothing is really insignificant. They are on their job even when we don't see or hear them (contrary to what most of us seem to believe), and, to avoid being caught off guard, coming up short, or having to improvise a quick lie or a quick getaway, we must be on our jobs even when we think we don't have to be.

6. Making the "need to know" principle part of our very being, should be understood to involve more than merely being vigilant with regard to clearly identifiable and visible repressive forces, and those kinds of situations and activity where the need is most obvious. The application of the "need to know" principle (basically, that no one needs to know any information other than that necessary to carry out their own activities), literally means that **NO ONE** inside organized structures know more than necessary, and it means absolutely no one outside organized structures know anything at all.

It often happens that, we begin working with people who are later uncovered as planted agents of the state, or who turn traitor. In such situations, we find ourselves faced not only with the exposure of names, addresses, details of actions, and other information that such persons acquired in the course of doing work that they were responsible for. We also usually find ourselves faced with the exposure of information that such people acquired from others who failed to practice "need to know."

7. Making "need to know" part of our being means getting into the habit of never volunteering information. **EXAMPLE:** A sister doing maintenance work at an office building is mopping the floor of one of the offices. An employee of the firm approaches the office, stops at the door upon seeing the wet floor, and asks, "Is that wax?" The sister says, "You can walk on it."

Now, if you ask this sister why she didn't say "Yes," it was wax, or "No," it wasn't: "Well, in the first place," she'll say, with the air of a worker-teacher, instructing a cadre-pupil, "i told him just what he needed to know. He **seemed** to need to know if he could walk on the floor. But then, too, he might have wanted to know if i **was** waxing it—which they say i'm to do three times a week, but i don't. So, he left, without finding out from me, whether it was wax or not. And, if tomorrow or next year, i **have** to say what it was, i can say whatever i like, or whatever i need to say. Yep, i make a habit outta tellin' 'em just what they need to know, and no more."

8. Serge: "…the immediate aim of the police is more to know, than to repress. To know, in order to repress at the appointed hour, to the extent desired—if not altogether."

The state and its repressive forces won't flash news bulletins each time they acquire a piece of information about revolutionary-mass forces. They won't publicize the names of those on today's surveillance sheet.

You may make a mistake, and in some cases you'll be, or become aware of it, before it results in tragic consequences. But, many times we make mistakes, but remain unaware of them—until the door is kicked in (and sometimes even then we won't know exactly what led them to us). The enemy won't let us know when we've made

mistakes and/or when they discover them. They assume that if we become aware of the mistake, we'll repair any cracks, or cover any traces, and learn from the experience so that the error won't be repeated.

The opposition assumes that if we learn that an agent has been exposed, or that a cadre has turned traitor, or that a comrad under torture has yielded information—the enemy assumes that in such situations we'll change whatever needs to be changed, and abandon whatever needs to be abandoned. If comrads are arrested and released, the enemy assumes that we will impose a "no contact" policy, whereby contact with that comrad by others above and below, are brought to an absolute minimum or stopped altogether. The enemy assumes that we know something about what we're doing, and that we take them, and ourselves, seriously.

They will get a piece of information and try to develop it to its deepest and widest limits, before deciding upon "the appointed hour." And, that's not always a pre-dawn raid. It's sometimes a stop by a traffic cop who "just happens" to notice a busted tail-light. Or, he may actually make the stop in ignorance, yet the grip of other branches seize the opportunity, when your info is run through the computer.

Sometimes the hour is seized when comrads carry out actions that run into obstacles. Under the cover of such mishaps, the enemy will move on names, faces, addresses, etc., that they already had, but they'll pretend to have only discovered them as a result of the failed action. In this way, the enemy tries to keep us in the dark about the extent of the information they already have, and they try to protect the sources of their information. They will always try to keep us ignorant as to how well they've been doing their job of infiltrating, turning, tapping, following, picture snapping, questioning, checking and cross-checking, indexing and cross-indexing…

Sometimes, the appointed hour arrives, but they deliberately "miss" someone. They throw the net only so far when making arrests… or, they release someone—but they're still interested in **KNOWING**. They hope that those "missed" by the net, and/or those released after an arrest, will become unconscious "breeders" and blind informers, by immediately becoming active again. In this way, we'd lead the state to more information on cadres they likely already knew about, and to names, faces, addresses, and methods, that they didn't know about, or didn't have the full scoop on.

They will also hope that **NEW** contacts will be made by unconscious breeders and blind informers; they will hope that **NEW** resources will be tapped, **NEW** networks established—all, exposed from the very beginning. They will hope that we won't perform what Lenin calls "the duty of a revolutionist to conceal from the eyes of the world the relationships and contacts which [he or she] maintains, which [he or she] is establishing or trying to establish."

9. Serge: "Faced by this wily adversary, powerful and cunning, a communist party lacking clandestine organization, a party which keeps nothing hidden, is like an unarmed [person], with no cover, in the sights of a well-positioned [hunter]. Revolutionary work is too serious to be kept in a glasshouse. The party… must organize so as to avoid enemy vigilance **AS FAR AS POSSIBLE**; so as to hide its most important resources **ABSOLUTELY**… so as to train our comrads in the behavior which is demanded by these imperatives."

"Clandestine organization" should be understood in at least two ways: 1) the organization of the type of political and military structures usually considered "underground"; 2) the type of political, economic, and socio-cultural activity which, while considered "public," or "legal," is nevertheless **REVOLUTIONARY** activity, and should be conducted with an attitude and methods characterized by the present reality of the war.

We must understand: It becomes a criminal act when cadres and activists continue to think and act as though they are protected by the U.S. constitution, state and local statutes, and the myths and lies fed the settlers and colonies of the empire about "amerikkkan democracy," and other nonsense. So-called bourgeois legality and morality died when the Portuguese landed on the African continent, and when Columbus landed in the "Indies." The most "innocent"/"public" or "reformist" activity, is actual, or potential, revolutionary activity, and real revolution is illegal in amerikkka, and too serious to be kept in a glasshouse.

There is no such thing as "legal, anti-imperialist struggle," or "legal, national liberation revolution." The opposition moves on the belief that there are, or that there will soon be, connections between "public" and clandestine anti-imperialist, revolutionary activity. It is their job to discover any such connections—and they take their job seriously. So, they tap anti-imperialist phones, tape anti-imperialist speeches and snap the pictures of those who deliver such speeches. They also follow "public" activists, and otherwise keep close tabs on **ALL** their activity, no matter how "legal."

This is exactly what's meant by "the party must organize so as to avoid enemy vigilance **AS FAR AS POSSIBLE**." Revolutionary cadres and the revolutionary masses organize all forms of activity—political, economic, socio-cultural—among all classes, groups, and strata. Enemy vigilance must be avoided **AS FAR AS POSSIBLE** in **ALL** mass, "public," and so-called "legal" work.

10. When it's said that "the party must organize so as to hide its most important resources **ABSOLUTELY**," this isn't limited to financial or material resources, nor to the stashing of such resources behind locked, secret doors.

What are our most important resources? Our cadres; supporters and sympathizers; networks; contacts and relationships. **THE PEOPLE ARE OUR MOST IMPORTANT RESOURCES.** The vast majority of our resources are "public"—they work nine-to-five; live in housing projects; attend school; receive some form of welfare payments; some (not enough as yet) hold sensitive positions in the enemy state apparatus, its academic, media, business and service institutions, and serve in its police and armed forces.

11. To say that "the party must organize so as to train our comrades in the behavior which is demanded by these imperatives," means that training in the consciousness and methods of "combating the political police" is part of the organizing process, beginning at the stage of cadre "spotting" and recruitment.

All organized structures must fashion an apparatus which specializes in such training, using detailed and systematic methods. This apparatus must be responsible for on-going study, drawing lessons from our own experience and from the experiences of others. It should also coordinate the periodic assessment of cadres, structures, from the standpoint of security, conducting and testing the training and raising its level, in the daily activities and struggles.

There must also be training of supporters and sympathizers, primarily through the conduct of political education. We shouldn't take for granted that people will know the enemy and the methods used to infiltrate, disrupt and divert mass organizations.

We must have a secure movement and struggle, not merely secure vanguard organizations, collectives, and units. We need an impenetrable wall of mass consciousness, an entire revolutionary class that knows about the purpose and methods of state repression, and how to defend against it, and how to turn defense into offense.

12. Some of the things we do, and some of the structures we build, must be "hidden" clandestinely, in the commonly understood meaning of the term. Other things we do, and other structures built, contacts made, relationships established, etc., while taking place in "public" view, must be done in a more-or-less clandestine manner, so that ultimate purposes aren't undesirably noticeable, connections aren't exposed, and contacts are subtle and unobserved.

PART TWO: GOOD PRACTICE IS THE RESULT OF GOOD PRACTICE

1. There was once a collective of aspiring New Afrikan revolutionaries, engaged in study, and one day the subject was "learning how to follow people and detect when you're being followed." One of the would-be revolutionaries saw no need for this type of study, got angry, and said that he was a revolutionary, and not an espionage agent.

Strangely, this study session took place in the late 1960s several days after the bloods had read an article which mentioned that the state was following such people as Stokely Carmichael, and placing beepers on their cars.

Other members of the collective tried to make the point that learning how to follow people, and to be able to detect and elude similar surveillance upon oneself, is an essential element in the training of all revolutionaries, whether they do "public" or "clandestine" work. Such training is part of the more practical side of the revolutionary **SCIENCE** practiced by the "professional" revolutionary.

2. Serge has a chapter on "Simple Advice To Revolutionaries," and he points out that his suggestions aren't "a complete code of the rules of clandestinity, nor even (a complete code) of the precautions to be taken by revolutionaries. They contain no sensational recipe. They are simply basic rules. Strictly speaking, common sense should be enough to suggest them. But unfortunately, long experience teaches us that it is not out of place to spell them out. Carelessness on the part of revolutionaries has always been the best aid the police have."

3. Serge's advice, sprinkled with a few bits of our comments: "At the start, all surveillance is from the outside. This always involves following the individual, getting to know their activities, movements, contacts, and then finding out their plans. 'Tailing' sections are developed by all police forces... In the most serious cases, two agents spied on the same person unbeknown to each other; their reports were cross-checked and used to complement each other... These daily reports were sent to the police to be analyzed by specialists. These officers... were dangerously perceptive. They would draw up tables showing a person's deeds and actions, the number of visits, their length, regularity, etc. Sometimes, these tables brought out the importance of one member's relationships and his probable influence... Every revolutionary must regard themselves as being permanently followed: on principle, the revolutionary should never neglect to take the necessary precautions to prevent being followed. The simplest rules are: 1) don't go directly to where you are going; 2) turn down a deserted street to check whether you are being followed; 3) when in doubt, turn back; 4) if you notice that you are being followed, jump on some kind of transport and then change."

Again, we must stress the importance of **CONSCIOUSNESS**. Security is not simply a matter of magical methods, especially when cadres only learn even the simplest methods in a mechanical manner, and by rote. Knowing the methods without having the theoretical perspective that allows them to be used in the most appropriate manner, is sometimes worse than not knowing the methods at all.

Another thing to keep in mind: It's not a matter of being paranoid when it comes to employing such methods, nor is it a question

of whether or not the opposition is actually following you. It's a matter of making a habit of being serious, apply science, being disciplined and vigilant. The enemy won't come up to you and say, "Watch yourself today, we're playing for real, and watching every move you make."

More on what we mean by stressing the importance of **CONSCIOUSNESS**: It happens that we got so-called vanguard forces who still—believe it or not—think that the time to get serious about "security" is after the state announces that "civil liberties" are being suspended, or that martial law is being imposed. But, by that time, it's too late to start employing security methods, or to begin developing a more developed consciousness. By the time such an announcement is made (assuming that it will be), the lists of those to be arrested have already been compiled!!!!

So, one aspect of what we mean by **CONSCIOUSNESS**, from the revolutionary perspective, is that, folks have lived in amerikkka all their lives, and studied and been part of the development of struggle against the state, but they still have the consciousness of bourgeois reformists, slaves, adventurists, and dilettantes. They still have the consciousness of the petty-bourgeoisie, even while claiming to wage revolutionary warfare.

4. Write down as little as possible. It's better not to write. Don't take notes on sensitive subjects: it's better sometimes to forget certain things than to take them down in writing. With that in mind, practice remembering addresses, names, etc. Where **NECESSARY**, take notes which are intelligible only to yourself. Everyone can invent ways of abbreviating, inverting, transposing… With correspondence, take into account that your mail **WILL** be opened. Say as little as possible and try to make yourself understood only by the addressee (and, the **BEST** way to do this is by pre-arrangement, i.e., during face-to-face discussions with comrads, discuss and decide upon the methods to be used). Mention no

third persons unless absolutely necessary (and, if this is to be done, it should be done according to pre-arranged methods, so that the third persons should be mentioned only by code names known only to the addressee)... Avoid all details about places, work, dates, and people... Learn to resort, even without prior arrangement, to what should always be very simple strategems for trivializing information. Don't say, for example, that Comrad Yusef has been arrested, but that Yusef has suddenly fallen ill. And, of course, "Yusef" will not be the comrad's real or work name, but a code name used only between yourself and the addressee. Each comrad should have as many names as necessary, and these names should be known only to those with a need to know.

In view of the fact that some correspondence between most comrads must take place, there must be face-to-face contact between such corresponding comrads so that the details of their exchanges can be arranged between them.

It's also much better that each comrad have different systems for corresponding with each comrad, than to have a single system for corresponding with each comrad. In the event of the state discovering the system used with one comrad, they won't be able to use that knowledge immediately against other comrads.

5. "Beware of telephones—**ALL** telephones. Never say **ANYTHING** over the phone that you wouldn't say to a police officer. Don't make appointments over the phone, except in pre-arranged, coded terms. And, when using such codes, make them sound as normal as possible, that is, don't have them sound as if they are obviously codes, or jagged parts of conversations, etc."

6. "Make it a principle that, in illegal activity (which is to say, in all activity), a revolutionary should know only what it is useful or necessary to know; and that it is often dangerous to know or to tell more. The less that is known, the greater the security. Be on guard

against the inclination to give away confidences. Know how to keep quiet; keeping quiet is a duty to the party and to the struggle. Know how to forget of your own accord what you should not know. It is a mistake, which may have serious consequences, to tell your closest friend, mate, or most trusty comrad a party secret which is not indispensable for them to know. Sometimes you may be doing them wrong; because you are responsible for what you know, and it may be a heavy responsibility. Don't take offense or get annoyed at another comrad's silence. This isn't a sign of lack of confidence, but rather of fraternal esteem and of what should be a mutual consciousness of revolutionary duty."

7. In the event of arrest: At all costs keep cool. Don't let yourself be intimidated or provoked. Don't reply to any question without having a lawyer present and without previously consulting with your lawyer. If possible, the lawyer should be a comrad, or at least someone who has a significant level of political consciousness. If it's not possible to have a lawyer, don't say anything without really thinking about it. As a matter of principle: **SAY NOTHING.** Trying to "explain" yourself is dangerous: you are in the hands of professionals who are able to get something out of your every word. Any "explanation" gives them valuable documentation. Lying is extremely dangerous: it is difficult to construct a story without its defects being too obvious, it is almost impossible to improvise. Don't try to be more clever than them: the relationship of forces is too unequal for that. **NEVER CONFESS.** When you deny something, deny it firmly. The enemy is capable of anything. Don't let yourself be surprised or disconcerted by the classic: "We know everything!" This is never the case. It is a bare-faced trick… Don't be intimidated by the eternal threat: "You'll pay for this!" What you'll pay for is a confession, or a clumsy explanation, or falling for tricks and moments of panic; but whatever the situation of the accused, a hermetically sealed defense, built up out of much

silence and few definite affirmations or denials, can only help. Don't believe a word of another classic ploy: "We know everything because your Comrad So-and-So has talked!" Don't believe a word of it, even if they try to prove it. With a few carefully selected clues, the enemy is capable of feigning a profound knowledge of things. Even if So-and-So did "tell all," this is a further reason to be doubly circumspect. Again: **SAY NOTHING. SIGN NOTHING.**

8. "Before the police and courts: Don't try to establish the 'truth'— there is no truth in common between the oppressed and the oppressor. Their truth is not ours. Before the judges of the oppressor, the Comrad does not have to account for any act. The Comrad can turn the courtroom into a school, or, the Comrad can keep silent."

9. "A supreme warning: Be on your guard against conspiracy mania, against posing, adopting airs of mystery, dramatizing simple events, or 'conspiratorial' attitudes. The greatest virtue in a revolutionary is simplicity, and scorn for all poses… including 'revolutionary' and especially conspiratorial poses…"

Re-Build!

first published in So That We Don't Fool Ourselves—Again: Study Notes on Secure Communication.

EVERGREEN E-390 $1.95

THE WRETCHED OF THE EARTH

BY FRANTZ FANON

A NEGRO PSYCHOANALYST'S STUDY OF THE PROBLEMS OF RACISM & COLONIALISM IN THE WORLD TODAY

Stop!

You Must Read This First

This is different from all other writings about Frantz Fanon, so there are things that you have to know before you start.

Frantz Fanon was one of the most influential revolutionary theorists of the anti-colonial rebellions, especially in the U.S.A., but today almost all of the thousands of books and articles on his work are by the careerist professors that Fanon so distrusted. Those he called the "wily intellectuals."

This is not. This study guide was written by one of those poor rebels for whom Fanon wrote his great book, *Wretched of the Earth*, in the first place. In his introduction to Fanon, Jean-Paul Sartre says that "…the Third World finds **itself** and speaks to **itself** through his voice." Because Frantz Fanon was a Black man from the French colony of Martinique in the Caribbean, who found himself as a French medical psychologist in Algeria during their anti-colonial war. Deserting to the side of the Algerian guerrillas, Fanon wrote *Wretched of the Earth* as a political guide for all those who were "Natives," the colonized like himself.

Fanon is most often spoken of by the middle-class intellectuals as a shocking political philosopher of racial violence against the white settler. Because in his writings he leapt over the heads of political parties and their ideologies, speaking directly to individuals on their need to personally take part in revolutionary violence;

as well as the need for the oppressed as a whole for the liberating psychological, cultural and political effects of that violence.

That layer of Fanon's thinking is real, but to Yaki it wasn't the center of Fanon's politics. In part because to Yaki it was, "been there, done that." One of those young "Natives" from the inner city streets who had picked up Fanon in the 1960s with careless eagerness, who had experienced armed expropriations and violence against white settlers, Yaki eventually found out that beneath the too-easy snapshot of Fanon as a race thinker was an underlying structure of Fanon's communalist/communist politics.

Here, Yaki is on a mission. To make up for the misunderstanding of Fanon's politics that he and so many of his young rebel comrades once had. To help guide the study by newer rebels of this complex and difficult reading. As part of his framework, Yaki chose a running critique of what is probably the most popular single book on Fanon, Deborah Wyrick's illustrated *Fanon for Beginners*. Wyrick's admiration for Fanon and her belief in his importance for people of color, gives her quick introduction to Fanon a fresh feeling. But, in his characteristic, bullet-on-target way, Yaki brushes all that aside to show how, over and over, in ways both crude and subtle, Wyrick's writing distorts and even lies about Fanon's basic politics. Yaki's study guide is a reminder that in studying we have to keep our eyes on the political answers being given.

Fanon's talk of "socialism" may seem outdated now, after the fall of bureaucratic state socialism around the world. But in really listening to Fanon's *Wretched*, we discover that his "socialism" is a communal rebellion of the grassroots villages against the capital, of the poor against the political parties that pretend to act in their name, of young armed rebels against officials and leaders, of communities against capitalism. It is still more than ever, our rebellion.

Much of this was written before Yaki left prison, and all of it—due to Yaki's untimely illness and death—before the phenomenon of "Obambi." Before the selection of some people of color to move so dramatically into top positions in the white settler power structure. Which has baffled many young rebels. Just as the popular enthusiasm over "one of our own" waving from Air Force One or leading White House Easter egg rolls, has made people soften their punches. It's what happens when anti-colonial rebellion is defeated, and new *neo*-colonial programs are installed by the ruling class. Although Yaki didn't get a chance to point this out, Fanon himself reminds us that capitalism massively turns to playing the race card (that it, itself, invented long ago, after all). In other words, capitalism turns to "Black" leaders and even "Black" political parties to sustain its hegemony over the now *neo*-colonized world.

Several important practical matters about this text: Yaki meant for his study guide to be read back and forth, side by side, with reading *Wretched* itself. But, he realized, there were *Wretched* editions of different sizes being sold. Which meant that the same passage would appear on different pages depending on whether you had the hardback, trade paperback, or mass market paperback edition. So he devised an intricate system of counting paragraphs within chapters, for letting his readers locate whatever *Wretched* passage he was discussing in whatever copy they had. Only, the original English translation in all versions that he and everyone else were using was replaced by the publishers with a different translation. The original editions with the translation Yaki uses became scarce books, hard to find and often expensive.

Starting a decade ago, a new edition was put out with a new English translation. A translation that is supposed to be less awkward and more up to date in its phrasing. Whatever its merits in that sense, it is also true that the "wily intellectuals" have taken over Fanon's own book. A big-name Harvard professor was appointed as the editor of the new edition, and he and the new translator both got to publish new individual introductions essentially promoting themselves inside the covers of Fanon's book. Even though it was now less available, Yaki continued to use the old translation because it was less academic, less literary, and because Yaki felt that it was truer to the rough spirit of Fanon's rebel stand. So, with no easy choices, the editors have left Yaki's numbering system for locating passages he is quoting or referring to just as it was. But, to help readers who don't have a copy of the now scarce earlier edition, in some cases where Yaki is talking about a key discussion in Fanon, the editors have added some more of Fanon's discussion from that passage. These quotations are set aside in shaded boxes running along the side of the page or at the page bottom.

The other thing is that *Meditations* is an unfinished work. Yaki wrote the different parts at different times, so in places his use of italics or bold text for emphasis was not consistent. He had completed the contents of the first three Parts—and Parts 1 & 2 were actually published as small pamphlets—but had not gone back over and standardized the style and grammar. The copy editors, not wanting to blur the individuality of his writing, only corrected typos but changed nothing else.

As for Part Four, it was never completed—it starts out as a rough first draft, where trial wordings are mixed with notes to himself to add this or say that. Often such notes to himself are marked by special brackets: {{like this}}. Soon enough, it is mostly notes and possible quotes to be used. The chapter is choppy, fragmentary, but still roughly completes an arc. The projected parts Five and Six that Yaki came to think were necessary, never, as far as the editors know, saw paper or were even in outline form. His cancer came on too rapidly and lethally for that. We will have to work without these. Still, *Meditations* is a major work, and in one sense it really is complete. Yaki never forgot how he first read Fanon but didn't really understand it. So, *Meditations* above all tries to teach us how to read seriously, critically, for ourselves. It was always our task to finish this path for ourselves. It is on us now.

the editors

Meditations on Frantz Fanon's The Wretched of the Earth

For NAC's and Other Activists Who
Struggle Against Racism
and Neo-Colonialism (Capitalism)
and for
the "Setting Afoot" of New People
(Socialist/Communist Humanism)

PART ONE

BY WAY OF INTRODUCTION

Comrads:

   Today, i started the fifth draft of this piece. My original intent had been to shape it for print and for distribution among a wide (and rather academic) audience. However, i've abandoned that aim, for two reasons. First, because i'm anxious to complete this project, and move on to others. Second, i want to return to a style of writing similar to that used to produce **Book One** of the *Journal*,[1] i.e., when i wasn't concerned about "style" or about meeting the assumed expectations of an (academic) audience. i hope that these "Meditations" will prove useful to you. They give me an opportunity to work out some ideas and to put some of them onto paper—as seeds, hopefully, for later development. i strongly suggest that none of you be content with merely reading these reflections. You should study and reflect upon your own copy of **Wretched**, the sources that i list, and any other related materials.

★ ★ ★

A NOTE ON CITATION

Because there are several editions of **Wretched** in print (i'm using the Grove Press, First Evergreen Edition, 1966), i'm not using the standard form of citation with reference to page numbers. Instead, i'm using a chapter-and-paragraph form. i've designated the chapters as follows:

Preface = "P"
Concerning Violence = "1"
Violence in the International Context = "1A"
Spontaneity: Its Strength and Weakness = "2"
The Pitfalls of National Consciousness = "3"
On National Culture = "4"
The Reciprocal Bases of National Culture
 and the Fight for Freedom = "4A"
Colonial War and Mental Disorders = "5"
Conclusion = "C"

i've also numbered each paragraph, separately for each chapter, so that, for example, (P.1) cites the first paragraph of the Preface; (2.5) cites the fifth paragraph of the second chapter; (4A.2) cites the second paragraph of "Reciprocal Bases..."; and (C.3) cites the third paragraph of the "Conclusion."

NB: From my reading of **Wretched**, i've determined that Chapter 1A ("Violence in the International Context"), is actually the first part of the "Conclusion"—that is, i believe they were separated by the editor/publisher, and not by Fanon. Nevertheless, i think they should be read as parts of a whole.

1. BACKGROUND ON
HOW AND WHY THE PROJECT WAS BEGUN

1A. The project was initially inspired by the reading of a paper by Ron Karenga, in which he cited Fanon and a number of others (e.g., Cabral, DuBois, Lenin and Gramsci), in support of his contention that petty-bourgeois intellectuals (or, the petty-bourgeois class as a whole—at some points he lumps these together), play "**the** decisive role in the theoretical and practical project of liberation."[2] (my emphasis) i believed that Karenga had distorted Fanon (and others) on this question. i happened to have a copy of **Wretched**, and i went to it to first check the lines that Karenga had quoted or paraphrased, and then to search the entire book for all references to the petty-bourgeoisie, and to intellectuals.

During this time, i mentioned to Amilcar that i was checking out **Wretched**, and that i had gained new insight into some of the issues that now confront us. He suggested that i write something that would help "unravel the book's complexity," because he had recently encountered young activists who'd picked up **Wretched** only to put it down before completing it, because they'd found it "too hard to read."

i didn't feel up to the task, nor did i want to put other projects to the side in order to give time to this. However, while not fully committed to writing on **Wretched**, i did begin to study it more meticulously, primarily for my own benefit, but also knowing that such study would be necessary should i decide to do a "breakdown" of sorts, for an audience of young activists, and attempt to emphasize the relevancy of the book's subject matter to our struggle, i.e., to strongly suggest that the book is relevant to contemporary issues, and that Fanon is as worthy of attention (if not more so) than most of the contemporary "public intellectuals" or "activist-scholars" feigning a radical or revolutionary stance these days.

As time passed, i began to feel as though i was experiencing something of a revelation, all the more so because i wasn't unfamiliar with the book. i'd read it for the first time in 1967 or 1968, and can't recount the number of times that i've opened its pages to check a reference or to read a few pages as a way of obtaining inspiration or orientation. i became convinced that i should write "something"—if only for myself and my comrads. That "something" is what you now hold in your hands.

1B. If you complete the reading of a (non-fiction) book today, you'll usually feel as though you know what it's about, that you've "got it" and don't have to return to it. However, if you pick up that book a month from now, or a year from now, you're bound to be surprised when it appears that you're reading lines that weren't there originally. You'll gain new insight into certain concepts that you thought you'd fully understood; you'll gain an understanding of propositions that had previously shot past you. What's happened between the first reading and the second? You've "grown"—had more experience, acquired more knowledge, become able to make more connections, grasp nuances that previously slipped through unnoticed or unappreciated.

It took me several readings before i was able to make out the outlines of the "forest" of **Wretched**. It was at this point that i could begin to distinguish sections within each chapter, and i then began to number the paragraphs of each chapter—and to read and meditate upon one paragraph at a time, then one section at a time. Sometimes i'd read through three or four paragraphs, or two or three sections, and then start over again. (For example, i divided "Concerning Violence" into eight (8) sections: paragraphs 1–6; 7–15; 16–30; 31–44; 45–66; 67–76; 77–87; and 88–99.)

Now, i know that some people will resist the adoption of a similar method, but i strongly suggest that anyone desiring to "fully" understand this book adopt a similar process. i've come across several references to **Wretched** made by academics (e.g. Cornel West), and it seems to me that they don't understand the book, and maybe a re-read would help them—assuming, of course, that they really want to be helped, since so many of them are representative of the "wily intellectuals" that Fanon scorches. (1.24)*

> EDITORS' NOTE: IN SOME CASES WHERE YAKI IS TALKING ABOUT A KEY DISCUSSION IN FANON, THE EDITORS HAVE ADDED SOME MORE OF FANON'S DISCUSSION FROM THAT PASSAGE. WHEN THE EDITORS HAVE DECIDED TO DO SO, ALL SUCH ADDED FANON QUOTATIONS ARE SET ASIDE IN SHADED BOXES RUNNING ALONG THE SIDE OF THE PAGE OR AT THE PAGE BOTTOM.

The proposed process is also time consuming, and some folks will feel that they could be reading other, more contemporary books, and not "wasting time" with this one. i'm reminded of a section of **Wretched** that somewhat applies here. (3.85)† It's not about being "fast" or reading everything that's published, or of reading whoever seems to be most popular at the moment. Don't let the market dictate your taste. Time taken to fully grasp this book will be made up in the better practice and the development of consciousness that result from adopting this method. Time taken to read and

---

* "But it so happens sometimes that decolonization occurs in areas which have not been sufficiently shaken by the struggle for liberation, and there may be found those same know-all, smart, wily intellectuals. We find intact in them the manners and forms of thought picked up during their association with the colonialist bourgeoisie. Spoilt children of yesterday's colonialism."

† "In an under-developed country, experience proves that the important thing is not that three hundred people form a plan and decide upon carrying it out, but that the whole people plan and decide even if it takes them twice or three times as long. The fact is that the time taken up by explaining, the time 'lost' in treating the worker as a human being, will be caught up in the execution of the plan. People must know where they are going, and why."

re-read **Wretched** will enable you to: 1) discern the b.s. in some of the other stuff that you read; 2) make more relevant connections to issues and concepts that you confront on a daily basis.

1C. The cover of my edition of **Wretched** says that it's Fanon's "study of the problems of racism and colonialism in the world today." Colonialism confronts us today, in a unique form (i.e., forms always differ from one country to another), shaping the context for OUR engagement with: racialized capitalist exploitation; internal class struggles; the nature and role of armed politics; relations between the people and the organizations that claim to represent them; Pan-Afrikanism/internationalism; the relations between our people and their allies in the imperialist state; the strengths and weaknesses in the theory and practice of nationalism; the struggle for socialism—all this, and more, is spoken to by Fanon in **Wretched**, and there are nuances and connections to our situation that We can't afford to ignore.

While reading **Wretched**, it's of course necessary to base ourselves on the concrete reality out of which it came and primarily speaks to. However, We must also be able to see the general in the particular (and, the particular in the general), and to recognize the extent to which OUR reality is being described and critiqued; the extent to which Fanon points the way forward for US.

It helps to know, going in, that Fanon speaks in several "voices," so to speak. He uses the "voice" of the "native" or "negro" who, during the colonial period (before the "fighting" starts), avoids confrontation with colonialism, and directs all physical and psychological violent impulses inwardly—while being envious of the position of the colonialist.

He speaks in the "voice" of the **ex-**"native" or **ex-**"negro" who—having decided to re-direct physical and psychological violence toward the colonialist—is not yet fully conscious, suffers setbacks, and allows the betrayals of the bourgeois forces that claim to speak for and to lead the struggle.

And, he speaks in the "voice" of the person who's overthrown *colonialism*, only to now confront *neo*-colonialism, realizing that "national independence" isn't the end of the struggle, and that the fully new people will develop only with the construction of the fully new social order.

Fanon is carrying us through a *process* of "decolonization"—through the stages of struggle for national independence *and* social revolution. However, he doesn't take us through a "linear progression" as (western) convention may have it. At one point he'll be talking about conditions and consciousness characteristic of the "period of colonization" or the "colonial period"—this is the "first voice" heard during the "peaceful" stage between colonial conquest and the beginning of the struggle to decolonize. He'll then move to some reference or discussion of the "decolonization" period—that between the beginning of the struggle and the winning of independence, and he may not always leave easily recognizable signs of transition. In the third chapter, he tends to move from the "decolonization" stage to the "post-independence" or neo-colonial stage—and then back again. Therefore, one must be able to distinguish the terms used to describe the several stages, because an inability to do so or a failure to do so can lead to confusion and a feeling that the book is "too complex."

Fanon treats the major themes in the same way, e.g., "violence" is not left to the first chapter, but actually runs from cover to cover; "spontaneity" (of "violence") is taken up initially in the first chapter; the "racism" and/or Manichean ideologies (i.e., those which are "dualistic," and present/view things in a "black and white" fashion) of both the colonizer and the colonized are treated, too, practically from cover to cover. How could these themes not be so treated, since We're dealing with the PROCESS and the stages in the evolution of peoples' consciousness, social revolution, and social development?

Maybe i should suggest that the chapters be read in the following order:

- First, read the Preface.
- Then, read chapters 1, 2, and 5, as parts of a whole.
- Then, read chapters 3, 4, and 4A, also as parts of a whole.
- Then, read 1A—which is not so much about "violence" as it is about reparations.
- and the Conclusion. (Again: 1A and the Conclusion are, i contend, parts of a whole.)

Chapter One introduces the themes of "colonial violence" and "revolutionary violence," i.e., that the violence of colonialism isn't merely physical or military, and that the violence of the oppressed peoples, once re-directed, must also take other than physical or armed forms. Ch. 2 is also on the theme of colonial and revolutionary violence, but focuses on the "spontaneity" of the initial forms of the people's violence—a spontaneity essentially characterized by its lack of coherence, consciousness, and foresight. Read Ch. 5 with Chs. 1 and 2 because it deals with violence and the need for the liberatory process to "concern itself with all sectors of the personality." (5.182)* Ch. 3 is about class struggle and what could be called Fanon's theoretical premises for the deconstruction of "race." Ch. 4

---

* "The Algerian's criminality, his impulsivity and the violence of his murders are therefore not the consequence of the organization of his nervous system nor of characterial originality, but the direct product of the colonial situation. The fact that the soldiers of Algeria have discussed this problem; that they are not afraid of questioning the beliefs fostered amongst them by colonialism... Once again, the objective of the native who fights against himself is to bring about the end of domination. But he ought equally to pay attention to the liquidation of all untruths implanted in his being by oppression. Under a colonial regime such as existed in Algeria, the ideas put forward by colonialism not only influenced the European minority, but also the Algerians. Total liberation is that which concerns all sectors of the personality."

and 4A deal with the formation of new (national) identity, with a focus on the need to deconstruct "blackness" or "niggerhood."

1D. i'm not sure that anything i say here will actually "unravel the complexity" of **Wretched** for anyone, but i am sure that if one sincerely wishes to understand what's being said by Fanon in the book, then one must read it, cover to cover, at least twice.

Don't, for example, read only the first chapter and then think that you know Fanon's position on "violence"; don't read the eleventh paragraph of the first chapter, without reading the last four paragraphs of the second chapter (or, the relevant lines in the third chapter), and think that you understand Fanon's position on "race" or "racism." An incomplete reading means superficial understanding and a distortion of your own development.

Moreover, i wouldn't suggest that one rely solely upon a book or paper by any author claiming to "explain" Fanon or **Wretched**, from any perspective, on any theme. Such material will probably prove useful, in one way or another, but it's no substitute for the real thing.

Shortly after our discussion, Amilcar sent me a copy of *Fanon for Beginners*, which has a chapter devoted to **Wretched**.[3] i found the book and the chapter in question to be informative. However, i also found the author to have certain biases which lent themselves toward an inaccurate appraisal of Fanon, and of **Wretched**.

Whatever one gets from an "easy read" (e.g., *Fanon for Beginners*), will be less rewarding than what will result from a personal venture through the "difficult" process of going to the source and struggling with whatever obstacles one may encounter. You'll come away with self-confidence, and an awareness appreciated all the more because it was achieved as part of a self-development undergone by mastering your fears, completing an intellectual process that you at first thought too difficult to attempt. Such a process of self-transformation and intellectual development is the central theme of **Wretched**, stated explicitly or implicitly on nearly every page (e.g., 3.85–96).*

Read **Wretched** (for) yourself. Study it. Take as much time as you think necessary. Don't be put off by any apprehensions or assumed "complexity," wanting everything to come to you easy and fast. You are equal to the task, and you'll get better as you go along. Dare to struggle—with your self. Dare to learn— and to apply what you learn to the transformation of your world.

2. SPEAKING TO THE SUBTITLE

2A. This piece is subtitled: "For NAC's and Other Activists Who Struggle Against Racism and Neo-Colonialism (Capitalism) and for the 'Setting Afoot' of New People (Socialist/Communist Humanism)."

i've come to think of these "Meditations" as an exercise in the process of creating a New Afrikan Communist "school of thought," developing, in part, through ideological struggle, theoretical development, the critique of past and present institutions, concepts, practices, etc.

Stretch yourself, and consider: Can We regard as an "historical necessity" that We are here today, calling ourselves "New Afrikan Communists," engaged, collectively, in the development of a shared world-view, in struggle for a socialist society? Are We not carrying on a tradition that, in one context, goes back thousands of years, to "communalism" or "primitive communism," and, in another context, ("modern") goes back, on these shores, at least to Peter H. Clark and the 1820s? Can We say that We've already begun to share the "school" as manifested by our practice—that the words We've produced, and the lines and ideas We've tested over the years, already lend themselves toward shaping a distinct body of thought? Can We pull from the *Journals*, from CROSSROAD, from the *New Afrikan Community Bulletin*, and from *The Grassroots*—from anything written by any of us—and say that We have examples of "New Afrikan communist thought"?

i'm not being purely rhetorical here. i'm suggesting that We should get more serious

---

* "In fact, we often believe with criminal superficiality that to educate the masses politically is to deliver a long political harangue from time to time. We think that it is enough that the leader or one of his lieutenants should speak in a pompous tone about the principle events of the day for them to have fulfilled this bounden duty to educate the masses politically. Now, political education means opening their minds, awakening them, and allowing the birth of their intelligence; as Cesaire said, it is 'to invent souls'."

about who We are and what We should be doing. i'm suggesting that affirmative answers can be given to the above, but We also have to work at it more consciously and systematically.

2B. Why call it "New Afrikan" communism, and not plain old "communism"? For much the same reason as We continue to say "Russian Communism" or "Chinese communism"; because "plain old communism" only exists as an ideal. There's theory, and there's practice... practice engaged on the base of the concrete conditions of one's own social situation. The actual construction of a communist society within any particular nation can only result in a form unique to that nation, no matter any similarities to the theory of communism held by other(s) nations.

Angolan, Russian, Algerian, Chinese, French, Vietnamese, Cuban, Korean, Tanzanian—these are nationalities. Our nationality is New Afrikan. We don't refer to ourselves as "black" because We don't base our nationality (nor our politics) on "race" or color or a biological element of our being. Social factors are the primary determinants of our national identity (and our politics).

Why not call ourselves "African-American" or "American" communists? For much the same reason that folks still talk about a "black America" and a "white America"—We are oppressed and exploited as a distinct people, and the particular development and present reality of "America" as a settler-imperialist state prevents any such identification. "Race" has been used to help realize and perpetuate the material and sociological factors that make us a distinct people. "America" (i.e., the United States) is an empire with a distinct nationality and world-view. So long as "America" means what it means, to people here and throughout the world, and so long as We're oppressed as a distinct people, it's hard for me to see us ever calling ourselves "Americans" of any political persuasion.

Why call it New Afrikan "communism" and not, say, "Marxism" or "Marxist Leninism"? Well, on one hand, because Marx wasn't a "Marxist," and Lenin wasn't a "Leninist"; because this kind of reductionism is part of the problem We face while sorting out what's relevant from the many other "schools," and trying to find our own way. Because "The struggle against narrow interpretations of Marxism, against West-centered reductionism, is part of the struggle for social and national liberation, of the struggle against ideological imperialism."[4]

We look back as far and as accurately as We can, into the social thought and practice of people on the planet, and We say that We can see an "original" socio-economic formation that We call "primitive communism" or "communalism": there was collective use of means and instruments of social production, prior to the development of huge surpluses, commodities and their exchange (value), and division of labor based on the exploitation of one group of people by another group of people; no concept of "ownership" or "private property" as We now know it; group interests were valued over individual ones, even while the individual was respected as an end in her or himself—yet, always within the context of collective work and responsibility, for no individual survived alone. The Bambara have a saying: "who am i without the others: In coming to life i was in their hands, and in leaving it i will be in their hands." We outline the primary characteristics of that type of formation—those kinds of social relations—and, together with a critique of the way We now live, We shape a vision of "modern communalism"—only these days We call it "communism."

Marx called it "scientific communism" or "scientific socialism," and he made particular contributions to that body of thought. However, We must remember that neither Marx nor anyone else singlehandedly "created" what We now regard as the theory of communism. From the communalism of the past, unto today, untold numbers of individuals and peoples have made and are making contributions to that body of thought. As they practice/struggle(d) to approximate the ideal in their actual social situations. (Nor can We overlook the roots of the philosophical base, i.e., dialectics, and a materialist world-view. That is, for example, as New Afrikan communists, when We begin to write our texts, We'll look to Egypt and other places along the south-eastern coast of Afrika as the source of understandings of the relation between thinking and being, from a materialist standpoint. If Marx, et al. claim to rest on the Greeks, then it must be understood that the Greeks rested upon the Egyptians. The fact is, the Greeks were unable to reconcile, to absorb or fully understand the system that they were "given", e.g., they were faced with a system that talked about the dialectical interaction of "four elements" as the source (earth, air, fire, water)—and Thales, for example, could only deal with water, and Democritus, as another example, could only deal with air. This disjointed system was, say, passed down to Hegel—it was thus "upside down" and when Marx made the switch on Hegel, he simply tried to right the distorted world-view of the Afrikans.)

Now, in case you missed it... The "four elements" are *material* elements... they are parts of a "creation mythology" that describes the origin of the world as arising from *within* the world, and not *outside* of it. You can call it a "primitive" materialism, if you like... and when you study, and notice the dialectics within the philosophical system of these early Africans, you can call that "primitive" dialectics, if you want. (Or, you can do as most of the so-called "Africanists" do and ignore these altogether.) But, *there* was the point of origin of what We today call "dialectical materialism"! Now, i know this subject needs more treatment, but it will have to be done at another time.

2C. The struggle against "racism" is, in the spirit of Fanon, one in which We struggle to become "anti-racist" in both our thought and our practice. It's also an attempt to approximate the communist ideal, transcending the boundaries of racialized discourse and practice that were erected by the oppressive apparatus, and which serve to reproduce, reinforce, and sustain it.

Because "race" and "racism" (like class and communism) will be discussed below, all i wanna say here is: No matter how We see the relation between "racism" and capitalism (e.g., that they arose simultaneously, or that one preceded the other), i think they should always be mentioned together. That is, i believe it's counterproductive to ever talk about "racism" without immediately and thoroughly linking it to capitalism, so that no one can be unmindful of the need to struggle against capitalism if they claim to be "anti-racist" or "against racism."

"Racism" is used to justify and facilitate the exploitation of peoples, and it's based on the false belief that humanity is divided into a plurality of "races" that stand in relation to each other as "inferior" or "superior" based on physical and/or cultural differences. There are no "races"—only people(s) and groups of people(s), united and distinguished by common history (social development), habits, interests, etc.—sometimes We call all of this "nationality" or ideology.

To be "anti-racist" is, first of all, not to hold the false belief in an alleged plurality of "races"; to be "against racism" is to combat all beliefs and practices that facilitate the exploitation of peoples, particularly when such exploitation is supported by the social construction of "race." Any attempt to destroy "racism" without an explicit link to the struggle against capitalism ultimately serves only to reinforce "racist" ideology and to shield capitalism from attack. On the other hand, an attempt to combat capitalism without an explicit link to anti-racist discourse and struggle allows capitalism to use the belief in "race" held by oppressed peoples, and appeal to the "racism" of citizens of the oppressive state, thus undermining all revolutionary initiative.

This combat also requires that We begin to de-link ourselves from the use of language that reinforces and reproduces racial ideology, e.g., the terms "white" and "black" in reference to the identity of peoples. This will be a difficult process, because: 1) the capitalist system depends upon continued use of such language, and its ideological apparatus is designed to oppose and undermine all attempts to de-link; 2) peoples oppressed through means of racial ideology have come to accept these terms as legitimate and as their own—even as they tend to acknowledge the constructedness of "race" and the terms used to make and perpetuate its "reality" (its reification):

> References to the realness of race are the means through which race as a reality is constructed.
>
> Abby Ferber

> ...[W]e always agree that "race" is invented, but are then required to defer to its embeddedness in the world.
>
> Paul Gilroy

Some of the seeds for my present perspective were given to me by Ngugi wa Thiong'o, in an article in which he discussed the thought and practice of writers under colonialism, who,

> ...did not always adequately evaluate the real enemy... Imperialism was far too easily seen in terms of the skin pigmentation of the colonizer. **Labor** was not just **labor** but **black labor**; **capital** was not just **capital but white owned capital**. Exploitation and its necessary consequence, oppression, were black. The vocabulary by which the conflict between colonial labor and imperialist capital was perceived and ideologically fought out consisted of white and black images sometimes freely interchangeable with the terms Europe and Africa.

> *The sentence or the phrase was "...when the white man came to Africa..." and not "...when the imperialist or the colonialist came to Africa..."; or, "...one day these whites will go..." and not "...one day imperialism or these imperialists will go..."! Except in a few cases, what was being celebrated in the writing was the departure of the white man, with the implied hope that the incoming black man—by virtue of his blackness—would right the wrongs and heal the wounds of centuries of slavery and colonialism.*
>
> *As a result of this reductionism to the polarities of color and race, the struggle of African people against European **colonialism** was seen in terms of a conflict of values between the African and European ways of perceiving and reacting to reality. But which African values? Which white values? The values of the European proletariat and the African proletariat? Of the European imperialist bourgeoisie and the collaborationist African petty-bourgeoisie? The values of the African peasant and those of a European peasant?*
>
> *An undifferentiated uniformity of European or white values was posited against an equally undifferentiated uniformity of African or black values. In short, the writer and the literature he/she produced did not often take and hence treat imperialism as an integrated economic, political and cultural system whose negation had also to be an integrated economic, political and cultural system of its opposite: national independence, democracy, and socialism...*[5]

Now, check this: Even as Thiong'o says all this, he himself defers to the embeddedness of "race" and its language, as he critiques the "reductionism to the polarities of race and color." More from habit, and failure to follow through on his own logic, Thiong'o (and so many others these days) continues to use "white" when he means "European" or "British" or "colonialism" or "capitalism"... he continues to use "black" when he means "African" or "Kenyan"...

2D. The "setting afoot of new people" is taken from Fanon. The last line in the book is: "For Europe, for ourselves and for humanity, comrades, we must turn over a new leaf, we must work out new concepts, and try to set afoot a new man." Of course, We read and say "new **people**," but the line captures, for me, what the book is really about—what the struggle for decolonization or for national independence... what the struggle for socialism is about.

To "turn over a new leaf" can mean, in this instance, the creation of a new set of social relations—socialist social relations. On the basis of these relations We seek the "attainment of so high a level of consciousness in all members of society that the norms of law and morality merge into a single code of conduct" for all members of the society.[6]

The phrase "new people" thus refers to the "immediate" (new) identity and social reality of the people as they struggle, and upon reaching a stage of independence and revolutionary seizure of power. It also refers to the on-going struggle and development of social relations that carry us toward that ideal code of social conduct, and economic arrangement.

Check this:

> *Decolonization... influences individuals and modifies them fundamentally... It brings a natural rhythm into existence introduced by new [people], and with it a new language and a new humanity. Decolonization is the veritable creation of new [people]... the "thing" which has been colonized becomes [human] during the same process by which it frees itself. (1.3)*

i think it's important to keep this concept of the "new people" in mind as We think and move all through each day, especially as it relates to the objectives of the struggle—objectives to be kept in mind no matter what the particular issue one deals with, because all issues are important, all are "revolutionary" and all are related to our need to help "modify individuals." Simply put: The objective of the struggle *is* to "modify" the people...

2E. "Humanism" is mentioned several times by Fanon in the book and, as i pointed to earlier, the book is about the struggle for a revolutionary, socialist, humanism, e.g.,:

> *The struggle for freedom does not give back to the national culture its former value and shapes; this struggle which aims at a fundamentally different set of relations between [people] cannot leave intact either the form or the content of the people's culture. After the conflict there is not only the disappearance of colonialism, but also the disappearance of the colonized [people].*
>
> *This new humanity cannot do otherwise than define a new humanism, both for itself and for others. It is prefigured in the objectives and methods of the conflict. A struggle which mobilizes all classes of the people and which expresses their aims and their impatience, which is not afraid to count almost exclusively on the people's support, will of necessity triumph... (4A.19–20)*

The humanism that We seek—a humanism that truly places its emphasis upon the social and political needs of the whole of the people—is the opposite of what passes as humanism under the bourgeois order. The bourgeois order claims to value the dignity and inherent worth of people, but its ideals of private property, individualism, and exploitation unmask the true concerns of capitalism's inhumane essence.

The revolutionary, socialist humanism that We seek has to be based on the collective/social ownership of the major means of production, the end of exploitation and all forms of oppression, because only on this basis can all people be allowed the conditions to fully develop **as individuals**, and to realize the ideals of humanism.

As We develop our new concept and practice of humanism, We'll need to keep the struggle against patriarchy and all forms of gender oppression also up front. How can We claim to seek to create a social environment that will allow the full and free development of each person, and not pull out all pillars of oppressive social relations?

3. A FEW WORDS ON THE PREFACE TO *WRETCHED*

You may be tempted, as i was, to skip the reading of the Preface, thinking it a poor substitute for the words of Fanon. Or, you may think it unnecessary to read what appears as one European's address to other Europeans, on purely European concerns. In either case, you'd be mistaken.

Sartre "says beforehand" essentially what Fanon says on most of the major themes of the book. i only take issue with one assertion made by Sartre, as you'll see below. Otherwise, the Preface is as good a place as any to begin one's study of, and meditation upon, **Wretched**.

3A. The struggle(s) against "racism" and colonialism (capitalism) involve struggle between classes (in both the objective and subjective senses of the term, i.e., as groups whose position is narrowly defined in economic terms, and as groups distinguished by their "stands"— their consciousness and their political and social practice). Sartre opens on the theme of class (struggle), i.e., the "manufacture" of a "native elite"—"a bourgeoisie, sham from beginning to end," which serves as intermediary between the people and colonialism, and is branded with "the principles of western culture." (P.1)

The contemporary decolonization process (our own, in particular), involves struggle between the class forces within colonized society, and is of central importance in the fight for liberation and social revolution. To paraphrase both Sartre and Fanon: In order to effectively engage and overcome the settler imperialist state, We must fight among ourselves—the two struggles forming parts of a whole, from beginning to end.

Some of the new concepts that We must work out involve "class"—to interpret or reinterpret the concept and break it free of definitions grounded in dogma, "west-centeredness," or the biases of other "schools of thought" and political tendencies. Our emphasis regarding the concept has to shift from the purely objective (i.e., relation to means of production, the size or source of income, etc.—all rather economistic), and begin to include the subjective criteria (i.e., the recognition of common interests and a common opponent; common organization to pursue those interests and defeat that opponent; a common vision of what We want the new society to look like; a common language—the medium for the new consciousness, etc.).

We also need to work out new concepts in relation to the major forms of class struggle, i.e., ideological, political, socio-cultural, as well as economic, and begin the efforts (theoretical and practical) to ground the new forms in a mass base, a "proletarian"/revolutionary/socialist line and class stand. i'd think that, overall, the most important form of mass-based class struggle would be ideo-theoretical—to promote the intellectual development of the majority of the people; to guide practice in all fields. It never hurts to raise these points, at every appropriate opportunity: The "anti-intellectualism" in the U.S. and the rest of the West (or, wherever) is about having the people hooked on a "what to think" program, rather than a "how to think" program. Everyone is or can/should be "intellectual," because We all have mental capacity and a need to develop and use it in the "collective mastery" of our society.

Fanon repeatedly points to the need for the people—not just the "intellectuals"—to be enlightened, to develop political and social consciousness; to accept responsibility for the entire social and political process. How can this be done if people don't think, question, develop their critical capacity, study the process of social development and know that they can change social reality?

And, as touched already, it's not just the "West," as We generally think of it, but "Marxism" in its predominant forms, which emphasizes economic elements (as does the bourgeois order itself) at the expense of ideological ones, superstructural ones. Thus, We overlook the importance of ideological struggle, the role of ideology (ideas) in the maintenance of capitalism—and in the struggle to overthrow it. If people are to struggle for a particular vision, they must make conscious decisions to do so... informed decisions.

When Sartre uses the term "manufacture" with respect to the colonized elite, he doesn't mean that no class structure existed in African societies prior to European colonization. Similarly, when he refers to the lack of homogeneity in the colonized world as being "born of colonial history" (P.6), that, too, needs clarification, because one would assume that any or all social, political, or economic divisions (i.e., class divisions and lack of "unity") in oppressed societies today are solely the result of imperialist oppression, and that's not the reality—even though some "elite" forces within oppressed societies find it in their interests to promote such a false image. Here's how Kwame Nkrumah attempted to correct the false image of "classless African societies":

> *Today, the phrase "African socialism" seems to espouse the view that the traditional African society was a classless society imbued with the spirit of humanism and to express a nostalgia for that spirit. Such a conception of socialism makes a fetish of the communal African society. But an idyllic, African classless society (in which there were no rich and no poor) enjoying a drugged serenity is certainly a facile simplification; there is no historical or even anthropological evidence for any such a society. I am afraid the realities of African society were somewhat more sordid.*
>
> *All available evidence from the history of Africa, up to the eve of the European colonization, shows that African society was neither classless nor devoid of a social hierarchy. Feudalism existed in some parts of Africa before colonization; and feudalism involves a deep and exploitative social stratification, founded on the ownership of land. It must also be noted that slavery existed in Africa before European colonization, although the earlier European contact gave slavery in Africa some of its most vicious characteristics. The truth remains, however, that before colonization, which became widespread in Africa only in the nineteenth century, Africans were*

prepared to sell, often for no more than thirty pieces of silver, fellow tribesmen and even members of the same "extended" family and clan. Colonialism deserves to be blamed for many evils in Africa, but surely it was not preceded by an African Golden Age or paradise. A return to the precolonial African society is evidently not worthy of the ingenuity and efforts of our people.

All this notwithstanding, one would still argue that the basic organization of many African societies in different periods of history manifested a certain communalism, and that the philosophy and humanist purpose behind that organization are worthy of recapture. A community in which each saw his well-being in the welfare of the group certainly was praiseworthy, even if the manner in which the well-being of the group was pursued makes no contribution to our purposes. Thus, what socialist thought in Africa must recapture is not the structure of the "traditional African society," but its spirit, for the spirit of communalism is crystallized in its humanism and in its reconciliation of individual advancement with group welfare...[7]

Pre-colonial African societies had their own "elites," their own classes and class struggles—imperialism merely arrested the <u>independent</u> development of these social formations, and stamped them with "the principles of western culture." Greed, exploitation, individualism, patriarchy—these weren't peculiar to the West, and they were among the indigenous traits looked for by colonizing agents as they sought out "promising adolescents" to join the first generation of "go betweens"—the very first "go betweens" were adult members of the colonized societies, whose pre-existing class consciousness and interests led them to serve the interests of imperialism, which found pre-existing African class structures and used them to serve its purposes. (P.1)

3B. Let's give some attention to the meaning of the "creation" of "native" elites—of course, not unrelated to colonialism's creation of the "native" (and, keeping in mind that Fanon makes an effort to point out that both the "native" and the settler, as "species," are creations of colonialism).

As Sartre describes the evolution of succeeding generations of the "elite" (also succeeding generations of "natives" or the changing structure of the colonized society under the impact of colonialism), he takes us from discussion of those who speak only when ordered to, through to the fourth generation, represented by Fanon: these are "**ex**-natives" (P.4–5), who begin to bend the language of the colonizer to the new requirements of the colonized people.

What is an "**ex**-native"? Essentially, the same as an **ex**-"colored," an **ex**-"negro" or an **ex**-"black"—even an **ex**-"African-American." Fanon gives the key when he points out that: *"Because it is a systematic negation of the other person, and a furious determination to deny the other person all attributes of humanity, colonialism forces the people it dominates to ask themselves the question constantly: 'In reality, who am I?'"* (5.6)

The "native" and the "negro," the "black" *and* the "African-American"—these are persons who are struggling for a new identity, which can only result when they attain—or, regain—freedom <u>as a people</u>. They are persons who have been denied independent development and the unfettered expression of their own ideologies. They haven't yet accepted the responsibility to develop a self-awareness, because they can't or won't de-link from the definition of "humanity" established by their oppressor—an oppressor constantly telling them that they aren't human.

Lets pick up Fanon:

> *The defensive attitudes created by this violent bringing together of the colonized [people] and the colonial system form themselves into a structure which then reveals* **the colonized personality.** *This "sensitivity" is easily understood if we simply study and are alive*

*to the number and depth of the injuries inflicted upon a native during a single day spent amidst the colonial regime. It must in any case be remembered that a colonized people is not only simply a dominated people. Under the German occupation the French remained men [i.e., people, human, and French]; under the French occupation, the Germans remained men. In Algeria there is not simply the domination but the decision to the letter not to occupy anything more than the sum total of the land. **The Algerians,** the veiled women, the palm-trees and the camels make up the landscape, the natural background to the human presence of **the French.***

*Hostile nature, obstinate and fundamentally rebellious, is in fact represented in the colonies by the bush, by mosquitoes, **natives** and fever, and colonization is a success when all this indocile nature has been finally tamed. Railways across the bush, the draining of swamps, and **a native population which is nonexistent politically and economically** are in fact one and the same thing. (5.7–8) (my emphasis)*

Reflect: The movie *Shaka Zulu*—the British "scouting party" is swept ashore by the storm. As they gather themselves on the beach, they're approached by a regiment of Zulu soldiers. Because he speaks the language of the Zulu, one of the party is taken to Shaka. In the next scene, Shaka asks him: "Of what tribe are you?," and the man answers, "Dutch."

When We cut to it, Shaka's question was about what We now call "nationality." Shaka asked the man, "of what **people** are you?" And, Fanon has just told us—what? That under German occupation, the French remained **French**; that under French occupation, the Germans remained **German**; that the **Algerians** made up part of the "landscape" to the "human" presence of **French** colonialism.

We'll get deeper into this below, but the point to be made here is that the problem arises when the colonized people "forget" who they are—"forget" that they **are** "human"—and succumb to the ideology of the colonizer which claims that only the settlers are "human." This results in the colonized people believing that they have to "prove their humanity" **to the colonizer**—but the standards are those of the colonizer, not those of the colonized. The colonized people simply fail to define—fail to continue to define—themselves... **for** themselves.

The "native," the "negro," the "colored," the "black," and the "African-American," have no identity apart from that given them by the colonizer—that is, not unless they RESIST colonialism, which entails: 1) their maintenance of an identity that is separate and distinct from that of the colonizer, and from that given them by the colonizer; 2) they begin to develop a NEW identity, through the process of "decolonization"—though having remained separate and distinct, colonized people aren't who they were prior to colonization, and they can't return to the past. Colonization has arrested their independent development, distorted who they are, and now they must become (a) NEW people during the process by which they regain their independence.

Now, the population native to the land under colonial domination is "nonexistent politically and economically." What exactly does that mean? In essence, it means that they aren't sovereign (which is why Fanon uses the phrase "the <u>restoration</u> of nationhood to the people"). It doesn't mean, in a strict sense, that they aren't "involved" in politics or that they aren't "involved" in an economic system. It means that the political and economic processes that they participate in are not of their own design, not under their control, and don't serve their interests.

This point is particularly relevant to us, and to neo-colonial situations generally, e.g., having a job and money and "being part of the American economy" doesn't mean that you're not colonized! Being able to vote in the **American** political process don't mean that you're not colonized! It all simply means that you've been tricked, and that you're still avoiding reality and confrontation with capitalism in its post-neocolonial form.

Here's another key point: It's not like i'm saying anything "new" here. DuBois was talking about this (the "double consciousness" and the need to make the choice between being a "negro" and being an "American"); Ralph Ellison talked about it in *Invisible Man* (when the guy was asking "WHO AM I?")

A "native"—or rather, an **ex**-"native"—is one who is "constantly in the making" (P.6; 1.22; 1.45 and 1.46) and who is cured of the "mental pathology which is the direct product of oppression" (5.9), and who claims an identity apart from that of the colonizer and the colonial system, and struggles to become a new person and to build a new society.*

* "In the period of colonization when it is not contested by armed resistance, when the sum total of harmful nervous stimuli overstep a certain threshold, the defensive attitudes of the natives give way and they then find themselves crowding the mental hospitals. There is thus during this calm period of successful colonization a regular and important mental pathology which is the direct product of oppression."

3C. Another important theme touched by Sartre in the Preface is that on the successive generations of "elites" (each generation also reflecting phases of colonial violence and the development of social/class structure and struggle, characterizing the fundamental contradiction, its aspects and forms), their roles and interests... the relations between the "elites" and the masses, and between the "elites" and colonialism.

As you read, stop now and then to meditate upon the similar development of generations of "elites" among our own people, and look for all of the implications and the need for re-interpretation of the Story. For example, was Phyllis Wheatley representative of the "promising adolescents" that were sought out among the Africans colonized by U.S. settler-colonialism? What she and others actually represented is, in one important respect, a matter of interpretation, i.e., from a "proletarian"/revolutionary (New Afrikan) and nationalist perspective, or from a bourgeois, assimilationist, colonialist perspective.

In Africa—and in New Afrika—the first generation of "elites" established under the colonial system, had little or no independent voice or initiative; they expressed little or no resistance to colonialism, and they didn't represent the revolutionary interests of the people. Who cares if Phyllis Wheatley was "the first negro to publish"—*What did she say?!!* Did she call George Washington a settler-colonialist/"slaveowner"? Did she call upon the newly-colonized Afrikans to rise up and throw off the chains? Did she bend the language to the new requirements of the people as they sought to regain independence and sovereignty?

The point is this: Even in 17th century "colonial America," (New) Afrikans were trying to regain their independence—that is, most of them were, while others were trying to accommodate themselves to the new colonial situation.

The 18th and 19th centuries, **here,** saw the rise of **our** second generation of "elites" (e.g., William Whipper), and there was also the rise of nationalist and socialist voices, speaking to the struggle to regain independence and create a new social system.

The third generation of "elites" was distinguished from those preceding it by a greater degree of frustration over their failure to be "included." They pushed the struggle for "integration" and "equality," while strengthening their base as a class. But again, there were "left" petty-bourgeois currents, the evolution of those earlier nationalist and socialist voices. Most importantly, there were the masses of the people, who had always maintained an identity and a set of interests that were (and remain) separate and distinct from those of the colonizer—without this base or foundation, the "elite" would have no standing.

Why are We not more aware of the social reality and political consciousness of the "lower classes" (the majority) of the people—not more aware of the existence of the nationalist and socialist currents in our social development? Because the tendencies that they represent haven't written (enough of) the "history" books or otherwise been legitimated as the propagators of OUR Story. The "elite" forces that write the books (especially those "marketable" or "acceptable" books), get time on talk shows and space in the U.S. press—they interpret our past and issue the commentary on current events through their own class perspective, and based on their own class interests—interests that they hold in common with their capitalist/colonialist masters.

Re-building requires re-orientation and re-interpretation. We don't yet have what could be called a revolutionary "people's history," because those doing the (media-promoted and legitimated) writing are part of the wrong class, and express the wrong interests. But, a reinterpretation of OUR Story is necessary, and there'll be no independence or socialism without it! The "intellectuals" who write what We need must represent a combination of those who "commit class suicide," and those who "come up from the people."

3D. These days it supposedly passes as common knowledge that a major consequence of—a major aim of—the counter-revolutionary initiative that went into high gear in the late 1960s and early 1970s was the thrust of pseudo-bourgeois and petty-bourgeois forces into "leadership"—and yet We claim to be confused and unable to explain the present absence of progressive and revolutionary momentum "from the bottom up."

i like to look to 1968—let's call it a "high tide" of our decolonization struggle. As symbols of the people's revolutionary-nationalist initiative, i see those Brothers standing with raised fists during the Olympic games—raised fists that were like raised flags of Red, Black and Green.

Look to 1968 and the establishment of the Kerner Commission, and its mandate: "To determine what happened; why it happened; what the U.S. needs to do to prevent it from happening again"!

The Kerner Commission was like any other body established by colonial powers (e.g., Kenya/Britain) to investigate "disturbances" in the colony, to divert the revolutionary drive of oppressed peoples into mere reformism; to grant "formal independence" and shape a neo-colonial solution. It can't be done without an alliance between colonialism and pseudo-bourgeois and petty-bourgeois forces among the oppressed people.

Underlying the "civil rights movement" and the "black power movement," the "riots," "rebellions," and "revolts," was a revolutionary (socialist) and a nationalist initiative. So, what did the settler-colonialist say? "Quick, quick, let's decolonize. Let's integrate, i.e., 'include' some of them, and make the rest of them believe that they are 'Americans,' too."

Reflect on this: It was in those same olympic games that George Foreman ran around the boxing ring waving the flag of the U.S.! Even symbolically this captures the reality of the moves made between 1968 and 1972: It represents the success of counter-revolution, the success of the neo-colonial solution (but it was really a post-neocolonial solution, because the first neo-colonial structure had been established one hundred years earlier), the ascendancy of the "new black middle class"—and the "black" liberation movement was turned into its opposite.[8]

Even Robert Allen's interpretation of the period can help to give sight to the blind:

> *In the United States today a program of domestic neo-colonialism is rapidly advancing. It was designed to counter the potentially revolutionary thrust of the recent black rebellions in major cities across the country. This program was formulated by America's corporate elite—the major owners, managers, and directors of the giant corporations, banks and foundations which increasingly dominate the economy and society as a whole—because they believe that the urban revolts pose a serious threat to economic and social stability, [and they are] attempting with considerable success to co-opt the black power movement. Their strategy is to equate black power with black capitalism.*
>
> *In this task the white corporate elite has found an ally in the black bourgeoisie, the new, militant black middle class which became a significant social force following World War II. The members of this class consist of black professionals, technicians, executives, professors, government workers, etc., who got their new jobs and new status in the past two decades. They were made militant by the civil rights movement; yet many of them have come to oppose integrationism because they have seen its failures. Like the black masses, they denounced the old black elite of Tomming preachers, teachers, and businessmen-politicians. The new black elite seeks to overthrow and take the place of this old elite. To do this it has forged an informal alliance with the corporate forces which run white (and black) America.*
>
> *The new black elite announced that it supported black power. Undoubtedly, many of its members were sincere in this declaration, but the fact is that they spoke for themselves as a class, not*

for the vast majority of black people who are not middle class. In effect, this new elite told the power structure: "Give us a piece of the action and we will run the black communities and keep them quiet for you." Recognizing that the old "Negro leaders" had become irrelevant in this new age of black militancy and black revolt, the white corporatists accepted this implicit invitation and encouraged the development of "constructive" black power. They endorsed the new black elite as their tacit agents in the black community, and black self-determination has come to mean control of the black community by a "native" elite which is beholden to the white power structure.

Thus, while it is true that blacks have been granted formal political equality, the prospect is—barring any radical changes—that black America will continue to be a semi-colony of white America, although the colonial relationship will take a new form.[9]

Remember: Allen published the above in 1970—take just a peep at what's happening today: George Curry, writing in *Emerge*, 11–99, that the attack on affirmative action "would essentially **wipe out the black middle class**. If **we** can't go to college in significant numbers, if **we** are not able to take **our** rightful place in the job market, and if **we** cannot take advantage of the tax dollars we provide to **our** government bodies, **we** will be relegated to a life of second-class citizenship." (my emphasis) He's talking to and for his class, not the people as a whole! Add to this Skip Gates, also speaking in *Emerge*, 3–99, as he talks about the role of his class and of his group of intellectuals at Harvard: "Our purpose is to get more black people to the middle class." Is this some sort of "black" "trickle down" theory? Do i really need to expound on this?

* "The starving peasant, outside the class system, is the first among the exploited to discover that only violence pays. For him there is no compromise; no coming to terms; colonization and decolonization are simply a question of relative strength."

† "It is within this mass of humanity, this people of the shanty towns, at the core of the lumpen-proletariat that the rebellion will find its urban spearhead. For the lumpen-proletariat, that horde of starving men, uprooted from their tribe and from their clan, constitutes one of the most spontaneous and the most radically revolutionary forces of a colonized people."

3E. Sartre's reference to the peasantry reminded me that Fanon's popularity among bloods in the U.S. in the 1960s rested, in part, upon his characterization of the peasantry and the lumpen as "revolutionary" and/or as the "vanguard." These characterizations have been widely and successfully challenged (or, clarified), over the years, and on an international level. While our practice has proven the unsoundness of prior beliefs, We've failed to put the premise to a thorough theoretical analysis, and put it to rest, which will allow this or similar incorrect views to surface again and to disrupt the momentum of the next revolutionary thrust.

A **revolutionary** class must: 1) recognize that it's a class, and that its members have common interests and enemies; 2) engage in conscious, unified action in pursuit of its interests; 3) act as the "vanguard" of the whole people. Fanon clearly described both the peasantry and the lumpen as initially absent these features. Why then did he refer to them as "revolutionary"? (1.49*; 2.45†)

These questions are all the more necessary because Fanon later described both the peasantry and the lumpen in different terms (e.g., 2.5–7; 2.59). And, his subsequent comments on the peasantry seem to confirm the observation that he saw in them a "force" that was "spontaneously" resisting certain "principles of Western culture," and that segments or strata of the peasantry sporadically resisted colonial occupation. Fanon "bends the stick" several times in **Wretched** in order to emphasize a point. In this instance, he bent it in order to contrast the "elite" and reactionary bourgeois classes and strata, against the "traditional," "patriotic," and progressive strata and class (embryonic) within the people as a whole.‡

Moreover, Fanon's characterization of the lumpen was also not uniform, i.e., he pointed to progressive and reactionary tendencies within the strata—leaving us to conclude that the lumpen is, essentially, of a petty-bourgeois character, i.e., vacillating, and illegitimate or would-be capitalists and parasites.

Keep in mind: Simply performing an objectively political or progressive act doesn't reflect a subjective class/revolutionary consciousness—just as consciousness alone is insufficient to change the world.

‡ "...we must remember that colonialism has often strengthened or established its domination by organizing the petrification of the country districts. Ringed round by marabouts, witch-doctors and customary chieftans, the majority of country-dwellers are still living in the feudal manner, and the full power of this medieval structure of society is maintained by the settlers' military and administrative officials." (2.5)

"Colonialism will also find in the lumpen-proletariat a considerable space for manoeuvring. For this reason any movement for freedom ought to give its fullest attention to this lumpen-proletariat. The peasant masses will always answer the call to rebellion, but if the rebellion's leaders think it will be able to develop without taking the masses into consideration, the lumpen-proletariat will throw itself into the battle and will take part in the conflict—but this time on the side of the oppressor." (2.59)

3F. Contrary to Sartre, Fanon's message to oppressed peoples **does** include important themes on the character and roles of citizens of settler-imperialist states. i'd like to think that Sartre was simply over zealous when, at (P.24), he says of Fanon: "If he had wished to describe in all its details the historical phenomenon of decolonization he would have spoken of us; this is not at all his intention."

That's simply not true, and Sartre even contradicts himself when, in (P.9), he says: "Why read it if it is not written for us? For two reasons: The first is that **Fanon explains you to his [people]** and shows **them the mechanism by which we are estranged from ourselves…**" And, in (P.10), he gives the second reason: That Fanon brings "the process of history into the clear light of day … the dialectic which liberal hypocrisy hides from you and which is as much responsible for our existence as for his." (my emphasis)

In the first pages of **Wretched**, Fanon introduces us to the Manichean ideology of the colonial system (of the West), and he makes it clear that the colonized people adopt this Manichean perspective in their evaluation of the settlers and themselves. However, as i pointed out above, Fanon is taking us through a process of development. By the end of the second chapter, he shows us how and why the colonized people begin to abandon that form of dualism.

In this connection, Deborah Wyrick asks: "How can a people wage an anti-colonial struggle without reinforcing and replicating the very categories that have organized its own oppression? Or, put another way, how can necessarily Manichean combat promote a post-Manichean world?"[10]

Fanon's answer, stated simply, is that the oppressed people must reject and abandon Manichean divisions if they want to avoid

reinforcing and replicating them. In a paragraph that should be reflected upon in its entirety, he points out that "Racialism and hatred and resentment... cannot sustain a war of liberation." (2.62)*

He then adds that the people reach a point in the struggle when they begin to "take stock of the situation, increase their knowledge and their political and social consciousness," and this allows them to: "pass from total, indiscriminating nationalism to social and economic awareness. The people who at the beginning of the struggle had adopted the primitive Manicheism of the settler—Blacks and Whites, Arabs and Christians—realize as they go along that the fact of having a national flag and the hope of an independent nation does not always tempt certain strata of the population to give up their interests or privileges... The people find out that the

---

* "Racial feeling, as opposed to racial prejudice, and that determination to fight for one's life which characterizes the native's reply to oppression are obviously good enough reasons for joining in the fight. But you do not carry on a war, nor suffer brutal and widespread repression, nor look on while all other members of your family are wiped out in order to make racialism or hatred triumph. Racialism and hatred and resentment—a 'legitimate desire for revenge'—cannot sustain a war of liberation. Those lightning flashes of consciousness which fling the body into stormy paths or which throw it into an almost pathological trance where the face of the other beckons me on to giddiness, where my blood calls for the blood of the other, where by sheer inertia my death calls for the death of the other—that intense emotion of the first few hours falls to pieces if it is left to feed on its own substance. It is true that the never-ending exactions of the colonial forces re-introduce emotional elements into the struggle, and give the militant fresh motives for hating and new reasons to go off hunting for a settler to shoot. But the leader realises, day in and day out, that hatred alone cannot draw up a programme. You will only risk the defeat of your own ends if you depend on the enemy (who of course will always manage to commit as many crimes as possible) to widen the gap, and to throw the whole people on the side of the rebellion. At all events we have noticed the enemy tries to win the support of certain sectors of the population, of certain districts and of certain chiefs. As the struggle is carried on, instructions are issued to the settlers and to the police forces; their behavior takes on a different complexion: it becomes more 'human'. They even go so far as to call a native 'Mister' when they have dealings with him. Attentions and acts of courtesy come to be the rule. The native is in fact made to feel that things are changing."

iniquitous fact of exploitation can wear a black face, or an Arab one, and they raise the cry of 'Treason'! But the cry is mistaken, and the mistake must be corrected. The treason is not national, it is social... In their weary road towards rational knowledge the people must also give up their too simple conception of their overlords. The species is breaking up under their very eyes. As they look around them, they notice that certain settlers do not join in the general guilty hysteria; there are differences in the same species. Such [people], who were before included without distinction and indiscriminately in the monolithic mass of the foreigner's presence, actually go so far as to condemn the colonial war. The scandal explodes when the prototypes of this division of the species go over to the [colonized people], become Negroes or Arabs, and accept suffering, torture, and death." (2.67)

Fanon continues: "The settler is not simply the [person] that must be killed. Many members of the mass of colonialists reveal themselves to be much, much nearer to the national struggle than certain sons [and daughters] of the nation. The barriers of blood and race prejudice are broken down on both sides... Consciousness slowly dawns upon truths that are only partial, limited and unstable..." (2.69)

Thus, We begin to refuse to identify ourselves—refuse to identify anyone—in "racial" terms. When Fanon says, early on, that "What parcels out the world is to begin with the fact of belonging to or not belonging to a given race, a given species"—he's not putting this forth as unalterable reality, but as something that needs to be changed. He's merely describing the Manichean world, the capitalist/colonialist world, the imperialist world; he's reflecting the state of consciousness of colonized peoples as they **begin** the struggle to become NEW PEOPLE.

When Fanon later talks about the "species" breaking up before our eyes (or, about "niggers disappearing", at (4.46)), he's talking about the break-up of "races" themselves—the "races" which were constructed as part of the construction of world capitalism, and which must be de-constructed along with the de-construction of capitalism. The break-up of the "species" now identified by skin color, becomes a new "species" to be characterized by what people think and by what they do... distinguished by social and political consciousness, and economic awareness.

Wyrick also notes that Fanon didn't separate **friends from enemies** by the use of any fixed notions, such as "race" or religion, and she cites a passage from Fanon's *A Dying Colonialism*: "For the F.L.N., in the new society being built, there are only Algerians. From the outset, therefore, every individual living in Algeria is an Algerian. In tomorrow's independent Algeria it will be up to every Algerian to assume Algerian citizenship or to reject it in favor of another."[11]

How did Fanon distinguish friends from enemies? Friends were those who actively worked for Algerian independence, i.e., the F.L.N. and its supporters in Algeria; anti-colonial people in France; formerly colonized nations throughout the world. Enemies were those who worked against Algerian independence, i.e., the colonial government in Algeria and its supporters; the government in Paris and its followers; developed nations with a vested interest in maintaining the imperialist status quo.[12] This is what allows "every individual living in Algeria" to be an Algerian. This is why friends and enemies are distinguished by the choices they make... the positions they take with regard to the struggle for independence and for socialism.

End of Part One

Notes to Part One

1. *Notes from a New Afrikan P.O.W. Journal/Vita Wa Watu*, Books 1 thru 12 (Combined), Spear and Shield Publications Collective.

2. "The African Intellectual and the Problem of Class Suicide: Ideological and Political Dimensions," *African Culture: The Rhythms of Unity*, ed. Molefi K. Asante and Kariamu Welsh Asante, Greenwood Press, 1985, pps. 91–106.

3. *Fanon for Beginners*, Deborah Wyrick, Writers and Readers Publishing, Inc., 1998.

4. *Class and Nation*, Samir Amin, Monthly Review Press, 1980, p. 4.

5. "The Writer in a Neocolonial State," *The Black Scholar*, July/August, 1986, pps. 2–10; pps. 3–4.

6. *Dictionary of Philosophy*, ed. Ivan T. Frolov, International Publishers, 1984, p. 76 ("Communist Public Self-Government").

7. "African Socialism Revisited," *Revolutionary Path*, International Publishers, pps. 438–445.

8. "On The Transition of the 'Black Liberation' Phrase, Concept, and Movement," *Vita Wa Watu*, Book Eight, Spear and Shield Publications Collective.

9. *Black Awakening in Capitalist America*, Doubleday, 1970, pps. 17–20.

10. Wyrick, op cit., p. 84.

11. *A Dying Colonialism*, Frantz Fanon, p. 152, Grove Press, New York, Evergreen Edition, 1967.

12. Wyrick, op cit., p. 85.

PART TWO

CONCERNING "VIOLENCE" AND THE DEVELOPMENT OF NEW PEOPLE

4A. In the first two chapters of **Wretched**, Fanon emphasizes that (armed) "violence" is essential to the initiation and maintenance of colonialism, e.g., "Their first encounter was marked by violence and their existence together—that is to say, the exploitation of the native by the settler—was carried on by dint of a great array of bayonets and cannon." (1.2) He also sets out to show how—and why—(armed) "violence" is also a necessary means for the successful pursuit of national and social revolution, because decolonization "can only triumph if we *use all means* to turn the scale, *including*, of course, that of [armed] violence." (1.5) (my emphasis)

Since the publication of **Wretched**, people have read those and similar lines, and come away with a narrow or one-sided concept of "violence"; they've read the first two chapters and come away with little more than a belief in the need to "pick up the gun." The people of Africa have suffered for this. We've suffered for it, and our children and grandchildren suffer for it today. Too many of us still fail to understand that the underlying aim of social revolution is to promote a *change in people* and to assist the development of political and social consciousness. Everything else that We usually associate with "revolution" or "national liberation" comes through and after change in people's consciousness!

Meditate on *"all means"*—most people read that line, and by the time they get to the last word in the sentence (violence), they've totally forgotten the "all means"! Consequently, what they come away with is something like: "Decolonization can only succeed if We use armed violence," and this reading and understanding leaves something out, and the absence proves itself in subsequent practice.

The use of **all means** demands theory and practice on all levels and in all social spheres. Our job is to determine how to do this based on the conditions that We find in our own social reality, especially as We want to move from a "low tide" to a "high tide." Our job is to acquire an understanding of the weak links in the system of oppression that binds us in the 21st century U.S.A., where revolution has "failed" not once, but several times before.

Meditate again, when you get to (1.6), as Fanon says that from the "actual formulation of the program," one must have decided to overcome *all* obstacles. Now, don't limit yourself and think that "all obstacles" will present themselves as only military phenomena. "All obstacles" means obstacles on the economic level, on the sociocultural level, and on the political level.

As you formulate a program, you must have a broad vision, a comprehensive social platform that addresses issues of mental and physical health, education, social services of all kinds, economic welfare, the production and distribution of food and clothing, adequate housing… You have to understand that you and the people are waging a struggle to fully control and administer your own society, and you must assume responsibilities beyond those of wanting to vent your frustration or act out your ideal conception of the heroic guerrilla and merely go out and shoot at someone. And, of course, this awesome responsibility, as James Boggs called it, requires united and coordinated effort, because no one person can do everything, but every person can do something—and all jobs are more or less equally important. That is, the "soldier" is no more important (may in fact be less important) than the person putting out the newsletter, or the person organizing the students, or the person agitating on issues such as no-rent housing, or people's control of the air-waves...

This need to understand that all means must be used is why Fanon quickly brings to our attention subjects which are meant to sharpen our understanding—and to broaden our concept—of "violence," (e.g., Manichean (dualist), white supremacist, and racial ideologies—and later points to the process of their deconstruction; forms of "avoidance" employed by oppressed peoples, and the ways that they/We exercise violence upon each other, while avoiding confrontation with the oppressive apparatus; narrow, bourgeois nationalism, and its pitfalls; the process of forming new, collective identity; relations between "leaders" and the people—class struggle—and the need for ever-greater people's democracy—all of this in the first chapter). He does this in order to show that *colonial* "violence" is a single process, which manifests itself in several forms (socio-cultural, political, economic, and military), and that "counter-violence"—the *revolutionary* "violence" of oppressed peoples—must also be exercised as a comprehensive process, assuming several forms. It's within this context that Fanon speaks of "violence" as he closes the second chapter: "Violence alone, violence committed by the people, violence organized and *educated* by its leaders, makes it possible for the masses to understand *social truths* and gives the *key* to them." (2.70) (my emphasis)

Meditate: What does it mean to "educate" violence—so that the people may thus understand **social** truths? How does the "education" of violence give the key to the people? Most importantly, what is the "key"?

Maybe We're not far enough into the book to begin answering these questions, or maybe We can go back to the Preface in the search: "...*In this violence which springs from the people... the military, political and social necessities cannot be separated.*" (P.22) Could it be that to "educate" violence We must increase our political and social awareness?

"Violence" is educated—the people are educated—via the development of theory and the conduct of practice in all areas of social life. "Violence" is "educated" as the people develop their political consciousness, and as they assume what Le Duan calls "collective mastery" of the society.

The "key" can't be a key to "violence" (narrowly speaking, mere armed forms), because an "educated" violence is that which provides the "key." Only when We understand "violence" (i.e., colonial and revolutionary) in a broad way can We begin to understand the "key" as: the awareness derived by the people of their role as the makers of history—"history" here being all of the activity of people in pursuit of their aims as a sovereign entity. Making history requires the making of informed choices, and the making of decisions to act in one way and not another. Choices must be made based on a particular interpretation of reality. Read **Wretched** carefully, and you'll see that Fanon talks much less about the use of arms than he does about the need for the people to develop their consciousness, and to learn to lead themselves...

Check it out: Here We are reading a chapter on "violence"—which most of us think of only in terms of arms or physical force—but how much does Fanon actually talk of arms or physical force? You might expect every page to contain some mention of guns, knives, armed encampments, guerrillas training in the forests, nightly raids on the farms of settlers, attacks on local police stations or military outposts—but how much of this is actually there, in this chapter on "violence"? Not much, you say? Well, **why do you think that is?**

Fanon doesn't talk much about guns or *armed* forms of violence because it's the other forms—rather, it's the whole—of colonial violence that most concerns him, e.g., "In the colonial context, the settler only ends his work of breaking in the native when the latter admits loudly and intelligibly the supremacy of the white man's *values*. In the period of decolonization, the colonized masses mock at these very values, insult them, and vomit them up." (1.16) (my emphasis)*

Many of us used to think that "Values" weren't important, and we thought this, in part, because some among us used to think (and some still think) that "Values" were the "whole" and they're not... they are an important part of the whole... we must give attention to all parts... of the whole.

Colonial violence must be negated by *revolutionary* violence, i.e., when the colonized mock Western and Euro-American values, insult them, and vomit them up, during the period of "decolonization"—a period, in fact, comparable to our 1960s and early 1970s, when We had, for example, a "black arts movement," and debated the need for, and the value of, a "black aesthetic," and

---

* "As soon as the native begins to pull on his moorings, and to cause anxiety to the settler, he is handed over to well-meaning souls who in cultural congresses point out to him the specificity and wealth of Western values. But every time Western values are mentioned they produce in the native a sort of stiffening or muscular lockjaw. During the period of decolonization, the native's reason is appealed to. He is offered definite values, he is told frequently that decolonization need not mean regression, and that he must put his trust in qualities which are well-tried, solid, and highly esteemed. But it so happens that when the native hears a speech about Western culture he pulls out his knife—or at least he makes sure it is within reach. The violence with which the supremacy of white values is affirmed and the aggressiveness which has permeated the victory of these values over the ways of life and thought of the native mean that, in revenge, the native laughs in mockery when Western values are mentioned in front of him. In the colonial context the settler only ends his work of breaking in the native when the latter admits loudly and intelligibly the supremacy of the white man's values. In the period of decolonization, the colonized masses mock at these very values, insult them, and vomit them up."

the poets rapped about new values as they mocked those of "the man"; the singers sang about new values as they insulted those of "the system"; the writers wrote novels and essays about new values as they vomited up those of "white america"... But today, We still send our children to the schools of *the* U.S., where they pledge allegiance to the U.S. and its flag, and in a thousand ways, every day, We and our children admit loudly and intelligibly the supremacy of Euro-American, *capitalist* values, and demonstrate the effectiveness of colonial violence and the absence of a counter-violence, a revolutionary violence, which negates the influence of "foreign" values (i.e. *capitalist* values) in our homes and in our minds...

We can take it backward, without a break, to, for example, the 1660s, and see that there and then, too, We mocked the settler's values even as he tried to suppress our new national identity and undermine our purpose of (re)gaining our (new) national independence—"What's your name, boy?" ***"Kunta Kinte,*** *motherfucker!"*

We seldom, if ever, think of ourselves as among those petty-bourgeois forces in need of committing "class suicide"—but We must remember where We are. Here, in the seat of empire, even the "slaves" are "petty-bourgeois," and our poverty is not what it would be if We didn't in a thousand ways also benefit from the spoils of the exploitation of peoples throughout the world. Our passivity wouldn't be what it is if not for our thinking that We have something to lose...

How much more necessary must it be for us to focus on the need to develop a revolutionary consciousness, here in the belly of the beast, where even the so-called radical left is little more than an appendage to bourgeois liberalism and in many cases serves as a buffer between capitalist-colonialism and a peoples' struggle for independence and socialism. All critical thought is suppressed by the media and the market—and, the educational process!

4B. Let's start with same questions and meditate on the first paragraph of the first chapter: "National liberation, national renaissance, the restoration of nationhood to the people … whatever may be the headings used or the new formulas introduced, decolonization is always a violent phenomenon … the replacing of a certain 'species' of [people] by another 'species' of [people]. Without any period of transition, there is a total, complete and absolute substitution … To tell the truth, the proof of success lies in a whole social structure being changed from the bottom up." (1.1)

I've meditated on this paragraph and, among the questions i've raised about it are: 1) What is "violence," and why is it (always) necessary?; 2) What is "decolonization"?; 3) What is "social structure," and why is change thereof a necessary criterion for the success of the struggle?; 4) What does Fanon mean by "species" and why does he put it within quotation marks in this paragraph?; 5) Why does he refer to the "restoration" of "nationhood"—and what is a "nation"?

Only after going through **Wretched** several times, and then returning to reflect on this paragraph, was i able to recognize the context (or, the "voice") in which Fanon was speaking here. That is: 1) He appears to be telling us what **is**, but he's actually telling us what **was**; 2) He seems to be speaking in absolute terms, suggesting, for example, that there will not be, or should not be, a "period of transition," and that instead there be a simple, mechanical, "substitution" of "species"—a mere change of place, one for the other. This is not the case.

Taking us through the process of struggle, Fanon starts at the "beginning" of the birth of revolutionary consciousness and confrontation; he gives us a look through the eyes and into the mind of the colonized person who stands in the colonial period and is only beginning to engage the process of decolonization. That is, it's in the colonial period that the people look ahead and tend to believe that there should be no period of transition, and they assume that there will be a simple substitution of themselves for the settlers. At the beginning of the struggle, the people don't understand, for example, the multiple meanings of the term "species" that causes Fanon to qualify it (in fact, the word is placed within quotation marks to warn us not to take it at its conventional meaning).

i know it's kinda like giving away the plot, but We need to jump to the second chapter for a moment, and try to unravel a bit of "complexity," because it's there that Fanon, then speaking in the voice of one who's matured a bit and suffered a few setbacks during the decolonization period, tells us that: "...While the native thought that he could pass without transition from the status of a colonized person to that of a self-governing citizen of an independent nation, while he grasped at the mirage of his muscles' own immediacy, he made no real progress along the road to knowledge. His consciousness remained rudimentary..." (2.61)

Now, i've chosen to make this connect between the first and second chapters... between the subjects of "violence" and "spontaneity" as a way of erecting my own flashing light, and to make the point that Fanon makes repeatedly throughout the book, but that We tend to miss: It's not a mere matter of using armed forms of struggle. To paraphrase Fanon, the people can't become self-governing citizens in a truly independent nation, without developing their consciousness, no matter how much or how well they "fight" or how skillful they are in the use of weapons. Failure to grasp this fact accounts for much of the backsliding among would-be activists, and for many of the failures of past attempts at revolutionary transformation on these and other shores. **"National liberation" or "revolution" is about the transformation of people and their consciousness.**

Fanon started by giving us a glimpse of the state of people at the beginning and We should reflect upon our own beginnings, past and present. In our present, We stand in what i call a "post-neocolonial" period, but no matter what it's called, it's a period of beginnings, a period "before the fighting starts" and We're engaged in building foundations for a renewed effort to decolonize... to de-link from the capitalist way. In this context, Fanon reminds us that as We look ahead, We must be able to determine "which is a true decolonization [i.e., one in which the people have developed a revolutionary consciousness and assumed 'collective mastery'] and which a false," and the importance of a coherent perception of appropriate means and tactics, i.e., "how to conduct and organize the movement." (1.45)

In order to determine the best means and properly conduct the struggle, We gotta ask questions... call into question everything about colonialism, post-neocolonialism, *and capitalism*. Some people may think that the raising of questions (such as those i raised above about the first paragraph) is unnecessary, or that the answers are obvious. i've read that first paragraph more times than i can remember, but the questions weren't always raised, and the answers weren't then, nor are they now, obvious. My understanding of **Wretched** and of Fanon's thought, and of the/our social revolutionary process always suffered for my failure to raise and properly answer these and similar questions. i know i'm not alone.

When Fanon implores us to "question everything," We must take that literally, and probe the meaning and implications. Underneath it all is a quest to share with Fanon "that obsession... about the need for effort to be well-informed, for work which is enlightened and freed from its historic intellectual darkness," (3.88) so that We may "hasten the growth of consciousness... a necessity from which there is no escape" if We wish to make progress. (3.75) Through the process of raising questions, We challenge ideas and structures, and We transform ourselves—all through reflection. Fanon wants us to raise questions because he wants us to think—critically. This is a simple, but fundamental point, one of the "keys" to a truly independent and progressive future.

Reflect a bit, too, on the phrase "intellectual darkness" and get away from the conventional, Western, Euro-American idea that "ordinary people" aren't, can't be or shouldn't be "intellectual." Get away from the idea that only certain people or groups can be "intellectual," and think about everyone as "intellectual." Even go back to the first paragraph and reflect on that question about the social structure being changed, from the bottom up, and connect this to the need for ALL of the people to develop and exercise their mental capacities in the effort to solve the theoretical and practical problems of the society. This reminds me of a line from George Jackson, re: the oppressive state has molded the people through a "what to think" program, and the task of the people is to develop a "how to think" program. To question. To imagine that things can be different and that the people themselves—that *you*—can make all necessary changes. There will be no revolution without theory or without mass participation and the assumption of responsibility by you/the people.

As We attempt to "re-build," it's fitting that We re-read and meditate on this book by Fanon, especially if We understand its relationship to the problems that We face forty years after it was written.

There are some who think that the slogan "re-build" means that We, in some mysterious way, "start where We left off," meaning the "high tide" of struggle in the 1960s and early 1970s. It's assumed that We can start to rebuild by miraculously producing an instant "high tide" which, of course, should include armed actions. It's assumed that the new high tide can be created by simply wishing for it, or calling for it. It's assumed that armed actions are appropriate simply because some of us are angry or frustrated, or mistake our consciousness for that of the people. It's also assumed that the high tide was arrested by the mere repression of the movement by the settler-imperialist state, and had nothing to do with our own shortcomings. My generation may remember Mao saying that, on occasion, when the revolution fails, it's the fault of the so-called "vanguard."

We need to understand: The *old* movement is dead, and *it* can not be rebuilt! We can not return to the past, or rebuild the past, nor can We build a NEW movement without sufficient *foundation*. If We consider that the late 1960s represented the "high tide" of a process, We have to know when and how that process was started—a "high tide" is the result of the kind of work that most of us shun as if it were a plague.

In this instance, We're like those "militants" Fanon refers to, who must go to the countryside and/or to the mountains, "toward bases grounded in the people." (1.21) and, i'm not even talking about what to do when one reaches those bases, just that those bases must be approached. Hopefully, We won't act like the Vietnamese cadre (see: CROSSROAD, Vol. 9, n. 4, Spring, 2001, pps. 9–11) who got to the base but didn't know what to do or how to do it, and blamed his shortcomings on the people. He merely cursed reality because he didn't fully appreciate that his job was to change reality—to take it as it was/is, and transform it into the pattern of new customs and the plan for freedom. (1.43)

We can even put it another way: If We wanna help to build a NEW revolutionary movement, among the things that We must do are: 1) thoroughly re-examine the past, learn the lessons, and begin to use what We learn while, 2) building bases grounded in the people, learning from them, sharing our knowledge with them, becoming one with them, and share with them as one of them the responsibility for leadership of the movement and for the new society that We're creating.

We have to start this process by finally admitting to ourselves that the old movement is dead. We have to acknowledge that, say, We didn't take George Jackson to heart when he told us what We needed to do in order to keep the people from becoming "Americans" again, after they left the marches and rallies… ten minutes after the success of the state's strategy to neutralize the movement, create new "buffer classes" of pseudo-and-petty-bourgeois "spokespersons/leaders"…

> The effectiveness of rallies and mass demonstrations has not come to an end. Their purpose has diacritically altered, but the general tactic remains sound. Today, the rally affords us the opportunity to effect intensive organization of the projects and programs that will form the infrastructure… If the mass rallies close, as they have in the past, with a few speeches and a pamphlet, we can expect no more results than in the past: two hours later the people will be americans again… But going among the people at each gathering with clipboards and pens, and painfully ascertaining what each can contribute to clear-cut, carefully defined political projects, is the distinction between organization and… sterile, stilted attempts…[1]

Today, the people ARE "Americans"—even most of the so-called "radicals" and "nationalists" ARE "Americans" at heart. They are consumers and proponents of consumption. They are taken by the "commodity fetish." They will not advocate real revolution and the armed forms of struggle that must be part of the process; they won't support any sincere attempt to generate such a process. These are the people about whom Fanon said, "their objective is not the radical overthrow of the system." (1.46)* In all the scholarly work that they do, they won't write about the Nat Turner's [rebellion] or hold seminars on the legitimacy of the counter-violence of oppressed peoples: "...and it sometimes even happens that they go so far as to condemn the spectacular deeds which are declared hateful by the press and public opinion in the mother country." (1.52) They will support Mumia because they think he's "innocent"—but they won't support Sundiata Acoli or Basheer Hamid or any of the other Political/Prisoners of War that languish behind the walls, years after the memories of "the struggle" have faded…

Would-be cadres think that all they should have to do is give a brief talk about how bad things are, and why the people should resist (i.e., take up arms), and think that this is all that's necessary—and then curse the people when they don't respond as We think they should… as if this is enough to **change a mindset that's reproduced**

---

* "What are the forces which in the colonial period open up new outlets and engender new aims for the violence of colonized peoples? in the first place there are the political parties and the intellectual or commercial elites. Now, the characteristic feature of certain political structures is that they proclaim abstract principles but refrain from issuing definite commands. The entire action of these nationalist political parties during the colonial period is action of the electoral type: a string of philosophico-political dissertations on the themes of the rights of peoples to self-determination, the rights of man to freedom from hunger and human dignity, and the unceasing affirmation of the principle: 'One man, one vote.' The national political parties never lay stress upon the necessity of a trial of armed strength, for the good reason that their objective is not the radical overthrowing of the system. Pacifists and legalists, they are in fact partisans of order, the new order—but to the colonialist bourgeoisie they put bluntly enough the demand which to them is the main one: 'Give us more power.' On the specific question of violence, the elite are ambiguous. They are violent in words and reformist in their attitudes. When the nationalist political leaders *say* something, they make quite clear that they do not really *think* it."

and reinforced by print media and soap operas, romance novels and ads for cosmetics and cars and gadgets that claim to solve all of our problems. We become confused when We find that the five minute talk isn't enough to *overcome the pressures that force people to conform—on the job, or to give in to the children who want the latest fashions, toys, and video games...* But then, we want those *things* ourselves, don't we? The consumers that We are... The "Americans" that We are...

Check it: All of this is about "values" and it's about the forms of colonial violence that creep into our homes and into our minds. The job of the would-be cadre is to begin to analyze and understand our concrete reality and to apply what We learn in the books to this reality. We have to be creative in shaping forms of "revolutionary violence" in order to negate colonial violence in all its forms, on all social levels.

But dig this: It's *always* about "concrete conditions"... You have to figure out exactly where We are **today**—"what is this place?"... how did We get here... sound too simple, really, which may account for our inability to grasp it in a timely manner... forcing us to have to start from scratch every thirty or forty years...

We study other revolutions... the struggles of other peoples... and We are inspired by them. However, We find it hard to generate a struggle of our own, because We still have, on one hand, that "great divide" among ourselves, i.e., those that wanna be free, and those that wanna accomodate themselves to "the fetish"...

These days, agitation is not to be based on the integration of a water fountain or a bus, but, say, the robbery of the people by the insurance companies and those that make the legal drugs that far more people are addicted to than those using the crack... The people are being stuck up every time they fill their gas tanks.

i would be irresponsible if i failed to note this essential point for any one serious about "change" these days (a few of you already practice this point): You cannot do the depth and breadth of "the work" if you **all** have to spend twelve hours a day working for IBM—because you have to pay rent and there are other bills… Some of us have to rethink the "collective," 21st century style… "contemporary" america style. Some of us will have to support at least one cadre!!! At least one **real** cadre…

Working for "change" is a full time job, and We can't continue to try to do this work solely from within 501(c)(3)'s… or by using the few hours per day "after work," that We say We're using for "the cause"…

4C. What is "violence," and why is it (always) necessary for successful decolonization? Since We're talking about the colonial (and capitalist) context, it will be necessary to know something about colonialism and how "violence" is manifested in the colonial context (i.e., colonial violence).

In my search for answers to the questions, i first went to the dictionary and then to the Thesaurus, and here is what i began to work with: Violence is that which INJURES (i.e., it does an injustice to; it wrongs, harms, impairs, and tarnishes the standing of; it gives pain to, as in "to injure one's pride"; it's detrimental, defamatory, and it violates others).

Violence is that which ABUSES (i.e., even with words—it reviles); it's that which puts to a wrong or improper use; violence is maltreatment. Check it: Every time you say "nigga," "bitch" or "ho," you're committing a violent act!

Violence is TREATMENT (i.e., behavior—to bear oneself toward; to act upon, especially to alter or manipulate), or PROCEDURES (i.e., action, conduct, process), that DISTORTS (alters out of original condition or situation; deforms or falsifies), INFRINGES (breaks, defeats, frustrates, encroaches upon in a way that violates another), or PROFANES (i.e., debases or defiles).

Colonialism (***and capitalism***), in the economic, political, and socio-cultural forms, brings "violence" into the home and into the minds of the people (1.7 & 1.8), and the process of decolonization (revolutionary counter-violence) is a battle to be waged in the media and in the marketplace, the sports arena, and the barber shops and street corners even as We select subjects to be discussed... (1.7–8)*

Colonialism is a form of imperialism, and imperialism is an international expression of capitalism—you don't fully understand colonialism, and you don't successfully attack it, without understanding and attacking capitalism.

---

* "The colonial world is a world divided into compartments. It is probably unnecessary to recall the existence of native quarters and European quarters, of schools for natives and schools for Europeans; in the same way we need not recall Apartheid in South Africa. Yet, if we examine closely this system of compartments, we will at least be able to reveal the lines of force it implies. This approach to the colonial world, its ordering and its geographical lay-out will allow us to mark out the lines on which a decolonized society will be reorganized.

"The colonial world is a world cut in two. The dividing line, the frontiers are shown by barracks and police stations. In the colonies it is the policeman and the soldier who are the official, instituted go-betweens, the spokesmen of the settler and his rule of oppression. In capitalist societies the educational system, whether lay or clerical, the structure of moral reflexes handed down from father to son, the exemplary honesty of workers who are given a medal after fifty years of good and loyal service, and the affection which springs from harmonious relations and good behavior—all these esthetic expressions of respect for the established order serve to create around the exploited person an atmosphere of submission and of inhibition which lightens the task of policing considerably. In the capitalist countries a multitude of moral teachers, counsellors and 'bewilderers' separate the exploited from those in power. In the colonial countries, on the contrary, the policeman and the soldier, by their immediate presence and their frequent and direct action maintain contact with the native and advise him by means of rifle butts and napalm not to budge. It is obvious here that the agents of government speak the language of pure force. The intermediary does not lighten the oppression, nor seek to hide the domination; he shows them up and puts them into practice with the clear conscience of an upholder of the peace; yet he is the bringer of violence into the home and into the mind of the native."

Colonialism is a comprehensive system, operating on all social levels (economic, political, cultural), and is not a mere expression of military aggression, i.e., "violence" in physical forms.

In most cases, colonial violence in armed/physical forms is preceded by unarmed and nonphysical forms of aggression, in the guise of traders, academics, missionaries—who seek not only to lay hold of the land and labor of the peoples, but also to lay hold of their minds, their customs, and their languages. These violent actions suppress, distort, injure, frustrate, infringe, profane and unduly alter the targeted peoples and their social orders, and cripple the people's ability to resist and to regain their independence!

Let's take a look at Wyrick's description of colonialism:

> Colonialism means the forceful occupation of another people's land in order to extract material benefits; thus it means compelling the colonized to work for the colonizer's economic interests. If there aren't enough suitable native workers, more can be imported. This is where slavery comes in handy. Fanon believes that colonialism depends on racism. Enslaving or oppressing another group of people is easier if they look different than you do. Colonialism also means imposing the cultural values of the colonizing nation upon the colonized; this is called "the civilizing mission" or "the white man's burden." Such phrases mask and justify the massive theft that drives the colonial project. Modern European colonialism began with Columbus. Voyages of discovery involved claiming "new" land for European powers.
>
> The growth of consumer capitalism mandated the growth of colonialism, and vice versa. "Exploitation colonies" had the sole purpose of producing wealth and extracting marketable commodities—Caribbean plantation colonies are prime examples.
>
> "Settler colonies" had the additional purpose of moving large groups of people from the colonizing nation to the colony—the United States was a settler colony, as was Australia...[2]

Colonialism is a single process, manifesting in several forms, and each of these forms "injures" oppressed peoples, i.e., colonialism is, as a whole, a form of: the exploitation of natural resources, and the prevention of the independent development of industry; the drawing of arbitrary national borders, and the implantation of alien political systems; the imposition of a Euro-centric educational system, and the distortion of the history of the colonized people; the daily psychological trauma—"the injuries inflicted upon a native during a single day spent amidst the colonial regime" (5.6 & 5.7)—or the use of arms to enforce all of the above.*

Therefore, colonial violence must be negated by revolutionary violence, that "violence" exercised by oppressed peoples *which contests for power by opposing the ideas which uphold the existing social reality and creates new ideas and a new social reality.* Revolutionary violence contests colonial rule on the streets, in the schools, in the homes, and in hospitals; it repairs what colonial violence has impaired; it renews the momentum and initiative that colonial violence has caused to stagnate; it liberates what colonial violence has arrested, e.g., "Colonialism is not satisfied with merely holding a people in its grip and

* "Because it is the systematic negation of the other person and a furious determination to deny the other person all attributes of humanity, colonialism forces the people it dominates to ask themselves the question constantly: 'In reality, who am I?'

"The defensive attitudes created by this violent bringing together of the colonized man and the colonial system form themselves into a structure which then reveals the colonized personality. This 'sensitivity' is easily understood if we simply study and are alive to the number and depth of the injuries inflicted upon a native during a single day spent amidst the colonial regime. It must in any case be remembered that a colonized people is not only simply a dominated people. Under the German occupation the French remained men; under the French occupation, the Germans remained men. In Algeria there is not simply the domination but the decision to the letter not to occupy anything more than the sum total of the land. The Algerians, the veiled women, the palm-trees and the camels make up the landscape, the natural background to the human presence of the French."

emptying [their] brain of all form and content... it turns to the past of the oppressed people, and distorts, disfigures and destroys it. This work of devaluing pre-colonial history takes on a dialectical significance today." (4.9)

The "dialectical significance" is that even today, We have to deal with the past as part of the process of shaping the future. It's also that here, for us, inside the belly of the beast, where the material dominates, We must begin to place greater focus on the non-material—ideas over things; help people to become aware of the workings of economic relationships by first helping them to develop their analytical skills and their ideo-theoretical capacities... their intellectual capacity. You must understand that THIS is "a necessity in any coherent program." (4.12)

Colonialism creates a "colonized personality" (5.7) and "total liberation is that which concerns all sectors of the personality." (5.183) Fanon says again:

> It is not only necessary to fight for the liberty of your people. You must also teach that people once again, and first learn once again yourself, what is the full stature of a [person], and this you must do for as long as the fight lasts. You must go back into history, that history of [people] damned by other [people], and you must bring about and render possible the meeting of your people and other [people].
>
> In reality, the soldier who is engaged in armed combat in a national war deliberately measures from day to day the sum of all the degradation inflicted upon [people] by colonial oppression. The [person] of action has sometimes the exhausting impression that [they] must restore the whole of their people, that [they] must bring every one of them out of the pit and out of the shadows. [They] very often see that their task is not only to hunt down the enemy forces but also to overcome the kernel of despair which has hardened in the native's being. The period of oppression is painful; but the conflict, by reinstating the downtrodden, sets on foot a

process of reintegration which is fertile and decisive in the extreme. A people's victorious fight not only consecrates the triumph of its rights; it also gives to that people consistence, coherence and homogeneity. For colonialism has not simply depersonalized the individual, it has colonized; this depersonalization is equally felt in the collective sphere, on the level of social structures. The colonized people find that they are reduced to a body of individuals who only find cohesion when in the presence of the colonizing nation.

The fight carried on by a people for its liberation leads it, according to circumstances, either to refuse or else to explode the so-called truths which have been established in its consciousness by the colonial civil administration, by the military occupation, and by economic exploitation. Armed conflict alone can drive out these falsehoods created in [people] which force into inferiority the most lively minds among us and which, literally, mutilate us. (5.141–143)

Now, let's meditate on some of this. It's not only necessary to "fight" so that you can raise your own flag and declare the existence of your own nation. You must also teach the people... once again... and first learn again yourself, what is the full stature/meaning of being "human"... of being sovereign and having the capacity to pursue your own aims... To define for yourself the content of your "humanity" and not have it defined by others—especially when those others are oppressing you, arresting your development, and restricting you to an environment that alienates you from yourself—from what you would or could be if not for their violence.

Why is it that We can only find cohesion when in the "presence" of the colonizing nation? In one sense, it's because that "presence" imposes itself upon us in a way that prevents us from concentrating our energies upon our own **human** needs. That "presence" is everything about the thought and practice of the colonizing nation and its influence upon us and our heretofore inability to de-link from it and create our own "presence" in the world. To a great degree, We do know who We are, and We're afraid to even try to fully manifest ourselves. (This brings to mind a line from Cornel West, which i wonder if he fully understands or has the courage to follow-through on: "*...black people will not succeed in American society if they are fully and freely themselves...*"[3]—my emphasis) We know that We aren't really "natives" or "negroes"... that We aren't "blacks" or "African Americans"—but We're afraid to cut the cord. It's safer and easier to continue to be "blacks," because We can do that without undergoing the discomfort and insecurity that comes with the effort to de-link.

To put it another way, focus on the last two sentences in the second quoted paragraph: We've not only been "depersonalized" as individuals, but as a people, "in the collective sphere, on the level of social structures." What does it mean for a people to be "depersonalized" on the level of "social structures"? It's very simple, really. It's about losing independence as a people; it's about not having "authentic" classes because the development of the nation/people has been distorted and frustrated by colonialism. Thus, all the social and political science of the colonizing nation says that either the colonized people don't have their own classes, or that they are in some strange way "unequal" members of the classes of the colonizing nation—"a body of individuals who only find coherence when in the presence of the colonizing nation." Reflect on that for a while...

Now, the third quoted paragraph takes us again to the issue of the forms of colonialism and the expression of its violence in each of these forms, i.e., its "civil administration," its "economic exploitation," as well as its "military occupation."

As colonialism causes the "death" and mutilation of the colonized people ("The appearance of the settler has meant...the death of the aboriginal society, cultural lethargy, and the petrification of individuals..." (1.95)), it also creates the "native" or the "negro"—which Fanon described as an "arrested image of *a type of relationship*"! (4A.13) Yeah, "niggerhood" is the same as being a "native," a "negro" or "black" and "African-American"—it's not really about the color of the skin, but about *a type of relationship* that We otherwise refer to as colonialism, or imperialism, or as capitalist exploitation... the relationship between the master and the slave, the settler and the native, the "white" and the "black"... the "bourgeoisie" and the "proletariat"... the oppressor nation and the oppressed nation... the exploitative ruling class and the revolutionary class... (my emphasis)

Colonial violence is that which "has ruled over the ordering of the colonial world, which has ceaselessly drummed the rhythm for the destruction of native social forms and broken up without reserve the system of reference of the economy, the customs of dress and external life..." (1.13) It attacks, as a whole, the colonized peoples' material and intellectual life.

We begin to see a direct connection between the forms and effects of the process of colonial violence, and the demand for an all-inclusive program of national and social revolution, at (1.31–1.42), where Fanon talks of muscular tension and begins to list the forms of avoidance along which the paths of revolutionary violence must travel, while negating colonial violence.

However, none of this is inevitable: "The immobility to which the native is condemned can only be called in question if the native **decides** to put an end to the history of colonization—the history of pillage—and to **bring into existence** the history of the nation—the history of decolonization." (1.30) (my emphasis)

4D. What were those questions again...
What is "decolonization"?

Let's say that from the NAC perspective, "revolutionary violence" and "decolonization" are the same—that the terms describe the same process. For example, Wyrick's definition of decolonization is that it is a *"process of changing from a colonial territory to an independent nation, occurring in social and cultural ways, as well as in political and economic ones."*[4] So, i'd say that this describes the process of revolutionary violence, as well as the process of decolonization.

Granted, simply pointing to "social and cultural ways" and to "political and economic" (and military) ways leaves out the kind of detail that most young activists and would-be cadres are quick to ask for. Most folks want blueprints handed to them.

The fact is, i don't have all the answers; i'm in prison and removed from the setting where the answers are most likely to be found. Now, i could talk in more detail on each of the areas, but it would all be more or less abstract, because only those out in the real world can locate and link themselves to the concrete realities in their environments that will allow motion to be made. My job is to help with the "how's" and the "why's"—you have to find the "what's" for yourselves, and then test the theory, test the lessons, find the appropriate ways to take reality as it is, and transform it.

My concern is that We more fully and firmly grasp the "how's" and the "why's," and begin to maintain some continuity from one generation to the next, and not continue to repeat the pattern of having to start from scratch every twenty or thirty years. This kind of continuity will help us to create social environments in our homes and neighborhoods that will allow entire families to be conscious and active, and not just one member of the family; allow entire communities to be conscious and active, and not just one family, on one block, surrounded by "Americans"...

So, We can't restrict our concept of "decolonization" to a narrow vision of merely "seizing power" or "regaining independence" while otherwise maintaining a rudimentary development of consciousness, and leaving the running of the society in the hands of relatively small, privileged groups.

To end the "static period" (1.64), brought on by colonial oppression, is not only to regain a certain physical or political independence, but to pursue a certain path of social development: "...*When the nation stirs as a whole, the new [people are] not an a posteriori product of that nation; rather [they] co-exist with it and triumph with it... Independence is... but an indispensable condition for the existence of men and women who are truly-liberated; in other words, who are truly masters of all the material means which make possible the radical transformation of society.*" (5.183)

Decolonization is the "renaissance" of the nation—a revival or rebirth; it's the "restoration of nationhood" (i.e., sovereignty) to the people. Think here in terms of dynamism and dialectical relationships. Think in terms of things either stagnating and passing away, or as in forward motion, newness rising. So, terms like "renaissance" and "revival," "rebirth" and "restoration" have to be understood not as static images, but as terms describing phenomena in motion and development; what's being "revived" is the people's ability to control their environment and shape their lives, their futures. It's not the "old" nation that rises, but a new one.

Decolonization is the establishment of new (social) relations between individuals; new names for (the) people, for schools and streets—and sometimes, even a new name for the (new) nation. At bottom, decolonization is the process which results in a new, revolutionary and socialist consciousness.

On the surface, it's easy to say what decolonization is: It "sets out to **change the order** of the world" (1.2) and it only appears, initially, to be a program of "disorder" because it opposes the "order" of the colonial system. Decolonization (revolutionary violence) requires an **ordering**, a discipline, a coherence—it's an "historical process" which can't be understood, become intelligible nor clear to the people unless and until We "discern the movements which give it historical form and content." (1.2)* (my emphasis)

Unfortunately, our clarity comes only after many setbacks and much suffering and loss of life. The understanding of a need for "ordering" has certain prerequisites, e.g.: "All this taking stock of the situation, this enlightening of consciousness and this advance in the knowledge of the history of societies are **only possible within the framework of an organization**, and inside the structure of a people. Such an organization is set afoot by the use of revolutionary elements coming from the towns at the beginning of the rising, together with those rebels who go down into the country as the fight goes on. It is this core which constitutes the embryonic political organization of the rebellion. But on the other hand the peasants, who are all the time adding to their knowledge in the light of experience, will come to show themselves capable of directing the people's struggle…" (2.67) (my emphasis)

Check: If there are to be guns, then there must first be "minds behind the guns"! Even "embryonic" consciousness/self-awareness is the prerequisite

* "Decolonization, which sets out to change the order of the world, is, obviously, a programme of complete disorder. But it cannot come as a result of magical practices, nor of a natural shock, nor of a friendly understanding. Decolonization, as we know, is a historical process: that is to say that it cannot be understood, it cannot become intelligible nor clear to itself except in the exact measure that we can discern the movements which give it historical form and content. Decolonization is the meeting of two forces, opposed to each other by their very nature, which in fact owe their originality to that sort of substantification which results from and is nourished by the situation in the colonies. Their first encounter was marked by violence and their existence together—that is to say, the exploitation of the native by the settler—was carried on by the dint of a great array of bayonets and cannon. The settler and the native are old acquaintances. In fact, the settler is right when he speaks of knowing 'them' well. For it is the settler who has brought the native into existence and who perpetuates his existence. The settler owes the fact of his very existence, that is to say his property, to the colonial system."

for the people's decision to call into question the colonial world. A "program" is a plan, and a plan means We must reflect upon our situation, and develop a vision of how We want to live—it's not enough to say that We simply don't wanna continue to live as We do.

Changing the way We live demands a vision of a new way, and We presently lack that vision. i say that We lack the vision because not enough of us understand the need for it; not enough of us put in the time to reflect upon the present reality in a critical way. We lack vision because not enough of us work on making the analyses of the concrete situation, and too many of us lack the ability to take our reality, as it is, and begin to transform it. We haven't yet learned to apply theory in—and through—the test of practice, and our shortcoming leads us to downplay the need for theory only because We don't know how to develop it, test it, evaluate and adjust it.

Decolonization is (but not quite simply), the "replacement" ("to put some thing new in the place of") of a certain "species" of people by a new "species" of people. Now here, only in one context, is there meant a "restoration" of the "native inhabitants" to their former position as an evolving, independent people, by and through the process of "removing" the colonizer. In a broader context, there are actually two "species" being "replaced," because the colonizer can't remain the same if colonialism truly comes to an end. There is no colonizer without the colonized. Both "species" are affected by the decolonization process; both "species" are "replaced"—transformed into something new.

Decolonization must have a period of "transition" (a period of development). From our studies, from our observations and our practice, We know that "leaps" don't happen all at once, in an instant. All the more need for the people to have knowledge of the laws of social development, and understanding of the process of social/revolutionary change; all the more need for the people to have an awareness of the phenomenon of spontaneity and its weaknesses, an awareness of the pitfalls of a narrow nationalist consciousness; all the more need for the people to be helped to realize that "everything depends on them and their salvation lies in their own cohesion, in the true understanding of their interests and in knowing who are their enemies" (3.82), and that if they stagnate, it's their responsibility; if they go forward, it's due to them, too: "there is no such thing as a demiurge...there is no famous man who will take responsibility for everything...the demiurge is the people themselves and the magic hands are finally only the hands of the people." (3.89)*

Decolonization is class struggle among the people—a struggle not simply between groups, but between [class] "stands," between forms and levels of consciousness; "class struggle" is struggle between visions of how the world works and of how We should live; it's a struggle between interests. So, Fanon tells us that **the people need to "have it out with each other"** (2.21), so they can avoid the creation of neo-colonialism, and not have to "realize two or three years after independence that they have been frustrated, that 'it wasn't worthwhile' fighting," and that nothing has changed but the form. (1.75) Why is this so? Because **the people didn't adequately**

---

* "In fact, we often believe with criminal superficiality that to educate the masses politically is to deliver a long political harrangue from time to time. We think that it is enough that the leader or one of his lieutenants should speak in a pompous tone about the principle events of the day for them to have fulfilled this bounden duty to educate the masses politically. Now, political education means opening their minds, awakening them, and allowing the birth of their intelligence; as Cesaire said, it is 'to invent souls'. To educate the masses politically does not mean, cannot mean making a political speech. What it means is to try, relentlessly and passionately, to teach the masses that everything depends on them...In order to put all this into practice, in order to really incarnate the people, we repeat that there must be decentralization in the extreme. The movement from the top to the bottom and from the bottom to the top should be a fixed principle, not through concern for formalism but because simply to respect this principle is the guarantee of salvation. It is from the base that forces mount up which supply the summit with its dynamic, and make it possible dialectically for it to leap ahead..."

change, advance in their knowledge, their political, economic and social awareness, etc. (my emphasis).

Check it again: "Decolonization... influences individuals and modifies them fundamentally. It transforms spectators... into privileged actors" and is "introduced by new [people], and with it a new language and a new humanity. Decolonization is the veritable creation of new [people]... the 'thing' which has been colonized becomes [human] during the same process by which it frees itself." (1.3)*

This is the heart of the book, the "key" to it all. Decolonization—the revolutionary process—is about "influencing" and "modifying" people. The revolutionary process aims to transform "spectators" into "actors"—the revolutionary process is introduced by "new people"—i.e., not until the people have made fundamental change within themselves do they begin the revolutionary process. The process includes "new language" which means the people have already begun to shape new meanings, new consciousness, and language is its medium. The revolutionary process exhibits a new humanity.

It seems that Fanon's thought is a bit contagious—i'm beginning to share his obsession with the need for consciousness developed by the people, so that they can use their "magic hands" to fully control their lives. Of course, i mean "the masses" or the "lower classes" or even the "proletarian masses" and not the "intellectual elements" as We generally think of them. How did We used to say it: All Power to the People!!? The aim is to turn all of the people into "leaders" and into "intellectuals."

---

* "Decolonization never takes place unnoticed, for it influences individuals and modifies them fundamentally. It transforms spectators crushed with their inessentiality into privileged actors, with the grandiose glare of history's floodlights upon them. It brings a natural rhythm into existence, introduced by new men, and with it a new language and a new humanity. Decolonization is the veritable creation of new men. But this creation owes nothing of its legitimacy to any supernatural power; the 'thing' which has been colonized becomes man during the same process it frees itself."

So, decolonization requires the use of ALL means; revolutionary violence must be exercised in all forms (cultural, social, political, economic and military). In order to "pick up the gun," the colonized person must first begin to challenge colonial violence by developing and employing an opposing consciousness. The people must gradually begin to question the legitimacy of the colonial (and capitalist)

"At the end of this massive collective struggle, we will uncover our new man, the unpredictable culmination of the revolutionary process. He will be better equipped to wage the real struggle, the permanent struggle after the revolution - the one for new relationships between men."   G.J.

world, and to believe in themselves, to assume responsibility for the institutions which, because they are theirs, stand as poles of opposition to the oppressive state and pillars to uphold the new people's state.

In other words, armed struggle is "started" when people begin to: re-define themselves, lose their fear and awe of the oppressive state and see it as illegitimate; to build their own socio-cultural, political and economic institutions; to de-link from the colonial/capitalist world, and their own anarchic myths and traditions.

Revolutionary violence (decolonization) is, as a whole, a form of "self-defense" (i.e., that slogan and concept most widely used these days, as part of a minimum program of agitation and propaganda), but a defense of the whole self, not just the physical body. The people's "self-defense" is an aggressive assertion of a new identity, a new self-awareness, and the acquisition and use of arms against the colonial system follows the spark of this new sense of self, a new sense of responsibility on the plane of morals.

The people's "self-defense" follows a certain awakening, during the colonial period, where they'd otherwise "fight among themselves" and "use each other as a screen, and each hides from his neighbor the national enemy." (5.179)* It's only after they realize their humanity that they begin to "sharpen the weapons" (all weapons) for use against colonialism, and to forge the new society. (1.15)

We know that our people are armed today, as never before (and in many respects, armed by the oppressive state), but their having arms doesn't signal a turn toward the left. Even when We consider efforts by the enemy to disarm the people, it's not the guns in their hands, as such, that's the source of the settler's fear, but the potential threat posed by an armed and politically conscious people.

* "…In the colonial context, as we have already pointed out, the natives fight among themselves. They tend to use each other as a screen, and each hides from his neighbor the national enemy. When, tired out after a hard sixteen-hour day the native sinks down to rest on his mat, and a child on the other side of the canvas partition starts crying and prevents him from sleeping, it so happens that it is a little Algerian. When he goes to beg for a little semolina or a drop of oil from the grocer, to whom he already owes some hundreds of francs, and when he sees that he is refused, an immense feeling of hatred and an overpowering desire to kill rises within him: and the grocer is an Algerian…

"The Algerian, exposed to temptations to commit murder every day—famine, eviction from his room because he has not paid the rent, the mother's dried-up breasts, children like skeletons, the building-yard which has closed down, the unemployed that hang about the foreman like crows—the native comes to see his neighbor as a relentless enemy. If he strikes his bare foot against a big stone in the middle of the path, it is a native who has placed it there; and the few olives that he was going to pick, X…'s children have gone and eaten in the night. For during the colonial period in Algeria and elsewhere many things may be done for a couple of pounds of semolina. Several people may be killed over it. You need to use your imagination to understand that…

"In Algeria since the beginning of the war of National Liberation, everything has changed. The whole foodstocks of a family or a mecha [a mountain village in Algeria] may in a single evening be given to a passing company. The family's only donkey may be lent to transport a wounded fighter; and when a few days later the owner learns of the death of his animal which has been machine-gunned by an aeroplane, he will not begin threatening and swearing. He will not question the death of his donkey, but he will ask anxiously if the wounded man is safe and sound.

"Under the colonial regime, anything may be done for a loaf of bread or a miserable sheep. The relations of man with matter, with the world outside and with history are in the colonial period simply relations with food. For a colonized man, in a contest of oppression like that in Algeria, living does not mean embodying moral values or taking his place in the coherent and fruitful development of the world. To live means to keep on existing. Every date is a victory: not the result of work, but a victory felt as a triumph for life. Thus to steal dates or to allow one's sheep to eat the neighbor's grass is not a question of the negation of the property of others, nor the transgression of a law, nor lack of respect. These are attempts at murder. In order to understand that a robbery is not an illegal or an unfriendly action, but an attempt at murder, one must have seen in Kabylia men and women for weeks at a time going to get earth at the bottom of the valley and bringing it up in little baskets … Who is going to take the punishment? The French are down in the plain with the police, the army and the tanks. On the mountain there are only Algerians. Up above there is Heaven with the promise of a world beyond the grave; down below there are the French with their very concrete promises of prison, beatings-up and executions. You are forced to come up against yourself. Here we discover the kernel of that hatred of self which is characteristic of racial conflicts in segregated societies." 5.179–182

4E. Violence Re-Directed

> *...the people have the time to see that the liberation has been the business of each and all, and that the leader has no special merit ... When the people have taken violent part in the national liberation, they will allow no one to set themselves up as "liberators." They show themselves to be jealous of the results of their action and take good care not to place their future, their destiny or the fate of their country in the hands of a living god. Yesterday, they were completely irresponsible; today, they mean to understand everything and make all decisions. Illuminated by violence the consciousness of the people rebels against any pacification. From now on the demagogues, the opportunists and the magicians have a difficult time. The action which has thrown them into a hand-to-hand struggle confers upon the masses a voracious taste for the concrete. The attempt at mystification becomes, in the long run, practically impossible. (1.99)*

Here We see the *ideal* result—a "true" decolonization. Read it again, carefully. Center your meditations upon "the consciousness of the people" and "they mean to understand everything and make all decisions." And, it never hurts to lay stress again upon the concept of "violence" that We're using, i.e., it relates to all aspects and levels of struggle, all areas of social life and the development of the people's consciousness, resting on their active participation in all areas of struggle. Keep in mind: It's not the mere use of arms by the masses that ensures that they become responsible, want to know everything, and make all decisions—including those decisions that dictate **that they remain armed after independence is won.**

However, the ideal outcome is not always what We get. Below, We'll see that: 1) The people's violence is re-directed, but it begins as a **spontaneous** process; its strength is that it's "voluntary," and its weakness is that it lacks coherence and deliberation. 2) It should be a violence that leads to the people assuming total responsibility for the struggle, and to their becoming fully conscious, new people.

3) However, the weakness of spontaneity also means that the people are restrained and not enlightened; independence becomes a farce—and a new struggle begins, now against neo-colonialism and, more directly, a struggle for socialism.

Fanon tells us that "Well before the political or fighting phase of the national movement," the people re-build their "perceptions." (4A.14)* These should be understood as perceptions regarding the world, the settler and colonialism and, most importantly, the people's self-perception. How does the colonized people—how do We—come to make the decision to begin the decolonization process, to develop and practice a program of revolutionary violence?

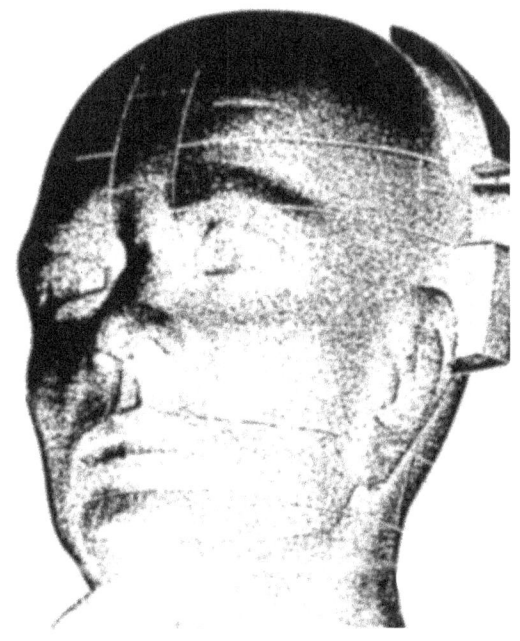

---

* "We might in the same way seek and find in dancing, singing, and traditional rites and ceremonies the same upward-springing trend, and make out the same changes and the same impatience in this field. Well before the political or fighting phase of the national movement, an attentive spectator can thus feel and see the manifestation of new vigour and feel the approaching conflict. He will note unusual forms of expression and themes which are fresh and imbued with power which is no longer that of invocation but rather that of assembling of the people, a summoning together for a precise purpose. Everything works together to awaken the native's sensibility and to make unreal and unacceptable the contemplative attitude, or the acceptance of defeat. The native re-builds his perceptions because he renews the purpose and dynamism of the craftsmen, of dancing and music and of literature and the oral tradition. His world comes to lose its accursed character. The conditions necessary for the inevitable conflict are brought together."

The "fighting phase" begins only after "the moment We decide to **embody 'history' in our own person**" (1.13)*; the decolonization process begins only after "the moment We realize our 'humanity'," and then "begin to sharpen our weapons" (1.15); the process of revolutionary violence begins only after We "vomit up bourgeois/Western values" (1.16), and only after "We discover that our lives, our breath, our beating hearts are the same as those of the settler; that his skin is of no more value than ours," and "this discovery shakes the world in a very necessary manner. **All the new, revolutionary assurance ... stems from it...**" (1.18) (my emphasis).

Before—and in order that—the "fighting phase" may begin, the people must begin to re-build their perceptions of themselves and of the social environment within which they live; they must re-build their perceptions of the world—a world now dominated by capitalism, and struggles against it.

It's simply (!) about the people asserting their (new) identity—asserting a form or concept of "humanity" that's distinct from that form or concept established by the colonial order and imposed upon the colonized, e.g., they say they're "human" and that We aren't; that if We wanna become "human" We must be like them—exploiters and oppressors and "individuals," Yet, the more We become like them, i.e., the

* "The violence which has ruled over the ordering of the colonial world, which has ceaselessly drummed the rhythm for the destruction of native social forms and broken up without reserve the systems of reference of the economy, the customs of dress and external life, that same violence will be claimed and taken over by the native at the moment when, deciding to embody history in his own person, he surges into the forbidden quarters. To wreck the colonial world is henceforward a mental picture of action which is very clear, very easy to understand and which may be assumed by each one of the individuals which constitute the colonized people. To break up the colonial world does not mean that after the frontiers have been abolished lines of communication will be set up between the two zones. The destruction of the colonial world is no more and no less than the abolition of one zone, its burial in the depths of the earth or its expulsion from the country."

more bourgeois We become, the more inhuman and inhumane We become, the more insane We become... the more We become alienated from ourselves...

During the colonial period—the so-called peaceful period—the people react to being "hemmed in" by "dreaming" of action, achieving freedom "from nine in the evening until six in the morning." (1.31) During the "peaceful" period, when colonialism is "in power and secure," it's rather difficult to notice any widespread, fundamental change in the self-perception of the people.

During the colonial period, the oppressive system keeps alive in us an anger which generally finds no external outlet, but rather takes the form of internally directed violence, in various forms, e.g., "the niggers beat each other up, and the police and [courts] do not know which way to turn when faced with the astonishing waves of crime..." (1.32)

Our "muscular tension finds outlet in bloodthirsty explosions—in tribal warfare, in feuds between sects, and in quarrels between individuals..."

> *...[A] positive negation of common sense is evident. While the settler or the policeman has the right the live-long day to strike the native, to insult him [or her] and to make him [or her] crawl to them, you will see the native reaching for his [or her] knife [or gun] at the slightest hostile or aggressive glance cast on him [or her] by another native ... By throwing [themselves] with all [their] force into the vendetta, the native tries to persuade [him or her self] that colonialism does not exist, that everything is going on as before [the conquest], that history [sovereign existence] continues... (1.35)*

During the colonial period, the mass of the people exercise violence through what Fanon describes as "behavior patterns of avoidance" (1.35), which are used to "by-pass the settler." These include: a belief in fatality, which removes all blame from the oppressive system, and attributes all misfortunes and colonial violence to "Fate" or to "God"; myths, spirits, and a magical/metaphysical superstructure which creates "a world of prohibitions, of barriers and of inhibitions far more terrifying than the world of the settler" (1.36); eroticism (1.40); dance (1.41), and seances (1.42). All of these forms of "avoidance" or internally-directed violence allow "the most acute aggressivity and the most impelling violence, to be canalized, transformed and conjured away." (1.41)

On the other hand, while the masses exercise their violence through these patterns of avoidance, the violence of the "elite" assumes other forms, i.e., "...The native intellectual has clothed his aggressiveness in his barely veiled desire to assimilate himself to the colonial world. He has used his aggressiveness to serve his own individual interests." (1.47)

As We read about this canalized violence, We should make an effort to uncover the forms of avoidance that are peculiar to us. Most of us read **Wretched** and fail to make the connections between the colonial situation that he describes, and the one that We are subject to.

Don't We exercise our aggressiveness against ourselves? Don't We witness bloodthirsty explosions in the form of "gang" warfare and "black-on-black crime"? On the individual and the collective levels, don't We evidence a positive negation of common sense as We, too, try to persuade ourselves that colonialism and capitalist exploitation and alienation don't exist? Don't We, too, grab hold of a belief in fatality (very common among young people these days)? And, what about OUR myths, spirits and magical/metaphysical superstructure? In our context, We employ conspiracy theories, the zodiac and numerology, Kente cloth and phrases from ancient languages; We invoke the power of a diet and the taboo of certain animals as food products. Without a doubt, We have our own prohibitions and inhibitions that We use to avoid a confrontation with the reality of colonial violence... our own barriers that We use to avoid de-linking from the colonial world.

So, We come back to the questions: How do We begin to rebuild our perceptions? How do We come to make the decision to engage the decolonization process? How—and why—do We begin to re-direct our violence? How do We come to make the decision to embody "history"? How do We **"realize our humanity"**? Again: It's only after We do this that the "fighting phase" begins. And yet, Fanon says that it's "**During** the struggle for freedom" that a "marked alienation" from the patterns of avoidance is observed. (1.43) (my emphasis) It's during the struggle that We come face to face with colonialism, discover reality, and transform it into the pattern of new customs and into the practice of revolutionary violence. But, how does this happen?

It happens under the influence of internal and external factors… under the influence of changed and changing objective and subjective conditions… under the influence of class forces inside and outside of the structure of the people—most of all, it happens more or less spontaneously.

One thing We must always keep in mind… one thing that Fanon and Cabral and so many others take pains to remind us: The people are the nation, and they maintain the national culture and identity, distinct from that of the oppressor, even when the oppressor appears "in power and secure." The period appears "peaceful" simply because the people don't see a viable alternative—but We never know when or in what form that alternative will make itself apparent and mark the shift to qualitative change, the "leap" to the beginning of a new stage.

However, when that situation emerges—spontaneously—the task will be to change the spontaneous character, and give the movement conscious and comprehensive direction, under the leadership of the people and a revolutionary or "proletarian" class stand.

At (1.44), Fanon says: "Now the problem is to lay hold of this **violence which is changing direction**. When formerly it was appeased by myths and exercised its talents in finding fresh ways of committing mass suicide, now new conditions will make possible a completely new line of action." (He uses somewhat different language to pose the same problem, at (1.67)) And, at (1.46), Fanon asks, "What are the [class] forces which, in the colonial period, open up new outlets and engender **new aims for the violence** of colonized peoples?" (my emphasis)

Here's how Fanon frames the examination:

> *Nowadays a theoretical problem of prime importance is being set, on the historical plane as well as on the level of political tactics, by the liberation of the colonies: when can one affirm that the situation is ripe for a movement of national liberation? In what form should it first be manifested? Because the various means whereby decolonization has been carried out have appeared in many different aspects, reason hesitates and refuses to say which is a true decolonization, and which is a false. We shall see that for a man who is in the thick of the fight it is an urgent matter to decide on the means and the tactics to employ: that is to say, how to conduct and organize the movement. If this coherence is not present, there is only a blind will towards freedom, with the terrible reactionary risks which it entails. (1.45)*

Let's stop here for a bit of orientation:

1) In a sense, the remaining chapters of **Wretched** are "previewed" in the first chapter—all of the themes are introduced and briefly treated there. That is, in the first chapter We encounter discussion of "spontaneity," "national consciousness," "culture" and "mental disorders"; We encounter discussion of "racism" and "class struggle". How could it be otherwise, if We recall our concept of revolutionary violence and decolonization? The first chapter provides an overview of all elements of both colonialism and anti-colonialism. If We confine ourselves to one theme, "violence" is the concern

of the first chapter, but it's also the concern of the second chapter...

2) As WE search for answers to the questions i've raised in this section, and as We focus particularly upon a brief examination of the "new conditions" and the class forces that open new outlets and create new aims for the people's violence, We're gonna encounter overlapping themes, e.g., spontaneity, and class struggle. We're gonna take up the theme of class struggle in **Part Three**, so here i wanna concentrate on the theme of spontaneity: It's the spontaneity of violence that's at issue—the strengths and weaknesses of a spontaneity that tends to characterize the beginnings of people's struggles and which, if not overcome, result in their failures, i.e., the failure to achieve "true" decolonization.

3) Now, let's go forward by going back to (1.45) [*"Nowadays a theoretical problem of prime importance is being set..."*], break it down just a bit, and look for points that will help to orient us as We proceed:

   a) National liberation revolutions have given rise to theoretical problems, on the historical plane, and on the level of political tactics;
   b) How do We determine whether or not a "revolutionary situation" exists within the colonial context?;
   c) What form(s) (i.e., political, economic, cultural, or military) are assumed by the first manifestation of the qualitative shift from the colonial to the anti-colonial period?;
   d) We've witnessed many national liberation struggles and the raising of many flags over newly "independent" nations. How do We determine which, if any, of these "independent" nations were or are truly decolonized, i.e.,

where "new people" have arisen and assumed collective mastery over a truly liberated society?;

e) How do peoples still suffering the capitalist/colonialist yoke answer all of the above questions, and decide upon the means and tactics to conduct and organize their revolutionary process? More to the point: How do they develop a "coherent" program—one that will allow them to avoid a mere "blind will" towards freedom (i.e., avoid the weaknesses of spontaneity), and thus also to avoid the "terribly reactionary risks" (i.e., neocolonialism) which the absence of coherence, and the presence of spontaneity, entail?

Yeah, We're still talking about how and why the people come to re-direct their violence. But, these questions lead into a discussion of "new conditions" and class forces which, in their turn, lead to discussion of the need for "coherence," and to overcome or avoid spontaneity, i.e., to avoid or overcome a mere "blind will" towards freedom, and its terrible consequences.

4F. Spontaneity and the Need for a Coherent Program

You turn to the second chapter and say: i've read about "violence," now i'll read about "spontaneity." Well, Fanon first raised the issue of spontaneity in the first chapter—and he's still talking about "violence" in the second chapter.

For example: At (1.26), he tells us that the people want and need "things explained to them; they are glad to understand a line of argument, and they like to see **where** they are going." (my emphasis) He then points out that, "...at the beginning of his association with the people, the native intellectual overstresses details," and "carried away by the multitudinous aspects of the fight, he tends to concentrate on local tasks," and "fails to see the whole of the movement all the time... He is occupied in action on a particular front, and... loses sight of the unity of the movement..."

Now, compare the above (from the chapter on "violence") with these lines (from the chapter on "spontaneity"): "...The elite will attach a fundamental importance to organization, so much so that the fetish of organization will often take precedence over a reasoned study of colonial society..." (2.1)

At (2.52), Fanon explains that "...During this period spontaneity is king, and initiative is localized... We are dealing with a strategy of immediacy" in which "the aim and program of each locally constituted group is local liberation. If the nation is everywhere, then she is here. One step further, and only here is she to be found. Tactics are mistaken for strategy. The art of politics is simply transformed into the art of war..."

As you begin to read the second chapter, notice that Fanon opens it on the subject of a difference of "rhythm" between the so-called "leaders," and the mass of the people. You know me... i went to the dictionary to see if i could get a better grip on "rhythm," and i did, basing it on: "an ordered, recurrent alternation in the flow of... that relates to forward movement; the aspect comprising all the elements that relate to forward movement; movement marked by regular recurrence of related elements; effect created by the elements that relate to development."

You'll have to pardon me if i'm a bit slow, or seem to take unusual and extended routes to points that you reach in more conventional and timely ways. To some of us, it's not immediately clear that a difference of "rhythm" implies difference in: class/consciousness; interests and tactics; ways and means of conducting and organizing the movement; "identity, purpose and direction"; true from false decolonization; "blind will" and "coherence". A difference of "rhythm" means that the elements are unrelated—like another way of saying "class contradictions" or contradictions between ideological world-views...

Next, notice how Fanon points up the distinction between those who want an "immediate bettering of their lot," and those who want to "limit and restrain" the former. Now, a "better lot" doesn't just mean, say, a higher wage; it also means the all-round development of the person/people... We're then shown that the "politically informed" person, under colonial domination, is one who "knows that a local conflict is not a decisive settlement" between the people and the system of colonialism. (2.1; also see 2.54)

No doubt, someone is asking: What does all this have to do with "spontaneity"?

True to form, i went to the dictionary and to the Thesaurus to check the word "spontaneity," and i began to work with: "the quality or state of being spontaneous; voluntary or undetermined action or movement." When i checked "spontaneous," i focused on: "1) proceeding from natural feeling or native tendency without external constraint; 2) arising from momentary impulse; 3) controlled and directed internally—self-acting; 4) not apparently contrived or manipulated." Synonyms are: impulsive; haphazard; instinctive. Antonyms are: studied, and deliberate. The shared meaning element of the synonyms is: acting or activated without deliberation, insight, forethought, or knowledge.

i then shifted my attention to the subtitle of the second chapter, and asked myself what may Fanon have meant by the "strength" and the "weakness" of spontaneity? Of course, i had to re-read and meditate on the chapter several times before it began to hit me. The "strength" of spontaneity (which i term its "objective" aspect) is its positive or progressive character—action that's self-motivated or unrestrained by external forces. The "weakness" of spontaneity (which i term its "subjective" aspect) is evidenced when the action is taken without sufficient deliberation or knowledge—without sufficient development of consciousness and conscious direction..."coherent" or comprehensive direction, which coordinates the movement as a whole… It's easy to notice that although Fanon often points (especially in the early stages) to the people's violence as "impatient" (1.52), spontaneous (1.69 and 2.17), and intuitive (1.72), he portrays this action in its "objective" aspect, as the manifestation of the "strength" of spontaneity. This comes across in one paragraph fairly clearly:

> *But it may happen that the country people, in spite of the slight hold that the nationalist parties have over them, play a decisive part either in the process of the maturing of the national consciousness, or through working in with the action of nationalist parties, or, less frequently, by substituting themselves purely and simply for the sterility of the parties… (2.15)*

However, for every reference to, or example of, the "strength" of spontaneity, there are two or three references or examples of spontaneity's "weakness"—a weakness which Fanon discusses primarily in reference to the character and activity of the "leaders," the bourgeois nationalist parties, or the "intellectuals."

The "weakness" of spontaneity (i.e., the weakness in the decolonization process), is revealed when the so-called leaders and/or the "intellectuals" fail to make an analysis of colonialism (and capitalism) from a revolutionary (i.e., "proletarian") perspective, rather than using the bourgeois models of political or social science, and suggesting reformist solutions. It's also seen in the failure of these forces to put themselves "to school with the people: in other words, to put at the people's disposal the intellectual and technical capital that [they have] snatched when going through the colonial universities." (3.6)

If these forces truly have the people's interest at heart, then they should go to the people and help to prepare them to lead the struggle and to govern themselves; they should help the people to shape a vision of the new society—a vision developed as they challenge and critique the capitalist-colonialist world.

The "new conditions" that help to open new lines of action—and which bear most directly upon the issue of spontaneity—are those involving the international situation (especially the struggles of other colonized peoples), and the repression of the people's rising by the colonial system, i.e., colonialism will "create spontaneity with bayonets and exemplary floggings." (2.60)*

With regard to the latter, Fanon shapes the context by first rephrasing, at (1.67), the questions that he first posed at (1.44): "But let us return to that atmosphere of violence, that violence which is just under the skin. We have seen that in its process towards maturity many leads are attached to it, to control it and show it the way out. Yet in spite of the metamorphoses which the colonial regime imposes upon it in the way of tribal or regional quarrels, that violence makes its way forward, and the native identifies his enemy and recognizes [the source of] all his misfortunes, throwing all

---

* "The enemy is aware of ideological weaknesses, for he analyzes the forces of rebellion and studies more and more carefully the aggregate enemy which makes up a colonial people; he is also aware of the spiritual instability of certain layers of the population. The enemy discovers the existence, side by side with the disciplined and well-organized advance guard of the rebellion, of a mass of men whose participation is constantly at the mercy of their being too long accustomed to physiological wretchedness, humiliation, and irresponsibility. The enemy is ready to pay a high price for the services of this mass. He will create spontaneity with bayonets and exemplary floggings. Dollars and Belgian francs pour into the Congo, while in Madagascar levies against Hova increase and in Algeria native recruits, who are in fact hostages, are enlisted in the French forces. The leaders of the rebellion literally see the nation capsizing. Whole tribes join up as harkis [*Editors note: Harkis were the Algerian mercenaries who joined the French military to fight against their own people.*], and, using the modern weapons that they have been given, go on the war-path and invade the territory of the neighboring tribe, which for this occasion has been labelled as nationalist. That unanimity in battle, so fruitful and grandiose in the first days of the rebellion, undergoes a change. National unity crumbles away; the rising is at a decisive turning of the way. Now the political education of the masses is seen to be a historic necessity."

the exacerbated might of his hate and anger into this new channel. But how do we pass from the atmosphere of violence to violence in action? What makes the lid blow off?..."

The lid blows off when "good natives" become scarce; the nationalist parties call for public meetings and mass demonstrations, and, "...the agitation which ensues, the coming and going, the listening to speeches, seeing the people assembled in one place, with the police all around, the military demonstrations, arrests, and the deportation of the leaders—all this hubbub makes the people think that the moment has come for them to take action," (1.62) and it's under such conditions that "the guns go off by themselves..." (1.68)

Colonialist repression follows, but "far from calling a halt to the forward rush of national consciousness, urges it on. Mass slaughter in the colonies at a certain stage of the embryonic development of consciousness increases that consciousness..." (1.69) (i find it striking that, here We are talking about "guns" going off, and Fanon chooses to characterize it as the forward rush of national consciousness.)

So, in the wave of repression and the rush of the people's embryonic consciousness, "daily life becomes quite simply impossible. You can no longer be a fellah, a pimp or an alcoholic as before," and the "recurring terror de-mystifies" the people. (1.91) A "point of no return" is reached, as repression engulfs all sectors of the population. (1.92)

Now, once this situation develops, We could say that We witness the manifestation of the "strength" of spontaneity. However, what happens after the guns go off... spontaneously? Having guns go off is no guarantee that the embryonic consciousness of the people will continue to develop, and to facilitate their assumption of leadership over the movement and the new society being fought for. Let's now take a look at those "forces"...

"What are the forces which in the colonial period open up new outlets and engender new aims for the violence of colonized peoples? In the first place, there are the political parties and the intellectual or commercial elites…" (1.46) There is also the peasantry (1.49) and the colonialist bourgeoisie. (1.50)

We've already seen how the colonialists create spontaneity with their repression of the people. They also create and/or take advantage of existing spontaneity by introducing the idea of "nonviolence" and by encouraging a "compromise" solution, which "signifies to the intellectual and economic elites of the colonized country that the bourgeoisie has the same interests as them." (1.50)

The spontaneous rising of the people, and the existence of other national liberation struggles "modifies" the approach of the colonialists, who then set out "to capture the vanguard, to turn the movement of liberation towards the right, and to disarm the people." (1.66)*

---

* "A colonized people is not alone. In spite of all that colonialism can do, its frontiers remain open to new ideas and echos from the world outside. It discovers that violence is in the atmosphere, that it here and there bursts out, and here and there sweeps away the colonialist regime—that same violence which fulfills for the native a role that is not simply informatory, but also operative. The great victory of the Vietnamese people at Dien Bien Phu is no longer, strictly speaking, a Vietnamese victory. Since July 1954, the question which the colonized peoples have asked themselves has been: 'What must be done to bring about another Dien Bien Phu? How can we manage it?' Not a single colonized individual could ever again doubt the possibility of a Dien Bien Phu; the only problem was how best to use the forces at their disposal, how to organize them, and when to bring them into action. This encompassing violence does not work upon the colonized people only; it modifies the attitude of the colonialists who become aware of manifold Dien Bien Phus. This is why a veritable panic takes hold of the colonialist governments in turn. Their purpose is to capture the vanguard, to turn the movement of liberation towards the right, and to disarm the people: quick, quick, let's decolonize. Decolonize the Congo before it turns into another Algeria. Vote the consitutional framework for all Africa, create the French Communaute, renovate that same Communaute, but for God's sake let's decolonize quick…And they decolonize at such a rate that they impose independence on Houphouet-Boigny. To the strategy of Dien Bien Phu, defined by the colonized peoples, the colonialist replies by the strategy of encirclement—based on the respect of the soverignty of states."

Towards this end of "dislocating or creating diversions around the upward thrust of nationalism," the colonialists take advantage of the ideological weaknesses and social divisions among the people. (2.24; 2.59; 2.60)†

As We look at the role of the bourgeois nationalist parties, We should note that Fanon is not questioning the principle of the "party," but rather "the make-up of their leaders and the nature of their followings." (1.47) This note is for those who, for whatever reason, don't (yet) appreciate the need for and the role of structured organizations for the people to use as both weapons in the struggle against oppression, and as tools in the construction of the new society.

To begin with, "the characteristic feature of certain political structures is that they proclaim abstract principles but refrain from issuing definite commands. The entire action of these nationalist political parties during the colonial period [because they model themselves on those parties and principles of the colonialist bourgeoisie and its world-view] is action of the electoral type: a string of philosophico-political dissertations on the themes of the rights of the peoples to self-determination, the rights of [peoples] to freedom from hunger and human dignity, and the unceasing affirmation of the principle: 'One [person], one vote.' The national political parties never lay stress upon the necessity for a trial of armed strength, for the good reason that

† "...And the oppressor, who never loses a chance of setting the niggers against each other, will be extremely skilful in using that ignorance and incomprehension which are the weaknesses of the *lumpen-proletariat*. If this available reserve of human effort is not immediately organized by the forces of rebellion, it will find itself fighting as hired soldiers side by side with the colonial troops. In Algeria, it is the *lumpen-proletariat* which furnished the harkis and messalists; in Angola, it supplied the road-openers who nowadays precede the Portuguese armed columns; in the Congo, we find once more the *lumpen-proletariat* in regional manifestations in Kasai and Katanga, while at Leopoldville the Congo's enemies made use of it to organize 'spontaneous' mass meetings against Lumumba." (2.59)

their objective is not the radical overthrowing of the system. Pacifists and legalists, they are in fact partisans of order—the new [neo-colonial] order—but to the colonialist bourgeoisie they put bluntly enough the demand which to them is the main one: 'Give us more power.' On the specific question of violence, the elite are ambiguous. They are violent in their words and reformist in their attitudes. When the nationalist political leaders **say** something, they make quite clear that they do not really **think** it." (1.46)

i hope We've said enough about "violence" so that as you read passages like the one above, you'll know that the opposition of the bourgeois nationalists to "violence" is an opposition to ANY form of fundamental change in the system of neo-colonialism, colonialism, imperialism, capitalism—and patriarchy. "Violence" to them is any talk about all power really being in the hands of the people; it's any threat to their interests and to the interests of their capitalist masters.

As you read (1.46), you should try to picture any and all individuals or groups... any voiced positions that seem to fit the bill, or that can be accurately characterized as narrow, bourgeois-nationalist/reformist/post-neocolonialist... as representative of the "intellectual or commercial elite." Farrakhan or Jesse? Manning Marable, Cornel West or Skip Gates? What about some of the other persons or groups that talk about "self-determination" or "empowerment" and sometimes even use the word "liberation"— but they really think "assimilation" or "parity" or "pluralism" or, as is common these days, a bourgeois-oriented "multi-culturalism"— what they're saying is, "Give us more power!"

The parties "show a deep distrust toward the people" (of the rural areas) and "pass the same unfavorable judgment" upon them as the settlers. (2.5) They fail to "direct their propaganda towards" the (rural) masses (2.9), and they don't try to organize them or to use "existing structures and [give] them a nationalist or progressive character... They do not go out to find the mass of the people.

They do not put their theoretical knowledge to the service of the people..." (2.12)

As the people spontaneously engage the colonial system, the bourgeois nationalist parties "make the most of the manna, but do not attempt to organize the rebellion. They don't send leaders into the countryside to educate the people politically, or to increase their awareness or put the struggle onto a higher level..." (2.18)

The difference in "rhythm" continues after independence, "precisely because the people now at the head of affairs did not explain to the people as a whole, during the colonial period, what were the aims of the party, the national trends, or the problems of international politics." (2.21)

Ironically, the reformist activity and bourgeois character of nationalist parties indirectly takes a progressive twist, because, "In their speeches [they] give a name to the nation. In this way the [people's] demands are given shape. There is, however, no definite subject-matter and no political or social program. There is a vague outline or skeleton, which is nevertheless national in form, what we describe as 'minimum requirements.' The politicians who make speeches and who write in the nationalist newspapers make the people dream dreams. They avoid the actual overthrowing of the state, but in fact they introduce into their readers' or hearers' consciousness the terrible ferment of subversion... and the imagination is let loose outside the bounds of the colonial order..." (1.60–61)

Consideration of the intellectuals should begin at (1.17), where Fanon first mentions them, e.g., as the masses begin to vomit up bourgeois values, the "phenomenon is ordinarily masked" because of the action of certain intellectuals and, as the masses demand "that the last shall be first," the intellectuals bring "variants" to the petition. (1.20)

We've already noted the tendency of intellectuals to contribute to the development of spontaneity by their fetish for organization and their focus upon the immediate environment rather than upon the movement as a whole—and their failure to make a reasoned study of the colonial system and of their own social structure.

> *In order to assimilate and to experience the oppressor's culture the native has had to leave certain of his intellectual possessions in pawn. These pledges include his adoption of the forms of thought of the colonialist bourgeoisie...* (1.25)
>
> *Thus there is very easily brought into being a kind of class of affranchised slaves, or slaves who are individually free. What the intellectual demands is the right to multiply the emancipated, and the opportunity to organize a genuine class of emancipated citizens...* (1.48)*

* "...On the other hand, the mass of the people have no intention of standing by and watching individuals increase their chances of success. What they demand is not the settler's position of status, but the settler's place. The immense majority of natives want the settler's farm. For them, there is no question of entering into competition with the settler. They want to take his place."

(Now, go back a few pages in these **Meditations** to my mention of George Curry and Skip Gates—especially Gates' stated aim "to bring more black people into the middle class"—yeah, that's them, the "affranchised slaves" who wanna multiply their class...)

"[T]he elites of the colonial countries, those slaves set free, when at the head of the movement, inevitably end up by producing an ersatz conflict [i.e., artificial and inferior substitute]... The truth is that they never make any real appeal" to the colonized people, "they never mobilize them in concrete terms..." (1.59)

Of course, there are individuals within the bourgeois classes who break from the class orientation and begin to make a contribution to the formation of a coherent and deliberate program. Fanon first mentions this tendency within the context of conditions which favor a "backward surge of intellectuals towards bases grounded in the people," and an "eradication of the superstructure built by these intellectuals from the bourgeois colonialist environment." (1.21)

When such intellectuals begin to live among the people, they, too, begin to vomit up bourgeois values, and individualism disappears (1.22), and they adopt the method of "communal self-criticism"; they abandon the "habits of calculation, of unwonted silence, of mental reservations ... and the spirit of concealment." (1.23)

Fanon picks up the same theme at (1.59):

> *Obviously there are to be found at the core of the political parties and among their leaders certain revolutionaries who deliberately turn their backs upon the farce of national independence. But very quickly their questionings, their energy and their anger obstruct the party machine; and these elements are gradually isolated, and then quite simply brushed aside. At this moment, as if there existed a dialectical concomitance, the colonialist police will fall upon them. With no security in the towns, avoided by the militants of their former party, and rejected by its leaders, these undesirable firebrands will be stranded in country districts. Then it is that they will realize bewilderedly that the peasant masses catch on to what they have to say immediately, and without delay ask them the question to which they have not yet prepared the answer: "When do we start?"*

These "left" petty-bourgeois elements haven't prepared an answer to the question because, despite their antagonism toward the "right" bourgeois elements, they, too, have traditionally ignored the masses and failed to analyze their own social structure and to develop a coherent plan. It's here that Fanon places this theme within the context of the decisive intervention of the people, i.e., "in certain circumstances the country people are going to intervene in decisive fashion both in the struggle for national liberation and in the way that the future nation marks out for itself." (2.35) This is a fundamentally important phenomenon, and he proposes to study it in detail, as will We.

Fanon sets the stage over the next several paragraphs, with a more detailed description of the process that was initially noted at (1.59), and here the focus is clearly upon the phenomenon of spontaneity.

We shouldn't be surprised to learn that there are "two wills" at play—a contradiction between progressive and reactionary tendencies within the party (tho, again, both tendencies have neglected to involve the masses), which reflects the broader contradiction within the movement and among the people as a whole. (2.36) Fanon uses the terms "legalists" and "illegalists," altho other terms could be used to describe the opposing tendencies.*

The "left" begins to raise questions about the movement's ideology, strategy and methods; they begin to suggest the use of "all other means"—which We should understand to include armed forms of struggle, but only as one among ALL other means. Here, "coherent" program means one in which all elements of social life

---

* "We have seen that inside the nationalist parties, the will to break colonialism is linked with another quite different will: that of coming to a friendly agreement with it. Within these parties, the two processes will sometimes continue side by side. In the first place, when the intellectual elements have carried out a prolonged analysis of the true nature of colonialism and of the international situation, they will begin to criticize their party's lack of ideology and the poverty of its tactics and strategy. They begin to question their leaders ceaselessly on crucial points: 'What is nationalism? What sense do you give to this word? What is its meaning? Independence for what? And in the first place, how do you propose to achieve it?' They ask these questions, and at the same time require that the problems of methodology should be vigorously tackled. They are ready to suggest that electoral resources should be supplemented by 'all other means.' After the first skirmishes, the official leaders speedily dispose of this effervescence which they are quick to label as childishness. But since these demands are not simply effervescence, nor the signs of immaturity, the revolutionary elements which subscribe to them will rapidly be isolated. The official leaders, draped in their years of experience, will pitilessly disown these 'adventurers and anarchists'.

"The party machine shows itself opposed to any innovation. The revolutionary minority finds itself alone, confronted with leaders who are terrified and worried by the idea that they could be swept away by a maelstrom whose nature, force or direction they cannot even imagine. The second process concerns the main leaders [of the "revolutionary minority"—editor], or their seconds in command, who were marked out for police repression under the

are systematically connected, and that struggle on each of the fronts is coordinated.

The "right" wants to compromise with colonialism, to "change the system from within" as We often hear it said. They claim that joining, say, the Democratic or Republican parties will solve the problem—even a "third" or "independent" party that plays by the rules of the oppressive state—is held out as a solution. So, the "intellectual elements" (2.36) and the "militants" (2.37) combine to form a new party (2.38) They declare a new line (e.g., "Black Power" or the claim to open the "armed front" or to launch the "foco"). They end up going underground, or in the countryside or the mountains, while also realizing that activity in the urban centers alone won't be sufficient to overthrow colonialism. As they join the people—who are "rebels by instinct" (2.40), **spontaneous** action soon follows.

> colonialists. It must be emphasized that these men have come to the head of the party by their untiring work, their spirit of sacrifice and the most exemplary patriotism. Such men, who have worked their way up from the bottom, are often unskilled workers, seasonal labourers or even sometimes chronically unemployed. For them the fact of militating in a national party is not simply taking part in politics; it is choosing the only means whereby they can pass from the status of an animal to that of a human being. Such men, hampered by the excessive legalism of the party, will show within the limits of the activities for which they are responsible a spirit of initiative, courage and a sense of the importance of the struggle which marks them out almost automatically as target for colonialist repression. Arrested, condemned, tortured, finally amnestied, they use their time in prison to clarify their ideas and strengthen their determination. Through hunger-strikes and the violent brotherhood of the prisons' quicklime they live on, hoping for their freedom, looking on it as an opportunity to start an armed struggle. But at one and the same time outside the prison walls, colonialism, attacked from all sides, is making advances to the nationalist moderates.
>
> "So we can observe the process whereby the rupture occurs between the illegal and legal tendencies in the party. The illegal minority is made to feel that they are undesirables and are shunned by the people that matter... But the repression of these wayward elements intensifies as the legal party draws nearer to colonialism and attempts to modify it 'from the inside'. The illegal minority thus finds itself in a historical blind alley." (2.36–2.38)

We should pay particular attention to (2.50), where We're given one of the reasons why, "in the beginning," there's a "veritable triumph for the cult of spontaneity"—a one-sided analysis of the thought and practice of the bourgeois parties and their leaders has caused a rejection of all "politics" rather than a righteous rejection of reactionary political thought and practice. The new "left" now substitutes its own superficial line for that of their former comrades which, in practice and over the long run, proves to be just as dangerous as the line that they repudiated—it's "right" in essence. The next paragraph captures this, as We see that there's still "no program." And, at (2.52), We see the circumstances under which "spontaneity is king" and revolutionary politics are abandoned for the "art of war"...*

The spontaneous action sparks a widespread feeling of solidarity and accomplishment, as the people "wills itself to sovereignty." (2.53) However, the enemy launches an all-out offensive (military, political and social), which calls the people's euphoria

---

* "...Every success confirms their hostility towards what in the future they will describe as mouth-wash, word-spinning, blather and fruitless agitation. They feel a positive hatred for the 'politics' of demagogery, and that is why in the beginning we observe a veritable triumph for the cult of spontaneity [...]

"They hold one doctrine only: to act in such a way that the nation may exist. There is no program; there are no speeches or resolutions, and no political trends [...]

"During this period spontaneity is king and initiative is localized. On every hill a government in miniature is formed and takes over power. Everywhere—in the valleys and in the forests, in the jungle and in the villages—we find a national authority. Each man or woman brings the nation to life by his or her action, and is pledged to ensure its triumph in their locality. We are dealing with a strategy of immediacy that is both radical and totalitarian: the aim and program of each locally constituted group is local liberation. If the nation is everywhere, then she is here. One step further, and only here is she found. Tactics are mistaken for strategy. The art of politics is simply transformed into the art of war; the political militant is the rebel. To fight the war and to take part in politics: the two things become one and the same." (2.50–52)

into question. (2.54) Soon, the "spontaneous impetuosity" is condemned to self-repudiation (2.55), not only with regard to the mobility of guerrilla warfare:

> ...the leaders of the rising realize that the various groups must be enlightened; that they must be educated and indoctrinated, and that an army and a central authority must be created. Those leaders who have fled from the useless political activity of the towns rediscover politics, no longer as a way of lulling people to sleep; not as a means of mystification, but as the only method of intensifying the struggle and preparing the people to undertake the governing of their country clearly and lucidly... They discover that the success of the struggle presupposes clear objectives, a definite methodology, and above all the need for the people to realize that their unorganized efforts can only be a **temporary dynamic** [and that the struggle can't be won, and] you won't change human beings if you forget to raise the **standard of consciousness** of the rank and file... (2.57) (my emphasis)

Fanon now points again to the enemy's creation of spontaneity by taking advantage of the people's ideological and social weaknesses, and asserts that "the political education of the masses is seen to be a historic necessity." (2.60)

What's happened to all the solidarity, the euphoria, the feeling of accomplishment as We thought We were riding the "high tide"? "That spectacular volunteer [spontaneous] movement which meant to lead the colonized people to supreme sovereignty at one fell swoop, that certainty which you had that all portions of the nation would be carried along with you at the same speed and led onwards by the same light, that strength which gave you hope: all now are seen, in the light of experience, to be symptoms of a very great weakness. While the native thought that he could pass without transition from the status of a colonized person to that of a self-governing citizen of an independent nation, while he grasped at the mirage of his muscles' own immediacy, he made no real progress along the road to knowledge. His consciousness remained rudimentary." (2.61)

Now, go back and read that again, because i'm sure that at least some of you have failed to notice the keys, e.g., what are the "symptoms" of the very great weakness? What is the "weakness"? What kind of "transition" is necessary?

More and more i come to believe that We periodically find ourselves having to start from scratch not because our job is hard, but merely because We don't know what our job is! Go back, now, to the close of (2.57): "...you won't change human beings..." That's our job; that's the aim of the national and social revolution. Although We're only two chapters into **Wretched**, if you haven't firmly grasped this point yet, then you need to stop here, go back to the first page, and start over... In fact, you also need to go back to the first page of these Meditations and start over.

Many of us really need to pick up on the key in the last section of (2.61), as Fanon points up the period as one in which the people oppose their own "duality" to that of the settler. That they do so is a symptom of the ideological weakness characteristic of "spontaneity," which Fanon sheds light on at (2.62) and (2.63). That is, "racialism" won't sustain a war for national and social revolution, and that such a war should not be waged to allow racialism to triumph. People who hold and depend upon "racialism" don't yet fully realize their own humanity, and, among other things, they easily fall into the trap of the settlers' treatment of them as "human" within the colonial context: **"The native is so starved for anything, anything at all that will turn him into a human being... His consciousness is so precarious and dim that it is affected by the slightest spark of kindliness..."** (2.63)

The message for all of us is that "explanation is very necessary," and that "the people must see where they are going and how they are to get there..." (2.64)

The message is in the last paragraph of the first chapter, and in the last paragraph of the second chapter—We get images of what happens if spontaneity is overcome, and of what happens if it's not.

If "spontaneity" is overcome, then the "left" petty-bourgeois forces will commit "suicide" and become "new" with/as one of the people; the people will become totally responsible for the governing and development of their society.

If "spontaneity" is not overcome, then "independence" will become a farce.

End of Part Two

Notes to Part Two

1. George Jackson, ***Blood In My Eye***, Black Classic Press, Baltimore, 1996.

2. Deborah Wyrick, ***Fanon for Beginners***, Writers and Readers Publishing, Inc., New York, 1998, pps. 62–63.

3. Cornel West, ***The Cornel West Reader***, Basic Civitas Books, New York, 1999, p. 105.

4. Wyrick, op cit., Glossary.

PART THREE

ON THE DE-CONSTRUCTION OF "RACE"

CONTENTS
5A. About This Exercise
5B. Did Fanon Regard "Race" As A "Minor Term"?
5C. The Key Category: "Race" or "Class"?
5D. Fanon on "Race," Racism, Class,
     and the Struggle for Socialism: Meditations
5E. Thoughts on The Deconstruction of "Race"

5A. About This Exercise

> *In combating racism we don't make progress if we combat the people themselves. We have to combat the causes of racism. If a bandit comes into my house and I have a gun, I cannot shoot the shadow of this bandit. I have to shoot the bandit. Many people lose energy and effort, and make sacrifices combating shadows. We have to combat the material reality that produces the shadow ... It is important to avoid confusion between the shadow and the body that projects the shadow...*[1]

If you've read **Part One** and **Part Two** of these **Meditations**, you expected to find here, in **Part Three**, reflections on *Wretched's* treatment of the pitfalls of class and (narrow, bourgeois) national consciousness. Moreover, you would expect to find, in **Part Four**, my reflections on "race" (i.e., a fictional and erroneous categorization of peoples based on actual or imagined social, physical, or biological differences), and racism (i.e., a belief that a plurality of "races" exist; that some of these so-called "races" are superior to others; discrimination and exploitation of peoples using this belief as a rationalization). As i worked on the drafts for **Part Three**, and as i began to outline **Part Four**, it occurred to me that i should switch the order of their subject matter, because i think that "race" should be discussed and reflected upon prior to the subjects of class and national consciousness.

We need to address ourselves to the de-construction of "race" (i.e., to disprove the authenticity of the concept) and We should begin the process of eliminating the word (and all racial language) from the vocabulary and consciousness of the world's peoples— all as part of the process of eliminating racism, and transforming the material reality that "race" serves. This has to be done because of the probability that no effective revolutionary movement (no meaningful transformation of the world) will be generated without incorporating the deconstruction of "race" process into our theory and practice. The probability exists because "race" and racism have been the shadows that have historically diverted people's energies and diffused their revolutionary thrusts. This applies particularly to the motion of peoples within what are now U.S. borders, but it is clearly a worldwide phenomenon.

None of us are free of the responsibility to uproot racialized thought and practice—within ourselves, and wherever We encounter it. As i see it, a "racist" is anyone holding the belief that the human species is divided into a plurality of "races," some of which are superior to others. If you employ a racial binary (e.g., "black" and "white," or "sun people" and "snow people") to categorize people, then you're a "racist" and you practice racism—at a minimum, you confuse the shadow for the body, and you're wasting energy.

As i read the third chapter of **Wretched**, i began to meditate upon Fanon's discussion of the racism practiced by the (neo)colonial bourgeois forces (i.e., those "blacks" or Africans who took the places of the European colonial powers at the state level)—a "racism of defense, based on fear," as he called it. (3.35) Their racism was adopted and practiced to defend their class interests, to "corner the positions formerly kept for foreigners," (3.17) and to become the new ruling class. Their fear was/is that the people will act in their own interests, topple the bourgeois forces, and pursue the development of revolutionary socialist societies.

At the same time, Fanon continues, other sectors of the nation "*follow in the steps of their bourgeoisie,*" and begin to practice racism against non-nationals: "*In the Ivory Coast, the anti-Dahoman and anti-Voltaic troubles are in fact racial riots. The Dahoman and Voltaic peoples, who control the greater part of the petty trade, are, once independence is declared, the object of hostile manifestations on the part of the people of the Ivory Coast. From nationalism we have passed to ultra-nationalism, to chauvinism, and finally to racism."* (3.18)

It occurred to me that We, too, engage in racist behavior, largely as a result of following the lead of our bourgeois forces (and i know that too many of you can't readily identify these forces). And, as i think about it: How naïve We all were to believe, back in the day, that just because folks were "black," that alone made them authentic representatives of truth and justice, and signified that they were true servants of the people. The pity is, tho, that even today far too many of us still think that way. It ain't the color of the skin but rather the content of the character, as Bro. M. L. King, Jr. reminded us.

It's in the third chapter of **Wretched** that Fanon tells us that racialized thought and practice is one of the pitfalls of narrow, bourgeois nationalist consciousness. It causes the bourgeois forces at the head of the people's struggle to develop a neo-colonial "shell" (game) whereby "the nation is passed over for the race, and the tribe is preferred to the state." (3.2) Later, Fanon describes it very succinctly as "a narrow nationalism, and representing a race." (3.33)

Fanon proposes, instead, a "revolutionary nationalist" (socialist) consciousness and program, incorporating attention to the elimination of racism, consciously avoiding all forms of racialism (the categorization of peoples in "racial" terms), while also defeating the bourgeois forces that stand in the way of the people's struggle for genuine independence and socialist development.

Wretched addresses the de-construction of "race" because Fanon clearly urges the abandonment of "racial" identities, and he proposes the adoption of identities based on "class," and/or "nationality"—he encourages us to begin to identify ourselves as "human."

Wretched is about the de-construction of "race" because Fanon calls for the elimination of racism as part of the process of transforming oppressed peoples into "new people," as they build new, socialist nations, and as they help to build a socialist world.

As i reflected upon all of this, i was taken back to my reading of Wyrick's *Fanon for Beginners*.[2] i felt the need to shape this Part in a way that i hadn't originally intended, by incorporating and challenging certain claims made by Wyrick with regard to Fanon's views on "race" and "class," and the alleged divergence that she claims to have existed between the thought of Fanon and the thought of Marx on this and other significant subject matter. Fact is, Wyrick has an obvious bias against "scientific socialism" ("Marxism"), which is linked to her desire to establish the priority of "race" over "class," i.e., to allege the irrelevance or inapplicability of socialism to the struggles of "under-developed" countries and peoples, while positioning bourgeois forces to "leadership."

My aim in making what may appear to be an excessive excursion into Wyrick's work is to shed light on the parallel between Fanon's treatment of bourgeois forces in **Wretched**, and what should be our treatment of the bourgeois forces in our midst. Points must be made... seeds must be planted for the development of theory and practice around this theme. The de-construction of "race" (and successful revolutionary struggle) requires that We deal with the role of bourgeois forces, especially those who feign a progressive, radical, or "nationalist" stand. It requires that all forms of national-class struggle (ideological, political, economic) be engaged with these allies of capitalism, whose fear of socialism causes them to use the shadow of "race" in defense of their class interests, while diverting the people from anti-capitalist struggle.

Recall: We're talking about the same bourgeois forces who, under a confused and militant guise, clouded the issue with "skin analysis" at the height of the last upsurge:

> The only reason we have to get together is the color of our skin. They oppress us because we are black, and we are going to use that blackness to get out of the trick bag they put us

in... We are going to build a movement in this country based on the color of our skin...³

Black people do not want to "take over" this country... They want to be in [the whites'] place because that is where a decent life can be had.⁴

What does Fanon say—"there is no native who does not dream at least once a day of setting himself up in the settler's place." (1.10)*

That is: The "native" that Fanon describes as wanting to "take the place of" the settler, is not yet the "**ex**-native"—the person who comes to realize that it's not his skin or the settler's skin that

---

* "The zone where the natives live is not complementary to the zone inhabited by the settlers. The two zones are opposed, but not in the service of a higher unity. Obedient to the rules of pure Aristotelian logic, they both follow the principle of reciprocal exclusivity. No conciliation is possible, for of the two terms, one is superfluous. The settlers' town is a strongly-built town, all made of stone and steel. It is a brightly-lit town; the streets are covered with asphalt, and the garbage-cans swallow all the leavings, unseen, unknown and hardly thought about. The settler's feet are never visible, except perhaps in the sea; but there you are never close enough to see them. His feet are protected by strong shoes although the streets of his town are clean and even, with no holes or stones. The settler's town is a well-fed town, an easy-going town; its belly is always full of good things. The settler's town is a town of white people, of foreigners.

"The town belonging to the colonized people, or at least the native town, the negro village, the medina, the reservation, is a place of ill fame, peopled by men of evil repute. They are born there, it matters little where or how; they die there, it matters not where, nor how. It is a world without spaciousness; men live there on top of each other, and their huts are built one on top of the other. The native town is a hungry town, starved of bread, of meat, of shoes, of coal, of light. The native town is a crouching village, a town on its knees, a town wallowing in the mire. It is a town of niggers and dirty arabs. The look that the native turns on the settler's town is a look of lust, a look of envy; it expresses his dreams of possession—all manner of possession: to sit at the settler's table, to sleep in the settler's bed, with his wife if possible. The colonized man is an envious man. And this the settler knows very well; when their glances meet he ascertains bitterly, always on the defensive, 'They want to take our place.' It is true, for there is no native who does not dream at least once a day of setting himself up in the settler's place." (1.9–10)

matters, and that merely being in the settler's place will not change the inherent exploitative character of the system of colonialism, i.e., capitalism. Let's be clear: To merely want to be "in the settler's place" means that you really like the system—you support the system—and you just complain because you think you're not getting your "piece of the pie"!

There's a direct link between, say, the "skin analysis" of the mid-1960s, and the reasons that "black power" went from a revolutionary slogan to an accomodationist one, taken up even by the rulers of capital, and reshaped as "green power" and "black capitalism" and what We today know as "empowerment" or as a call for "a piece of the action." It's no accident that the mass consciousness today is heavily "racialized," and not revolutionary, just as "black nationalism" became "ethnic pluralism" and "cultural equality" in the form pushed by the rightist tendency of Afrocentricity. The real revolutionaries were disrupted and fell by the wayside; the bourgeois forces filled the vacuum, and today the people think that "racial feeling" is the same as revolutionary thought and practice.

As i began to think through the writing of this Part, it also occurred to me that i should begin by re-asserting the point that these meditations constitute an "exercise" for all of us. The exercise is something like a field, strewn with seeds, to which We must return and cultivate. That is, We should begin to initiate deliberate, on-going studies, debates, public discussions, and mass-based struggles. We should adopt new "stands," and new styles of work—all with the aim of changing ourselves, helping to change other people, and to change the world.

Within the context of the present subject matter:

- We should, ideally, study everything written by or about Fanon, to draw from the strength and relevancy of his analyses of "the problems of racism and colonialism" as We battle them in the forms that they assume today, in our social environment.

- We should, ideally, study and critique everything ever written on the origin and development of the word and concept "race," and the practice of racism. These should be linked to the engagement of public discussions that help to shape new anti-racial and non-racial (and pro-socialist) concepts and social relations. We should take up studies and struggles that re-examine presently held so-called "truths" about "race," while raising new questions on the relation between "race"/ism and capitalism, e.g., how did differences in social custom and physical characteristics become racialized bases for the class and national exploitation of peoples, and, subsequently, become the fetishized forms for discrimination in their own right?

- We should study everything ever written on the subjects of "class" and "class struggle," approaching the study critically, and help to create new concepts and language that gives them an immediate meaning to people—people who may not know the name "Marx," but who need to know that they are members of a "class" (conscious, "for-itself," or unconscious, "in-itself"), and they and their fellow class members are either leading or being led, active or passive participants in struggle with other classes for control of their lives and futures.

People need to know that "class"—like "race"—is a socially constructed concept. But, unlike "race," the concept of "class" arises from an observation of the actual contradiction resulting from the unequal appropriation of the social wealth by one group, at the expense of others. We use the concept to help us understand the processes and mechanisms of social divisions, and social (revolutionary) change.

People need to know that "class struggle" is taking place every minute, in every sphere of their lives, and that it can be understood as struggle between regression (capitalism) and progress (socialism), no matter what terms We use to identify the opposing forces, e.g., "Decolonization is the meeting of two forces, opposed to each other by their very nature." (1.2)* That is, terms such as "settler" or "bourgeois" can be used to identify the regressive, pro-capitalist forces, and terms such as "native" or "proletarian" can be used to

---

* "Decolonization, which sets out to change the order of the world, is, obviously, a programme of complete disorder. But it cannot come as a result of magical practices, nor of a natural shock, nor of a friendly understanding. Decolonization, as we know, is a historical process: that is to say that it cannot be understood, it cannot become intelligible nor clear to itself except in the exact measure that we can discern the movements which give it historical form and content. Decolonization is the meeting of two forces, opposed to each other by their very nature, which in fact owe their originality to that sort of substantification which results from and is nourished by the situation in the colonies. Their first encounter was marked by violence and their existence together—that is to say, the exploitation of the native by the settler—was carried on by the dint of a great array of bayonets and cannon. The settler and the native are old acquaintances. In fact, the settler is right when he speaks of knowing 'them' well. For it is the settler who has brought the native into existence and who perpetuates his existence. The settler owes the fact of his very existence, that is to say his property, to the colonial system."

identify the progressive, revolutionary forces—those most representative of the struggle for socialism.

i don't doubt that We may need new terms (i.e., other than "bourgeois" and "proletarian"), but it won't matter what terms We use if We don't know what it is that We struggle against and what it is that We struggle for—if We can't relate the terms to the concrete ways that We live, and to the ways that We want to live.

Let me try to illustrate the point (which is that We need to shape and share a vision of the kind of socialist society that We want to build; a vision developed, in part, through the critique of the bourgeois/capitalist order that now oppresses us all).

Fanon made the crucial point that:

> Under the colonial system, a middle-class which accumulates capital is an impossible phenomenon. Now, precisely, it would seem that the historical vocation of an authentic national middle-class in an under-developed country is to **repudiate its own nature in so far as it is bourgeois,** that is to say, in so far as it is the tool of capitalism, and to make itself the willing slaves of that revolutionary capital which is the people. (3.6)* *(emphasis added)*

We don't have to engage in industrial productivity, or live below the poverty line, in order to be "proletarian" (revolutionary) or to begin developing a "proletarian" (revolutionary/socialist) consciousness. It is, however, necessary that We "repudiate" our own nature, "in so far as it is bourgeois."

* "In an under-developed country an authentic national middle-class ought to consider as its bounden duty to betray the calling fate has marked out for it, and to put itself to school with the people: in other words to put at the people's disposal the intellectual and technical capital that it has snatched when going through the colonial universities. But unhappily we shall see that very often the national middle-class does not follow this heroic, positive, fruitful and just path; rather, it disappears with its soul set at peace into the shocking ways—shocking because anti-national—of a traditional bourgeoisie, of a bourgeoisie which is stupidly, contemptibly, cynically bourgeois."

Amilcar Cabral

With the paragraph at (3.6) (also see 1.21–22), Fanon planted a seed that was later cultivated by Amilcar Cabral. Fanon was expressing what's now commonly referred to as the concept and process of "class suicide," which is most associated with Cabral, and rarely, if ever, with Fanon. Cabral's elaboration held that:

> ...*to truly fulfill the role in the national liberation struggle,* **the revolutionary petty bourgeoisie must be capable of committing suicide as a class in order to be reborn as revolutionary workers, completely identified with the deepest aspirations of the people to which they belong.**
>
> *This alternative—to betray the revolution or to commit suicide as a class—constitutes the dilemma of the* **petty bourgeoisie** *in the general framework of the national liberation struggle. The positive solution in favor of the revolution depends on what Fidel Castro recently called the* **development of revolutionary consciousness.** *This dependence necessarily calls our attention to the capacity of [those engaged in] the national liberation [and socialist revolution] struggle to remain faithful to the principles and to the fundamental cause of the struggle. This shows us, to a certain extent, that national liberation [and socialist revolution] is essentially a political problem, the conditions for its development gives it certain characteristics which belong to the sphere of morals.*[5] *(emphasis in original)*

Although Fanon and Cabral spoke on "class suicide" with particular reference to (petty) bourgeois class forces, We should understand that the concept: 1) speaks to individuals rather than (or, more than) to an entire class; 2) speaks to individuals within all classes within oppressed (and oppressing) societies. The masses, or the majority of the people within both oppressed and oppressor nations must develop revolutionary consciousness ("proletarian"/socialist), which doesn't happen spontaneously. Moreover, "racial" deconstruction must be an integral component of a viable revolutionary (class-national) consciousness, particularly for all people within U.S. borders.

To "commit class suicide" means to "kill" the (class) consciousness of the bourgeois/capitalist order that exercises hegemony in our lives and minds. We tend to think of revolutionary activity as that which takes place outside of ourselves—as overthrowing of capitalist institutions and property relations—but We seldom think of the need to uproot the bourgeois ideas in our own minds, to repudiate the values, morals, and the entire range of beliefs that We now hold "in so far as they are bourgeois."

When Cabral calls us to be "reborn as revolutionary workers," most of us don't get beyond the tired images of the "industrial proletariat" or "working class." But Cabral actually suggests images of any and all men and women who strive to become "completely identified with the deepest aspirations of the people to which they belong"—to become people who "work" to produce revolutionary transformations in their society and within their individual selves.

- We need to critically study everything ever written on the origin of the word and concept "nation," and on the evolution of "nationalism." While engaged in this study, We must avoid the quagmire of both bourgeois and doctrinaire "Marxist" interpretations.

Like "race" and "class," the word and concept "nation" has also been socially constructed by peoples as they've made their own history, and defined from the perspective of their own needs and interests.

In one respect, We need to treat the question of "nations" similar to the way Cabral treated the question of the motive force of history with respect to the "class struggle."[6] By such treatment, We're likely to realize that "nations" existed in the world prior to their appearance in Europe. We must come to distinguish "modern" from "pre-modern," capitalist from pre-capitalist, nations—sovereign from oppressed nations. And, just as there is pro-capitalist, bourgeois nationalism, there is also pro-socialist, revolutionary nationalism, whereby peoples shape a new nationality "in the implacable struggle which opposes socialism to capitalism." (1.79)*

We must also cultivate a new "stand" (i.e., the philosophy, methodology, and theory underlying socialism—or better said, revolutionary humanism; new consciousness of the fundamental interests of the revolutionary "class"—We'll talk later on why i put that word within quotation marks—and the methods to be used by its organizations and institutions to realize its objectives), and begin to test/practice new styles of work.

For example, cast off those "mental reservations" that Fanon mentions (1.23)† and begin to talk to people—especially talk to them about socialism, the subject that Fanon says is most feared by the masters of capital. (1.82)

However, We need to learn to introduce the socialist alternative to people without always having to use the word (that is, until We've proven ourselves to people, gained their trust, and overcome their fear of the anti-communist propaganda spread

---

* "All the jacqueries and desperate deeds, all those bands armed with cutlasses or axes find their nationality in the implacable struggle which opposes socialism and capitalism."

† "Self-criticism has been much talked about of late, but few people realize that it is an African institution. Whether in the djemaas of Northern Africa or in the meetings of Western Africa, tradition demands that the quarrels which occur in a village should be settled in public. It is a communal self-criticism, of course, and with a note of humour, because everybody is relaxed, and because in the last resort we all want the same things. But the more the intellectual imbibes the atmosphere of the people, the more completely he abandons the habits of calculation, of unwonted silence, of mental reservations, and shakes off the spirit of concealment. And it is true that already at that level we can say that the community triumphs, and that it spreads its own light and its own reason."

by those who rule). We need to learn how to discuss socialist alternatives so that people don't rush to push the panic button, and can come to recognize these alternatives as reasonable and feasible. We need to begin to build "communalist" transitional structures wherever possible, so that the people can experience "socialism" in their lives, and break loose of the grip of the capitalist propaganda.

We need to begin to fight for socialism, here and now. If (as so many of us say, in defense of our own "laziness") the people around us aren't talking about socialism, it should be easy to see that part of the reason for their silence on the matter is our silence on it.

Moreover, talking about socialism, using examples or scenarios drawn from our own immediate circumstances, demands that We talk about building a non-"racial" socialist society, as does, for example, Julius Nyerere, who held that the basis of socialism is a belief in the oneness of humanity and its common historical journey. To paraphrase him: Socialism is not for the benefit of "black," "brown," "yellow" or "white" people—its purpose is the service of all people, and there can be no socialism without the acceptance of human equality.[7]

This exercise is about more than our desire to read and understand **Wretched** (as if it were about some abstract world, and not our own); it's about more than our need to understand (the failures of) the anti-colonial struggles on the African continent. This exercise is also about us, and about some of the things that We need to understand and to change in ourselves and our world. It's about our need to begin a mass-based and mass-oriented debate on "race" and "class," and on capitalism and socialism. This exercise is about us, because too many of us still think that the enemy is "white people," or that the problem is "white" racism (i.e., as if only "white" people can be "racists"). There are too many of us who fail to target the capitalist system as the enemy and as the problem; too many of us who equate "racial equality" with "liberation." In this instance, however, We fail to equate "liberation" with an end to all forms of the social alienation and economic exploitation that are characteristic of capitalist society; We fail to equate "empowerment" with the kind of power held by the people in a genuine people's democratic order.

As i read **Wretched** and come across Fanon's discussion of the (petty) bourgeois orientation of "Negro-ism" (Negritude), i can't help but make connections to "Afrocentricity," and realize that the predominant character of the latter leads up the same kind of "blind alley" entered by "the men of African culture" of which Fanon spoke. (4.18)

As Fanon discusses Manicheism and racialized binary thinking, i can't help but make connections to those among us who want to discuss "race treason" or "treason to 'whiteness,'" without also discussing treason to the very idea of "race" or, of a treason to "blackness"—as if it's sufficient to dismantle only one side of the racialized binary construction. "Blackness" is no less an unnatural social construction than is "whiteness," and is no less in need of deconstruction.

Connections can also be made to the use of "black" as a "political" and not a "racial" term—without defining the politics. "Black" is not truly de-racialized in this instance. What's needed is analyses of the political spheres that one has reference to, and the adoption of one or more new terms to describe the politics that We previously termed "black," e.g., "revolutionary humanist" politics.

Forms of the racism and colonialism that **Wretched** addressed when it was published remain obstacles to our efforts to overthrow capitalism, and will continue to be so unless and until We dismantle them. We need to fully understand what they are, how they manifest themselves today, what accounts for their "realness" in our lives, and how We can eliminate them. This exercise is about us because We must be able to clearly define the nature of our struggle and come to have the definition shared by the majority of the people. We must name what We struggle against, and name what We struggle for. That is: Are We merely struggling against "white" people? Are We merely struggling against racism, and for a non-racial but capitalist society? Are the principal relations that We need to uproot mere "race relations"?

> ...so-called race relations had very little to do with "race"— initially it was an historical accident that the peoples encountered in the European expansion differed in shared physical characteristics of an obvious kind. But once the racial ideologies had been formed and widely disseminated, they constituted a powerful means of justifying political hegemony and economic control.[8]

> A non-racial society can only be achieved by socialist revolutionary action of the masses... For it is impossible to separate race relations from the capitalist relationships in which they have their roots.[9]

At bottom, so-called "race relations" are economic relations between groups of people(s), better distinguished as classes and/or as nationalities. Just as Fanon pointed to "competition" as the motive for the practice of racism in the newly independent countries of Africa (3.17–36), contemporary research reveals a similar motivation for the development of the very concept "race," and racialized exploitation.*

---

* "We have said that the native bourgeoisie which comes to power uses its class aggressiveness to corner the positions formerly held by foreigners. On the morrow of independence, in fact, it violently attacks colonial personalities: barristers, traders, landed proprietors, doctors and higher civil servants. It will fight to the bitter end against these people 'who insult our dignity as a nation'. It waves aloft the notion of the nationalisation and Africanisation of the ruling classes. The fact is that such action will become more and more tinged with racism, until the bourgeoisie bluntly puts the problem to the government by saying 'We must have these posts'. They will not stop their snarling until they have taken over every one.

"The working-class of the towns, the masses of unemployed, the small artisans and craftsmen for their part line up behind this nationalist attitude; but in all justice let it be said, they only follow in the steps of their bourgeoisie. If

The differences that We now know as "racial" (i.e., perceived fundamental biological differences), were initially derived from social and cultural differences between localized and self-conscious groups of people that began to interact. Physical differences between them meant little or nothing, in themselves, unless and until the interaction began to involve "competition," and one group meant to begin taking "unfair advantage" of the labor and resources of another.

The kind of economic "competition" that would have an individual or class character within the localized, homogeneous social setting of a single group, came to take on a We-They character—as the competition came to involve socially and nationally distinct peoples. Differences in custom and physical appearance were then interpreted as biological, ranked hierarchically; group or national relations became "race" relations, as "race" became a shadow used to divert attention from the actual motive and process of economic relationships. In other words, the development of the concept "race" and the practice of racism rest on a particular (material) reason for elevating social or physical differences to the level of bio-genetic ideology and rationale for the exploitation of peoples.

> the national bourgeoisie goes into competition with the Europeans, the artisans and craftsmen start a fight against non-national Africans. In the Ivory Coast, the anti-Dahoman and anti-Voltaic troubles are in fact racial riots. The Dahoman and Voltaic peoples, who control the greater part of the petty trade, are, once independence is declared, the object of hostile manifestations on the part of the people of the Ivory Coast. From nationalism we have passed to ultra-nationalism, to chauvinism, and finally to racism. These foreigners are called on to leave; their shops are burned, their street stalls are wrecked, and in fact the government of the Ivory Coast commands them to go, thus giving their nationals satisfaction… We observe a permanent see-saw between African unity, which fades quicker and quicker into the mists of oblivion, and a heart-breaking return to chauvinism in its most bitter and detestable form." (3.17–18)

5B. Did Fanon Regard "Race" As A "Minor Term"?

> One of Fanon's most lasting insights is that race is not a "minor term"—indeed, that race not only changes the equation but may call for an entirely new calculus...[10]

In **Part Two**, i set out a number of questions that i later realized could be used to frame this exercise. The questions in **Part Two** were:

What is "violence," and why is it (always) necessary? What is "decolonization"? What is "social structure," and why is change thereof a necessary criterion for the success of the struggle? What does Fanon mean by "species" and why does he put it within quotation marks in (1.1)? Why does Fanon refer to the "restoration" of "nationhood"—and what is a "nation"?

The question for this Part was to have been: What does Fanon mean by the term "species"? To that i now add: What was Fanon's position on the subjects of "race," racism, and "class"? Did he regard colonialism as primarily a racial, or primarily an economic, relationship?

The answers drawn from my reading of **Wretched** and Fanon, seem to be at odds with those drawn by Wyrick.

If you've read **Wretched** (especially if done along with this exercise), then you may have concluded, as i have, that Fanon regarded Manichean and racist ideologies as means used to rationalize the oppression of peoples, and to legitimize their exploitation. Further, you may have concluded, on a broader scale, that "race" and racism help to create, reproduce, and reinforce hierarchies that are rooted in class and national relations of economic exploitation.

In Fanon's view, Manicheism and racism serve the interests of colonialism. The colonized persons who adopt these forms of thought lack an understanding of the nature of the "true" decolonization process, and its vision of the future nation and world.

For example, when Fanon says that the line and methods of the struggle prefigure humanist goals (4A.20), he's reminding us that, among other things, the colonial order is based on a racist dualism, and the new society must not rest upon or otherwise include this form of thought and practice.

In **Wretched**, We easily see that Fanon encourages us to abandon and to deconstruct racist Manicheism, which must involve the deconstruction of the concept "race" and all racialized thought. i also think it's clear that Fanon does not subordinate "class" to "race," nor oppose (revolutionary) nationalism to socialism, as, i think, Wyrick would have us believe.

Wyrick describes **Black Skin, White Masks (BSWM)**,[11] as Fanon's study of group "racial" identity, with its fundamental assumption being that the juxtaposition of the so-called black and white "races" created a form of collective mental illness:

> **Both** *races are locked within the constraints of color, but Fanon's emphasis here is on the formation, meaning, and effect of "blackness."*[12] (emphasis added)

i hasten to point out, first, that We are all (still) collectively mentally ill, evidence of which is our use of the language of "race."

The phrase "both races" shouldn't be used to describe the groups in question. This usage shows that the deconstruction of the concept of "race" has to be based on the elimination of racial language.

Go back to **Part One** and meditate on the discussion of Ngugi wa Thiong'o's treatment of the thought and practice of colonized intellectuals, who "did not always adequately evaluate the real enemy," and continued to see things in terms of "skin pigmentation," clinging to a "reductionism to the polarities of color and race."

Too many of us continue to use the language of "race," even as

We claim to be engaged in the struggle against racism, racial ideology, and for a new, collective identity.

> References to the realness of race are the means through which race as a reality is constructed.[13]

Have you really thought about that line since you first read it? How much thought have you given to this one?:

> We always agree that "race" is invented, but are then required to defer to its embeddedness in the world.[14]

We aren't really "required" to make such deferrals; it's more a matter of our own consciousness, conviction, and courage. This is one of those seeds that We gotta come back to and cultivate. We're actually required to decide upon new terms, to form new definitions, to engage and become consistent in their use and application.

In my last reference to Wyrick, i emphasized the word "both" to help point up that We're locked within the constraints of color, which is one of the "effects of 'blackness,'" and of accepting it as an authentic identity.

Fanon's examination of "blackness" was attention given to one side of the racialized binary construction that needs to be dismantled. It wasn't done to authenticate or perpetuate the use of the term "black" to identify a people. As We'll see below, Fanon actually sought to show the spurious nature of "blackness." As Wyrick herself says in this regard, our task is, in part, to free ourselves from the constraints of color, and to "reject the categories through which others seek to imprison us."[15] Yeah, "Black" people are a creation of colonialism ... and as an identity, it's really a form of imprisonment.

In her Glossary, Wyrick defines racism as "institutionalized assignment of values to real or **imaginary** differences in order to justify aggression and protect privilege." (emphasis added)

i couldn't find a definition of racism, as such, in **Wretched**, but Wyrick provides a useful passage when describing Fanon's response to the claim that European civilization wasn't responsible for colonial racism: "Colonial racism is no different from any other racism... All forms of exploitation are identical because all of them are applied to the same 'object': Man."[16]

Is Fanon defining racism as (a form of) exploitation, or is he, like Wyrick, saying that (all forms of) racism is used to facilitate exploitation? If he's saying the former, it would seem to be a definition of racism similar to those promoted here, post-1970, which tend to conflate racism and colonialism, or, mask colonialism by defining racism as a system of exploitation, rather than as a tool used by exploitative systems. This confuses us and leads us to struggle against racism, but not necessarily against capitalism, and for socialism.

Moreover, if Fanon is saying that racism is used to facilitate exploitation, doesn't that raise questions at least about the context within which to view Wyrick's claim that Fanon didn't regard "race" as a "minor term" in colonial situations?

The questions are important, because We must be able to distinguish Fanon's thought from Wyrick's. And, We must be able to understand—in general, and with regard to Fanon's thought, and **Wretched**—the relation of "race" to class (and nation)... the relation of "race" to the overthrow of capitalism and the construction of socialism.

Wyrick uses a discussion of Negritude, to not only set the stage for her claim that "race" wasn't a "minor term" for Fanon, but also that he regarded "race" (as opposed to class or economic relationships) as the key categorical term in colonial situations.

She says that Fanon was, in **BSWM**, ambivalent toward Negritude, on one hand holding that it exposed "gifts worthy of celebration," and, on the other hand, that it was "capable of drowning people of color in a tide of regression... Fanon is skeptical of reversing racist stereotypes by assigning positive instead of negative values to them."[17]

(Wyrick discusses Negritude again in her chapter on **Wretched**—i've looked but couldn't find any use of the term "Negritude" in my copy/translation of **BSWM**. What i did find is use of the term "Negroism." Based in part on my readings of the excerpts from **BSWM** that i use below, i think Fanon used "Negroism" in **Wretched** to indicate development of his thought on the "disappearance" of "negroes"—as when he says, at (4.46), that "niggers are disappearing," and at (4A.13), that "niggerhood" is a relationship that's on the way out, as is the disappearance of the colonized personality.)

Wyrick continues:

> *Fanon sees that Negritude is an important tool for finding meaning and worth in a hostile world, even if it does not ultimately provide an adequate foundation for black identity. It is on this point that he disagrees with Sartre...*[18]

i can't help myself—because every opportunity must be taken to point up the contradictions: Fanon, We're told, sees Negritude as an important tool "even if it does not ultimately provide an adequate foundation for black identity."

Fanon didn't seek an adequate foundation for "black" identity! He sought a foundation for national identity; or, for identity as a revolutionary class; or, for identity as "new people"—a new humanity... a new "species" of humanity not in any way characterized by or as "race"...

Now, why was it necessary to bring Sartre into a discussion of Fanon's thinking on Negritude? i contend that it was done to give us a false lead... to set up a false contradiction between (revolutionary) nationalism, and socialism.

According to Wyrick, Sartre claimed that Negritude was "the moment of negativity in a Marxist-Hegelian historical dialectic, the predetermined stage necessary to the victory of the proletariat, where race will not matter. Fanon is outraged."[19]

What are We to believe that Fanon was "outraged" about? That Sartre allegedly held that a society could be built where "race" wouldn't matter? We could, i guess, read Sartre (as presented by Wyrick) as claiming that Negritude itself represented a stage at which "race" no longer mattered. Or, We could read that the arrival of Negritude represented the beginning of a process that would lead to a society where "race" wouldn't matter. Or, is it simply that Fanon was supposedly outraged over a claim that "race" did not then matter, or would not matter at some point in the future?

According to Wyrick, Fanon's alleged outrage is expressed here: "At the very moment when I was trying to grasp my own being, Sartre, who remained the Other... was reminding me that my blackness was only a minor term... Without a negro past, without a negro future, it was impossible for me to live my negrohood."[20]

Well, maybe my interpretative ability is faulty, but i don't think there's only one way to read this passage. What do you think?

Here is Fanon, saying that when he was trying to grasp his being as "black," Sartre reminded him that "blackness" or "race" was/is only a "minor term"—or, a shadow—and that it's really not a question of living a "negrohood," but something more...

It could be that if Fanon had written in a style like mine, the words "blackness" and "negro" would have been accented so as to clearly suggest that he, too, had come to agree that his identity

should be something other than "negrohood" or "blackness"...
Wyrick then continues:

> One of Fanon's most lasting insights is that race is not a "minor term"—indeed, that race not only changes the equation but may call for an entirely new calculus. **A just and classless society may be possible, but it is not the same as a raceless one**, nor can it be achieved without each race "disalienating" itself. As long as one race is defined by its differences from the other, both will be fettered by racist formations. Their jobs, however, are not to enlighten or redeem each other. In this early work, even as he recognizes the reciprocal effects that racism has, Fanon emphasizes individual will and existential autonomy. No matter what a black man has been taught to want, Fanon is clear about what he should do. He must act to release himself from the tyrannies of past exploitations and present degradations. He must cast off his mask, break the deforming mirror, look at himself steadily, and see a free human being.[21] (my emphasis)

Again: Note the deference to the embeddedness, e.g., "each race," "one race," etc. All this argument for the importance of "race" from a person who says that racism sees the world in "unreal categories" and is "inherently unreasonable."[22]

Unlike Wyrick, i hold that a truly just and classless society is the same as a "raceless" one. But, let's look again at the last sentence of that paragraph: A just and classless society can't be achieved without each "race" disalienating itself! Precisely the objective! i thought that this is what Fanon was saying all along—especially because the concept of "disalienation" is one that he used to describe the process of each "race" becoming free "human beings"—even though, at times, they may also identity themselves as, say, Algerians. For clarity: alienation was caused by the creation and adoption of "racial" identities; thus, disalienation seeks to dismantle and abandon such identities.

Fanon's own words in **BSWM** tend to throw a different interpretation upon the passage in which Wyrick claims Fanon's "outrage," and the theme of his longing for a "negrohood."

Though extensive, i'm using most of the excerpts, in order to give you as much information as possible upon which to base your own interpretations:

> "The negro, however sincere, is the slave of the past ... Face to face with the white man, the negro has a past to legitimate…"

> "Those negroes and white men will be disalienated who refuse to let themselves be sealed away in the materialized Tower of the Past. For many other negroes, in other ways, disalienation will come into being through their refusal to accept the present as definitive."

> "I am a man, and what I have to recapture is the whole past of the world. I am not responsible solely for the revolt in Santo Domingo…"

> "In no way should I derive my basic purpose from the past of the peoples of color."

> "In no way should I dedicate myself to the revival of an unjustly unrecognized negro civilization. I will not make myself the man of any past. I do not want to exalt the past at the expense of my present and of my future…"

> "In this world, which is already trying to disappear, do I have to pose the problem of black truth?"

> "Do I have to be limited to the justification of a facial conformation?…"

> "There is no negro mission; there is no white burden."

"My life is caught in the lasso of existence. My freedom turns me back on myself. No, I do not have the right to be a negro…"

"I find myself suddenly in the world and I recognize that I have one right alone: That of demanding human behavior from the other."

"One duty alone: That of not renouncing my freedom through my choices."

"I have no wish to be the victim of the Fraud of a black world…"

"There is no white world, there is no white ethic, any more than there is a white intelligence…"

"I am not the slave of the slavery that dehumanized my ancestors…"

"The disaster of the man of color lies in the fact that he was enslaved."

"The disaster and the inhumanity of the white man lies in the fact that somewhere he has killed man…"

"I, the man of color, want only this: That the tool never possess the man…"

"The negro is not. Anymore than the white man."

"Before it can adopt a passive voice, freedom requires an effort at disalienation…"

"It is through the effort to recapture the self and to scrutinize the self, it is through the lasting tension of their freedom that men will be able to create the ideal conditions of existence for a human world."

> "Superiority? Inferiority? Why not the quite simple attempt to touch the other, to feel the other, to explain the other to myself?"[23]

Does it sound as if Fanon would truly be "outraged" at a reminder (by Sartre) that his "blackness," his "negro past," his "negro future," his "negrohood"—his "race" or racial identity—was only a "minor term"?

Fanon himself called for the disalienation of both "races." He pointed to the "black" people and urged them not to accept their present as definitive—including their present identity as "blacks."

So, did Fanon regard "race" as a "minor term"? In my opinion, yes—which doesn't mean that he didn't regard "race" or racism as "salient."

5C. The Key Category: "Race" or "Class"?

> *In general, Fanon agrees with Marx that history runs dialectically, through the struggle of faction against faction. But whereas Marx categorized factions in terms of economic* **class**, *Fanon claims that* **race** *is the key categorical term in colonial situations.*[24] (*Wyrick's emphasis in original*)

i mentioned earlier that the front cover of my copy of **Wretched** says that the book is Fanon's study of "racism and colonialism in the world today." i've had to remind myself that this description of the book was probably one developed by Grove Press, and not by Fanon.

It may be that the publishers chose to use the word "racism" as a kind of selling point aimed at a Western audience. Nevertheless, its use on the cover gives the impression that "racism" is a major, running theme in **Wretched,** which ain't necessarily so.

i mean, Fanon never uses the word "racism" until he reaches the third chapter, and then in connection with the racism and racialized thought of the colonized bourgeois forces and other sectors of the colonized population that take their lead from these forces. Again: Fanon understood racism as a tool of colonialism and of bourgeois rule.

We can speculate as to what Fanon would have written as a "selling point" for the cover. We're left to read the book for ourselves to determine whether or not Fanon truly regarded "race" as the "key categorical term" in the process of decolonization; left to read for ourselves to uncover Fanon's own description of the principal relationships and objectives of colonized peoples, and his own articulation of the relation of "race" and racism to the struggle against colonialism.

However, the key point is this: For him to have regarded "race" as the key categorical term in colonial situations, he would have to have understood "race" or racialized relations as the essential or universal relation between people, and not an incidental or contingent relation. i doubt that he did so.

i take it that Fanon knew that racism, as a means of discrimination, is based on a belief in the existence of "race"—a belief that it's a real, legitimate, natural way of categorizing people. That is, there'd be no racism without a belief that there are biologically identifiable and distinguishable "races," which stand in relation to each other as inherently superior or inferior. Thus, to combat racism, We must also combat the belief in "race"—We must assist

the slow dawning of our consciousness upon "truths that are only partial, limited and unstable."* (2.69)[25]

Fanon actually wastes no time to tell us what **Wretched** is about: "National liberation, national renaissance, the restoration of nationhood to the people... decolonization..." (1.1) There's no "race is the key" here. And, what does Fanon list as the fundamental tasks for colonized peoples? He says that "the defeat of colonialism is the real object of the struggle." (1.26) He also offers "the liberation of the national territory; a continual struggle against colonialism in its new forms; and an obstinate refusal to enter the charmed circle of mutual admiration at the summit." (4.49)

It doesn't seem to me that the Fanon whom Wyrick claims held "race" as the key categorical term, was the same man who held that the governments of newly independent nations must "give back their dignity to all citizens, fill their minds and feast their eyes with human things, and create a prospect that is human because

---

* "The settler is not simply the man that must be killed. Many members of the mass of colonialists reveal themselves to be much, much nearer to the national struggle than certain sons of the nation. The barriers of blood and race-prejudice are broken down on both sides. In the same way, not every Negro or Moslem is issued with a hallmark of genuineness; and the gun or knife is not inevitably reached for when the settler makes his appearance. Consciousness slowly dawns upon truths that are only partial, limited and unstable. As we may surmise, all this is very difficult... These politics are national, revolutionary and social, and these new facts which the native will now come to know exist only in action. They are the essense of the fight which explodes the old colonial truths and reveals unexpected facets, which brings out new meanings and pinpoints the contradictions camouflaged by these facts. The people engaged in the struggle who because of it command and know these facts, go forward, freed from colonialism and forewarned at all attempts at mystification, innoculated against all national anthems. Violence alone, violence committed by the people, violence organized and educated by its leaders, makes it possible for the masses to understand social truths and gives the key to them. Without that struggle, without that knowledge of the practice of action, there's nothing but a fancy-dress parade and the blare of trumpets. There's nothing save a minimum of readaptation, a few reforms at the top, a flag waving: and down there at the bottom, an undivided mass, still living in the middle ages, endlessly marking time."

conscious and sovereign [people] dwell therein." (3.96)* This is the same man of whom Wyrick had earlier said: "Revolutionary struggle is ultimately a humanistic project encompassing all people."[26]

Recall: We earlier used Wyrick's definition of colonialism, which she said is "the forceful occupation of another people's land in order to extract material benefits; thus it means compelling the colonized to work for the colonizer's economic interests... Fanon believes that colonialism depends on racism. Enslaving or oppressing another group of people is easier if they look different than you do," and that "theft" drives the colonial project.[27] It would seem

---

* "...We have seen in the preceding pages that nationalism, that magnificent song that made the people rise against their oppressors, stops short, falters and dies away on the day that independence is proclaimed. Nationalism is not a political doctrine, nor a program. If you really wish your country to avoid regression, or at best halts and uncertainties, a rapid step must be taken from national consciousness to political and social consciousness... On the level of underdeveloped humanity there is a kind of collective effort, a sort of common destiny. The news which interests the Third World does not deal with king Baudouin's marriage nor the scandals of the Italian ruling class. What we want to hear about are the experiments carried out by the Argentinians or the Burmese in their efforts to overcome illiteracy or the dictatorial tendencies of their leaders. It is these things which strengthen us, teach us and increase our efficiency ten times over. As we see it, a program is necessary for a government which really wants to free the people politically and socially. There must be an economic program; there must be a doctrine concerning the division of wealth and social relations. In fact, there must be an idea of man and the future of humanity... But if nationalism is not made explicit, if it is not enriched and deepened by a very rapid transformation into a consciousness of social and political needs, in other words into humanism, it leads up a blind alley. The bourgeois leaders of under-developed countries imprison national consciousness in a sterile formalism. It is only when men and women are included on a vast scale in enlightened and fruitful work that form and body are given to that consciousness. Then the flag and the palace where sits the government cease to be the symbols of the nation. The nation deserts those brightly-lit, empty shells and takes shelter in the country, where it is given life and dynamic power. The living expression of the nation is the moving consciousness of the whole of the people; it is the coherent, enlightened action of men and women... The national government, if it wants to be national, ought to govern by the people and for the people, for the outcasts and by the outcasts..."

to me that if "theft" drives the colonial project, then "theft" would more likely be the key categorical term.

Someone could make the argument that Wyrick's definition of colonialism—her belief that colonialism "depends" on racism—doesn't negate her claim about "race". Yet, We must recall her definition of racism: "Institutionalized assignment of values to real or imaginary differences, in order to justify aggression and protect privilege."[28]

Fanon does discuss racism, and the need to uproot it. Taking **Wretched** as a whole, i think We have to conclude that Fanon didn't regard "race" as the key categorical term upon which colonized peoples should base their struggles to regain national independence. Fanon saw the struggle against racism in colonial situations not only as part of the process of ousting the colonizer, but also as part of the struggle between the bourgeois and the revolutionary class forces of the colonized people—as part of the process of deconstructing the concept of "race," while transforming its material base and building a non-racial, socialist society.

At the center of everything else happening around us, We still confront what Robert Allen identified as the "longstanding unresolved problem" confronting Afrikans (and others) in the U.S.: "finding the proper relationship between a purely national (or racial) analysis and program on the one hand, and a purely class analysis and program on the other."[29]

i've always had a problem with the way Allen's proposition is phrased because it suggests ways of perceiving "race," "nation," and "class" which in themselves disallow easy resolution of the contradiction.

If We call these "errors of perception," then the first one is made when We forget that "race" is a fiction. Even tho We tend to say things like "racism is real," "race" is still a fiction, and any sense of "reality" that We think it assumes through the practice of racism or colonialism, remains a "shadow" of the material reality that produces it and which it serves. Yeah, "race" is "real"—as an idea—as a phenomenon operating through numerous spheres and institutions on the level of the superstructure. The "reality" of "race" is only relative—just as the independence and influence of all superstructural phenomena are relative vis-a-vis the base.

The next error is made whenever We equate "nation" with "race," e.g., when We think that making a "national" analysis is the same as making a "racial" one, or vice versa. i know that most people don't seem to know the difference between the two, and in the first place because they think that "race" is real. However, the difference is also hard to distinguish because the peculiarity of racialized capitalist and colonialist exploitation throughout the world (but particularly in the U.S.) has caused us to become accustomed to using racial frames of reference as We actually analyze national, and class, phenomena.

Now, the third error is made whenever We think that there are such things as "pure" national and class analyses within the context of the issue under discussion. That is, We can't analyze "nation" without giving attention to the classes within it, and nor can We analyze classes outside the boundaries provided for them by the nation. Moreover, a "pure" class analysis, as most people perceive it, is impossible without engaging all the other social activity that influence and are part of "class" formation and function.

What happens, then, if We avoid making these errors? Or, what happens if and when We dispense with all inherited dogma, no matter the source, and begin to use the methodology as it should be used, and make concrete analyses of concrete situations and uncover what's really around us, and not try to make the reality fit someone's preconceived notions or models?

If i'm reading Fanon correctly, he's saying that the people aren't/shouldn't struggle simply to achieve "national liberation," but to build socialism—that the struggle for national independence remains incomplete so long as the construction of a socialist society is incomplete.

It's within a similar context that i view the struggle(s) inside the U.S. For example, New Afrikans are waging a struggle for socialism! We struggle as a people ("nation") within the political borders of a capitalist-settler-colonialist society that uses "race" to distort the minds and divert the energies of the masses of both the colonized and the colonizing nations. Ours has always been a "class struggle"; ours has always been a "national" struggle—and it has always served the interests of the oppressive society to characterize our struggle as one based merely on "race relations."

Much of this is simply about perception, or about consciousness. Imamu Baraka wasn't too far off the mark when he said that within U.S. borders, "black" is a country—that New Afrikan people have been separated and made to live in our own "country of color."[30]

Imamu Baraka

Of course, "black" ain't a color in that context, but a racialized name of a "country," a people, a nationality. Under racialized capitalist and colonialist oppression, especially in the U.S., color marks the boundaries of subjugated national territory. And, color becomes a unique element in the "class" relationship to the colonizing nation. That is, in the era of imperialism, "class struggle" manifests itself as struggle between oppressed ("proletarian") and oppressor ("bourgeois") nations/peoples—the colonized ("proletarian") and the colonizing ("bourgeois") nations/

peoples/"classes" are the opposing poles in "proletarian socialist world revolution" against the "world capitalist/bourgeoisie."

At the moment, it's as if We hold an unarticulated concept of "class" that doesn't transcend "race," but incorporates it as one of its peculiar distinguishing characteristics. Sometimes, We say "race" when We actually mean to say, or should say, "class" or "nation." Something like that distinction which underlies the way Fanon opposes "racial feeling" to "racial prejudice." (2.62)* Or, something like that which underlies Wyrick's statement, as she draws from Fanon's **BSWM**, that "the white man makes the black man by recognizing only his skin."[31] What really happened is that the "white man" was made in the same process, and by the same means, so that even today We tend to recognize ourselves and others, by skin, color, "race"—and it's all a fiction, social construction, and a particular form of, or element of, consciousness. We find ourselves resting on this foundation even when We use the word "race" to mean "the group" or "the people" as in "He's a 'race man'."

Because "race" has come to function on the superstructure, it's become part of our distinct way of life and cultural existence. "Racial" interests have become part of the group interests that We share, and which stand as antagonistic to the interests of other

---

* "Racial feeling, as opposed to racial prejudice, and that determination to fight for one's life which characterises the native's reply to oppression are obviously good enough reasons for joining in the fight. But you do not carry on a war, nor suffer brutal and widespread repression, nor look on while all other members of your family are wiped out in order to make racialism or hatred triumph. Racialism and hatred and resentment—'a legitimate desire for revenge'—cannot sustain a war of liberation...At all events as we have noticed the enemy tries to win the support of certain sectors of the population, of certain districts and of certain chiefs. As the struggle is carried on, instructions are issued to the settlers and to the police forces; their behavior takes on a different complexion: it becomes more 'human'. They even go so far as to call a native 'Mister' when they have dealings with him. Attentions and acts of courtesy come to be the rule. The native is in fact made to feel that things are changing."

groups of people—classes and nations. "Race"—as a characteristic of the peculiar class and national social relations of capitalist and colonialist exploitation—has helped to provide us with an understanding of being a distinct community which extends across local and regional boundaries, constituting part of our national bond; it's part of the collective consciousness that We have of ourselves—which informs the creation of the organizations and institutions that We use in pursuit of our aims. Now, all of this is, really, less about "race" than about class and national formation and consciousness. Rather, not about "race," since that's a fiction…

Because "race" is a fiction, what We have to do is resolve the theoretical problem posed by our being a uniquely constituted oppressed people which, depending upon the context of the analysis, can be understood as: 1) an oppressed "nation," and/or 2) a potentially revolutionary/proletarian "class."

Now i know there'll be all kinds of objections, from all quarters, and among them the claim that i can't have it both ways. All i can say is that this ain't my way, it's the way that it is. What it becomes is up to you, i.e., what you do or fail to do, to transform yourself and the present reality.

For example: Whether New Afrikan people struggle to create a separate socialist existence on distinct territory depends—upon what New Afrikan people do or fail to do. Whether New Afrikans join with others to make a socialist revolution in/for the whole of the U.S. depends—upon what New Afrikans and others do or fail to do…

Let me hasten to point out: By "New Afrikans" i don't mean "black" people. i mean those who come to identify their nationality as "New Afrikan," and who thus exhibit the consciousness and embrace the values and philosophy… those who pursue the goals of "New Afrikans." To me, being a "New Afrikan" is not about the color of one's skin, but about one's thought and practice. i know that not everyone agrees with this, but that's their problem…

As i mentioned earlier, Fanon doesn't mention "racism" until the third chapter of **Wretched** (esp. 3.17–36), where he makes the connection with his critique of the colonized bourgeois forces. (But, also notice the references to the racialized thought of the intellectuals in Chapter Four.) He shows how they uphold the concept of "race" and promote racialized thought and practice in order to block the advance of national and social revolution—to prevent the radical unity of the people from averting the rise of the neo-colonial state. Underlying all references to "racism" (to "race") are the economic and political relationships between, on the one hand, the colonized bourgeois forces and the forces of colonialism and, on the other hand, the colonized bourgeois forces and the mass of the people. Put another way: "At the foundation of racism is a system of savagely unequal economic and political relations."[32] It matters not whether We're talking about the form of colonial relations between Algeria and France, or between New Afrikans and the U.S.

Wyrick devotes an entire section of her chapter on **Wretched** to set up what i consider to be a false polemic between Marx and Fanon. She succeeds in announcing her bias toward, and her ignorance of, socialist thought. She also reveals herself as one of those wily intellectuals that Fanon warns us against. That is, Wyrick engages in an exercise to cloud the revolutionary socialist methodology underlying Fanon's analysis, and in order to do so she takes a few of his statements out of context. She provides us with an example of some of the means used by New Afrikan bourgeois forces who seek power "in the name of a narrow nationalism and representing a race." (3.33)

Those who seek to truly oppose and uproot racial thought and racism have to do so by basing their efforts on a struggle to decompose the belief in "race," and unveil the capitalist motives underlying the practice of racism. Racism will continue to exist so long as the belief in the concept of "race" and the material reality underlying it exist. It's this belief which allows racism to appear as totally autonomous of the economic relations that it serves. Unless and until it's uprooted, its forms will change, and the pervasiveness and intensity of its practice will ebb and flow, following the needs of its base, the political requirements of the oppressive state, and the forms and levels of struggle engaged by the people.

Must racism be challenged? Yes. Does "race" have a certain kind of "reality"? Yes. But, what We fail to focus on is that "race" is only as "real" as our consciousness and our practice allow it to be.

Those who try to make us believe otherwise are either deluded, or have the conscious motive of not wanting us to shift our attention from the shadow to the robber—for fear that our attention will be focused on them. Their motives are to join in the robbery; they want to pursue the capitalist way, and they only oppose the efforts of the rulers of capital to exclude them from the spoils and the positions. And, they do it in the name of "opposing racism"— but you never hear them shout, seriously, against capitalism. You surely never hear them proclaim a belief in socialism, nor do they urge the people to study socialism and to join them in its pursuit.

Wyrick sets up her false polemic by saying that colonized peoples need a coherent political philosophy, and that:

> *Fanon advocates socialism as both a practical and ethical "solution" for emerging countries. Many nationalist parties in Africa, however, couch socialist goals in what Fanon considers to be misleading, even dangerous, Marxist language. It's not that Fanon necessarily disagrees with Marx's critique of industrial capitalism, analysis of European society, and dialectical theory of history. Instead, he recognizes that economics and social organization in "underdeveloped countries" bear little resemblance to conditions in highly developed ones... and that the pressures of the colonial situation must be dealt with as well.*[33]

Let's not even touch that sarcastic use of "solution"...But We have to deal with the implied contrast between "socialist goals" and "Marxist language." Where, i'd like to know, does Fanon discuss this alleged misleading, dangerous, "Marxist language"? What is Fanon supposed to have said about the use of such language to "couch socialist goals"? Finally, she seems unable to make the distinction between the method, and any particular results derived from the application of that method to concrete situations, in terms of both place and time. Naw... it's Wyrick who's trying to mislead here, starting by accenting "solution," as if to say that Fanon advocated something less than scientific socialism. In one of his clearest statements on the issue:

> ...Of course we know that the capitalist regime, in so far as it is a way of life, cannot leave us free to perform our work at home, nor our duty in the world. Capitalist exploitation and cartels and monopolies are the enemies of under-developed countries. On the other hand the choice of a socialist regime, a regime which is completely oriented towards the people as a whole and based on the principle that [people are] the most precious of all possessions, will allow us to go forward more quickly and more harmoniously, and thus make impossible that caricature of society where all economic and political power is held in the hands of a few who regard the nation as a whole with scorn and contempt. (1A.6)

What is it that Wyrick wants us to believe? That Fanon advocated a form of socialism that couldn't be described in some of the language used by Marx—an "African socialism," maybe? That Fanon didn't think that the methodology used by Marx to analyze and critique industrial, capitalist/Western/European societies is applicable to colonial, African societies? Maybe this is why she thought it apt to cap off the section with Fanon's oft-quoted suggestion that "Marxist analysis should always be slightly stretched every time we have to do with the colonial problem."[34]

Walter Rodney

i say that the language Fanon would have considered dangerous and misleading is that used by those who couched bourgeois goals under the banner of, say, "African" socialism. Walter Rodney told us that some of those waving this banner were under the illusion that they could find a "third way" between capitalism and doctrinaire "Marxism," while others were "blatantly dishonest from the beginning... cheap tricksters... attempting to hoodwink" the people—because the people were "no longer willing to accept anything that is not put to them in the guise of socialism."[35]

However, in either case, "They failed because their conception of what was a variant different from bourgeois thought and different from [doctrinaire] socialist thought inevitably turned out to be merely another branch of bourgeois thought."[36]

Kwame Nkrumah told us that it was because the people wanted socialism that the phrase "African socialism" became "a necessity in the platform diction" and the political writings of African activists, intellectuals, and heads of parties and states. However, the phrase lost legitimacy as it became identified with policies that didn't promote genuine socialist economic and social development.[37]

Kwame Nkrumah

We should be quick to note that Fanon urged us to "stretch Marxist analysis," not abandon the methodology of revolutionary socialism! When We "stretch" something We must maintain or even tighten our grip on it. In this case, WE must recall that revolutionary socialist philosophy, theory, and methodology don't require us to fixate on prior conclusions, nor to turn any prior conclusions into dogma. Rather, We are to use them as tools in the analyses of concrete situations, and use the conclusions that are thus drawn as guides to action.

When Wyrick says "stretch," she really means "abandon"—her aim is to dissuade colonized peoples from adopting and adapting socialist methodology.

Wyrick seems to doubt—and seems to want us to doubt—the applicability of "Marxist analysis" to the struggles of non-European peoples. Her reasoning is a variant of the dominant objection to the study and use of scientific socialist methodology made in the 60s and 70s in the U.S., particularly among New Afrikans, i.e., that Karl Marx was a "white boy" and a racist, and thus unworthy of study by "people of color." Among the most appropriate responses to such claims was that given by Huey Newton of the Black Panther Party:

> If you are a dialectical materialist... Marx's racism does not matter. You do not believe in the conclusions of one person, but in the validity of a mode of thought; and we in the Party, as dialectical materialists, recognize Karl Marx as one of the great contributors to that mode of thought. Whether or not Marx was a racist is irrelevant and immaterial to whether or not the system of thinking he helped develop delivers truths about processes in the material world.[38]

Walter Rodney suggests that the question of the relevance of revolutionary socialist thought to the struggles of African peoples is most often raised by those who operate from within the bourgeois framework: "*One starts out located within the dominant mode of reasoning, which is the mode of reasoning that supports capitalism, and which questions the logic and relevance of socialism, and even opposes its study.*"[39]

Rodney holds that revolutionary socialism is valid for peoples in this period, not only in Europe, but also in Africa, the Caribbean, and the U.S., because it retains its potential as a tool and set of conceptions that operate across time and space:

> A methodology which begins its analysis of any society, of any situation, by seeking the relations which arise in production between [people]. There are a whole variety of things which flow from that: [people's] consciousness is formed in the intervention in nature; nature itself is humanized through its interaction with [people's] labor; and [people's] labor produces a constant stream of technology which in turn creates other social changes.
>
> So this is the crux of the Scientific Socialist perception. A methodology that addresses itself to [people's] relationship in the process of production on the assumption—which I think is a valid assumption—that production is not merely the basis of [people's] existence, but the basis for defining [people] as a special kind of being with a certain consciousness [which is] a very powerful force, and one that even some Marxists have been tempted to underestimate.[40]

Rodney also says that the methodology and ideology of socialism have been "utilized, internalized, domesticated in large parts of the world that are not European," and that revolutionary socialism "is already the ideology which was used by Cabral, which was used by Samora Machel, and which is in use on the African continent itself to underline and underscore struggle and the construction of a new society."⁴¹

Wyrick suggests that the "Marxian"/scientific socialist categories and concepts that need "stretching" are:

 1) "CLASS STRUCTURE," BECAUSE:

- "race" and not "class" is the key category in colonial situations. Or, as she also puts it, economic relationships are secondary to racial ones. To support this claim, she quotes Fanon (1.11), but appears to take the quote out of context, while also distorting it by omission: "…Economic reality, inequality, and the immense difference of ways of life never come to mask the human realities. When you examine at close quarters the colonial context, it is evident that what parcels out the world is to begin with the fact of belonging to or not belonging to a given race…"⁴²

- there's a fundamental distinction between European "class structure" and colonial "race structure." To support this claim, she quotes Fanon (1.12), but again, i think, somewhat out of context, and distorts by omission: "…The governing race is first and foremost those who come from elsewhere, those who are unlike the original inhabitants, 'the others.'"⁴³ We're to believe, first, in the existence of a "race structure" that negates or subordinates the existence and relevance of "class structure" and economic relationships—and why? Because the colonialists are "those from elsewhere"? This "geographical difference," as she calls it, actually marks the distinction between two nation-classes, and "race" is used to mask the economic-material basis. There is no "race structure," only a racialized national-class structure unique to colonial (and capitalist) relationships.

  When Fanon talks about the colonial bourgeoisie as "a true branch of the bourgeoisie of the mother country, that derives its legitimacy, its force and its stability from the bourgeoisie of the homeland" (3.65), i get no sense of his seeing this class (structure) in racial terms. The "others" are the representatives of a class (and nation), not a "race"—they are a "species" in the socio-economic framework, not the biological one. Even when the context of (3.65) is taken into account, the point goes to the nature of the contradiction—the "key category" in colonial situations. An analysis of colonialism doesn't begin with the binary opposites "black" and "white" ("race"), but with economic, political, and social analyses of the class/national opponents. The points of contention between colonizer and colonized are sovereignty and economics, not "race."

+ colonialism grafts "a weakly imitative class structure onto a colony, but it is always an alien system and one that affects urban areas only," leaving the rural areas and the peasantry "outside the class structure."[44] Thus, it's the "classless masses" (a twist of Fanon's use of "classless idlers" in reference to lumpen elements, at (2.48)) that make the decolonization struggle.[45]

We can't ignore, as Wyrick seems to do, the fact that the peoples subjected to colonial oppression had their own classes and class structures prior to colonial contact, and these continue to exist, even if not allowed independent operation and development. **Wretched** is full of examples and references to counter Wyrick's implication that the only class structure in colonized countries is that imported and grafted onto them by colonialism.

It may be that the proper way to interpret Fanon's remark about the peasantry being "outside the class system" (1.49) is the very interpretation that he seems to make at (2.10), when discussing the differences between the people in the towns and those in the rural areas, and the old/new "town and country" contradiction. That is, it may be that being "outside the class system" actually means being "excluded from the advantages of colonialism." If truth be told, this is the only reading that makes sense, because Fanon is clearly aware of the class structure "native" to the colonized country, e.g.,

> ...colonialism has often strengthened or established its domination by organizing the petrification of the country districts. Ringed round by marabouts, witchdoctors and customary chieftains, the majority of country-dwellers are still living in the feudal manner, and the full power of this medieval structure of society is maintained by the settlers' military and administrative officials. (2.5)

> ...the native peasantry lives against a background of tradition, where the traditional structure of society has remained intact. (2.9)

 2) "HISTORICAL MATERIALISM" (OR, THE MATERIALIST CONCEPTION OF HISTORY), BECAUSE:

- the majority of colonized people are not engaged in industrial production;
- colonized people are engaged in "resistance" to colonialism, and not "class struggle," which is said to prove that "material forces" aren't the base of "history" for colonized peoples!

 3) THE CATEGORIES BASE AND SUPERSTRUCTURE, BECAUSE:

- on one hand, she claims, Fanon didn't believe that the "model" or, that these categories, applied to colonial situations. Yet, she also claims that Fanon had adopted Althusser's division of the superstructure into "repressive" and "ideological" apparatuses, and believed the former was operative in colonial situations.

  It appears that Wyrick's idea of "stretching" these concepts and categories is to simply replace them with "race" or to claim that Fanon replaced them with "race." If We believe her, not only is there a fundamental discontinuity in the thought of Marx and Fanon, but there's also no basis for the applicability of revolutionary socialism to the struggles of colonized peoples. i think her claims require a bit more attention.

With regard to her claims on class (structure), let's start with the statement of hers that i used to open this section:

> *In general, Fanon agrees with Marx that history runs dialectically, through the struggle of faction against faction. But whereas Marx categorized factions in terms of economic **class**, Fanon claims that **race** is the key categorical term in colonial situations.*

i don't think Wyrick has studied socialism, nor done extensive or critical reading of the works of Marx. If she had, i doubt she'd use the phrase "economic class," because it's a sure giveaway of a superficial, economistic, and bourgeois orientation. Marx didn't perceive class formation and function in purely economic terms. Wyrick's phrase is the kind that Fanon would find dangerous and misleading.

Contrary to popular belief, Marx didn't write on the subject of class in the definitive or detailed manner in which We too often believe that he did. It's said that he was about to define "class" in the third volume of *Capital*, but the work breaks off before he could do so.

However, We find a useful example of Marx's concept of class in *The 18th Brumaire of Louis Bonaparte*, where he holds:

> *In so far as millions of families live under economic conditions of existence that separate their mode of life, their interests and*

> their culture from those of other classes, and put them in hostile opposition to the latter, they form a class. In so far as there is merely a local interconnection among these small-holding peasants, and the identity of their interests begets no community, no national bond, and no political organization among them, they do not form a class.[46]

Clearly, Marx didn't see "class" in purely economic terms, and it isn't the mere objective economic similarity of interests that make class formation and function. While economic conditions are surely part of the criteria for class formation, Marx gives us other indispensable criteria, which could be listed as: 1) that class members must share a common position in their relation to the means of production, i.e., common economic conditions, relative to their labor and the appropriation of the social surplus; 2) that they must share a separate way of life and cultural existence; 3) that they must share a set of interests which are antagonistic to other classes; 4) that they must share a set of social relations, i.e., a sense of unity which extends beyond local boundaries, and constitutes a "national" bond; 5) that they must share a corresponding collective consciousness of themselves as a "class," and; 6) they must create their own political organizations, and pursue their interests as a "class."

Present in this passage from *The 18th Brumaire*, is a distinction between a "class-in-itself" and a "class-for-itself" which Marx also made in *The Holy Family*.[47] There, he used the term "in-itself" to capture the contingent character of that group which merely met the first of the criteria listed above. That is, the group which only

shared an objective, common relation to the means of production wasn't a "real" or "complete" or revolutionary class—it wasn't the gravedigger of capitalism that We tend to equate with the term "working class" or "proletariat." The transformation of the group into a class "for-itself" depends upon the acquisition and development of the remaining elements, i.e., the group must develop consciousness of itself as a class; create political organizations; engage in unified action to oppose and defeat its class enemies; begin to build a society free of all forms of exploitation and oppression, and eliminate all class divisions.

Wyrick says that Fanon and Marx agree that "history" develops through the struggle of "faction against faction," and that Marx calls these factions "classes"; and, allegedly, Fanon calls them "races." It seems to me that Wyrick doesn't even want to use terms like "class" and "class struggle" unless she can do so in a disparaging manner. i mean, why else avoid saying that Fanon and Marx agreed about the role of class struggle in the history of class societies?

However, what questions come to mind after reading her statement? The first question for me was: Is this an accurate representation of Fanon's thought? Next, i asked whether she was setting before us questions on the constitution of "history" and/or its motive force. Is Wyrick saying that the motive forces underlying "race" and "racial struggles" are somehow different from those that apparently underlie class and class struggles? Is she saying that for Fanon, the motive force of history for colonized peoples is "race struggle" and not "class struggle"?

What truly underlies the seeming opposition between "race" and "class"? Or, We can even ask, again: What is the "relation" between "race" and "class"? That is, what is there other than that the concept of "race" prevents us from seeing that it masks the economic relation between groups of people that We'd otherwise categorize as classes, nations, or nationalities? On the other hand, the narrow concept of class prevents us from seeing that groups of people that have been racialized are in fact "classes," most often circumscribed by national boundaries, in this era of racialized capitalist-imperialist and colonial exploitation.

i'm gonna address the questions i've raised, and try not to lose my focus on the statement and the theme of "stretching" the concept of class struggle. But i have to link these tasks with two related statements (altho the first will be dealt with on its own, below). The first is Wyrick's remark that, for Marx, "history" concerned "the material relationship of people to the means of production." This is significant here because her aim is, again, to show a divergence between the thought of Marx and Fanon on this question.

Second, Wyrick asserts that: "for Marx, all history is the history of class struggle," while "for Fanon, the history of colonized peoples is the 'history of resistance' [1.30] to colonial invasion and domination. Marx therefore totalizes history and in so doing removes from consideration entire historical narratives. Fanon realizes that Marx repeats Hegel's error of confusing Europe for the world. 'History [is] written by the Westerners... to serve their purposes' [4.25], so non-Westerners must make their own history."[48]

Now, Wyrick advances a difference between the "history of class struggle" and the "history of resistance"; the history "written" by Westerners, and the history "made" by non-Westerners. She also commits an injustice to her readers by repeating the charge—long ago made and laid to rest—that Marx (and, by implication, socialist methodology) is irrelevant to non-Western peoples, because he "totalizes history" and leaves out of it, or without it, the non-Western world.

Amilcar Cabral

To help me tie all of this together, i have to bring Amilcar Cabral into the mix, with his **"The Weapon of Theory."** This piece was, in the 1970s and 80s, often cited by petty bourgeois intellectuals and bourgeois nationalists as an example of Cabral's alleged divergence from Marx on the question of class struggle as the motive force of history. In fact,

"*By far the sharpest fighting ideologue in Portuguese Africa – and indeed in the whole continent – is Amilcar Cabral....*"
John Gerassi

Cabral did stretch doctrinaire "Marxism" in that he made even more explicit what had already been asserted by Marx...

"The Weapon of Theory" was delivered by Cabral at the first Tricontinental Conference of the Peoples of Asia, Africa and Latin America, held in Cuba, in 1966. His purpose was to present an "opinion of the foundation and objectives of national liberation in relation to the social structure."[49] The relevant points and parts of the speech are as follows:

> *Those who affirm—in our case correctly—that the motive force of history is the class struggle, would certainly agree to a revision of this affirmation to make it more precise and give it an even wider field of application, if they had a better knowledge of the essential characteristics of certain colonized peoples, that is to say, peoples dominated by imperialism. In fact, in the general evolution of humanity and of each of the peoples of which it is composed, classes appear neither as a generalized and simultaneous phenomenon throughout the totality of these groups, nor as a*

finished, perfect, uniform and spontaneous whole. The definition of classes within one or several human groups is a fundamental consequence of the progressive development of the productive forces and the characteristics of the distribution of the wealth produced by the group, or usurped from others. That is to say that the socio-economic phenomenon "class" is created and develops as a function of at least two essential and interdependent variables—the level of productive forces, and the pattern of ownership of the means of production. This development takes place slowly, gradually, and unevenly, by quantitative and generally imperceptible variations in the fundamental components; once a certain degree of accumulation is reached, this process then leads to a qualitative jump, characterized by the appearance of classes and of conflict between them.[50]

Cabral then poses the question: Does "history" begin only with the development of classes and class struggle?:

To reply in the affirmative would be to place outside history the whole period of life of human groups from the discovery of hunting and later of nomadic and sedentary agriculture, to the organization of herds and the private appropriation of land. It would also be to consider—and this we refuse to accept—that various human groups in Africa, Asia and Latin America were living without history, or outside history, at the time when they were subjected to the yoke of imperialism...[51]

Class struggle is the motive force of history only in specific historical periods, i.e., after the development of classes "within one or several human groups," thus:

...This means that before the class struggle—and necessarily after it—one or several factors was and will be the motive force of history. It is not difficult to see that this factor in the history of each human group is the mode of production—the level of productive forces and the patterns of ownership—characteristic

> *of that group. Furthermore, as we have seen, classes themselves, class struggle and their subsequent definition, are the result of the development of the productive forces, in conjunction with the pattern of ownership of the means of production. It therefore seems correct to conclude that the level of productive forces, the essential determining element in the content and form of class struggle, is the true and permanent motive force of history.*[52]

Cabral concludes, therefore, that "history" exists before the rise of classes and class struggle, and, that each human group has/makes "history" and will continue to do so, because "history has continuity, even after the disappearance of the class struggle or of classes themselves." People will "outlive classes and will continue to produce and make history," since We can never be free of the burdens of our needs of mind and of body, "which are the basis of the development of the forces of production."[53]

(i must pause here to say: 1. The question here involves "class struggle" bounded by capitalism. There was class struggle prior to the rise of the capitalist state; 2. The question here involves the relation between nations—nations either dominated by capitalist relations, and on the other hand, nations dominated by imperialist/colonialist relations. There were nations on the planet prior to their rise in Europe under the capitalist impulse.)

i wanna continue with other key points made by Cabral in **"The Weapon of Theory,"** because they'll help us to see the complete picture and the steps taken, as well as help us to exercise greater facility in the use of the tools:

1) Prior to the private appropriation of the means of production, in the communal era, there were no classes, and no state.

2) As productive forces developed, so did private appropriation of the means, the development of "conflicts of interest"

within the society, and the appearance of classes, in "feudal or assimilated agricultural or agro-industrial" societies, and then there was the appearance of state structures, class struggle being "the social expression of the contradiction in the economic field between the mode of production and private appropriation of the means of production."[54]

3) Imperialism makes its appearance, as "a worldwide expression of the search for profits and the ever-increasing accumulation of surplus value by monopoly financial capital ... piratry transplanted from the seas to dry land, piratry reorganized, consolidated and adapted to the aims of exploiting the natural and human resources of our peoples."[55]

4) "...the essential characteristic of imperialist domination" is "the negation of the historical process of the dominated people by means of violent usurpation of the freedom of development of the national productive forces..."[56]

5) National liberation is the process and result of people's rejection of the negation of their historical process, regaining their "historical personality," and "returning to history" through the destruction of imperialist domination, i.e., "to free the process of development of the national productive forces."[57]

6) However, "...the principal aspect of national liberation struggle is the struggle against neo-colonialism," i.e., the struggle against the native agents of imperialism and the would-be new ruling class of the "liberated" nation. Thus, genuine national liberation "necessarily corresponds to a revolution within the dominated or newly independent society."[58]

7) "...there are only two paths for an independent nation: to return to imperialist domination (neo-colonialism, capitalism, state capitalism), or to take the way of socialism."[59]

8) That is, genuine national liberation is evidenced by changes in the relations of production (ownership of the means), which free the development of the productive forces (people). The increase in the development of the productive forces allows the elimination of private appropriation of the means, the eventual elimination of classes, class struggle, and the state: "New and hitherto unknown forces in the historical process" are unleashed, "the social structure returns to horizontality, at a high level of productive forces, social relations, and appreciation of human values."[60]

One of the keys is to remember that at the center is the concept "productive forces," and at the center of that concept is PEOPLE! Combine this with an understanding that "history" was and is made by PEOPLE… people producing… to satisfy their needs of body and of mind.

i think We should note that Cabral makes no reference to "race" or "racial groups," but instead talks about "human groups." Note, too, that the piece is about classes and class struggles, drawn from the particular experience of the people of Guinea-Bissau, but with applicability to all other colonized and exploitative social settings. Finally, note that he opens the topic by affirming that, "in our case," the motive force of history is, now, the "class struggle."

Is Cabral "revising" Marx, or is he "revising" certain elements of so-called "Marxism"—and claims made by imperialism, e.g., that colonized peoples had no history? Did Marx actually hold that history began with classes and class struggle? Why were questions about history and class struggle, with reference to African and other colonized peoples, even raised?

To believe Wyrick, We have to believe that colonized peoples have no productive forces and no mode of production (prior to European contact); that their societies somehow developed outside of the material world and the social and productive relations that arise from their historical activity. We'd have to believe that the concepts and categories of socialist methodology don't apply to non-Western peoples because of some biological factors. We'd have to believe that Africans and other non-European peoples somehow avoided the development of classes and states, through essentially the same means and process that led to the development of classes and states in Europe.

Classes are a consequence of historical development, and We can't claim that Africans have (made) history, and then try to deny that they had classes and states before contact with Europeans—deny that classes arose among African peoples as a natural consequence of their struggles to produce, and the gradual and unequal appropriation of social wealth by "groups" within the societies which came to be called "classes."

Africans had and made history because they had modes of production—because they had and developed their productive forces—and the level of productive forces is the true and permanent motive force of history.

Does "race" factor into the character or level of "productive forces"? Does "race" supersede or replace productive forces as the motive force of history? Does "race" take priority over satisfaction of our needs of body and mind to become the basis for the development of history and productive forces? Maybe We can begin to tie all this together by going back to some of the questions that i raised above.

- What constitutes "history" and its "motive force"? History is the activity of people engaged in production to satisfy their material and spiritual needs. The motive force of history is the level and development of the productive forces (people).

- What motive force underlies "class struggle"? The contradiction between the productive forces and the relations of production, i.e., the pattern of ownership of the means of production. The people struggle to replace existing relations of production—to change the existing pattern of ownership of the means and the appropriation of surplus value—in order to allow the productive forces to freely develop and establish a new set of property relations.

- What motive force underlies so-called "race struggle"? Actually, the same motive force that underlies class struggle—only "race" disguises the material/economic relations and the essential struggle to free and develop the productive forces. Imperialism and colonialism (and racialized capitalism or forms of "domestic colonialism") has transformed "classic" class relations within single societies into national-class relations between peoples.

- What's the "distinction" between "race" and "class"? Both are social constructions, but class helps us locate and understand the source of social contradictions and the bases of social development. "Race," on the other hand, serves no useful or progressive social role—it obscures the source of social contradictions, and obstructs the progressive development of the human species, i.e., the productive forces of humanity as a whole.

- What is the "relation" between "race" and "class"? In this context, it's the material base. Again: "Race" serves the base, in this instance by hiding it, while class (analysis) reveals it. "Race" obscures "class."

- What is a/the "history of resistance"? The answer can be found, in part, through examining the context in which the phrase is used. That is, Wyrick opposes it not only to a "history of class struggle," but to the very notion that colonized peoples have a "material relation" to the means of production. In this context, the phrase "history of resistance" is a petty-bourgeois camouflage of class/struggle to free the national productive forces and to develop a socialist revolutionary process. The image that the petty-bourgeois forces present before the people is that claiming the ideal of a grand unity cemented by skin color and superficial understanding of "culture." The petty bourgeois forces want to govern and to acquire wealth—they do not want opposition to these aims to come in the form of an enlightened and self-motivated people, who move forward screaming "Stop, Thief!!" and "All Power To The People!!"

Now, was Cabral "revising" or diverging from Marx/scientific socialism, when he "refined" the relation of class struggle to history? Not necessarily. That is, altho Cabral's formulation seemed "original" to some, Lenin, for example, had earlier stated that, "Just as material causes underlie all natural phenomena, so the development of human society is conditioned by the development of material forces, the productive forces."[61]

However, Marx's oft-quoted remarks on the material base of society also go to the point of defining history, and of the productive forces being the true and permanent motive force of history. That is, from the beginning of human social living, people must first produce, and from this everything else arises:

> *History does nothing, it 'possesses no immense wealth,' it 'wages no battles.' It is man [people], real living man [people], that does all that, that possesses and fights; 'history' is not a person apart, using man [people] as a means for its own particular aims; history is nothing but the activity of man [people] pursuing his [their] aims.*[62]

In *The German Ideology*, Marx (and Engels) held that the underlying basis of social development ("history") was the progress of the productive forces and productive relations:

> *The first premise of all human history is, of course, the existence of living human individuals. The first historical act of these individuals, distinguishing them from animals, is not that they think, but that they begin to produce their means of subsistence.*[63]

Why did Cabral have the need to "stretch Marxism" on this question? First, because he believed, with Lenin: "We do not regard Marx's theory as something complete and inviolable; on the contrary, we are convinced that it had only laid the foundation stone of the science which socialists must develop, *in all directions*, if they wish to keep pace with life."[64] (my emphasis)

Cabral directed his words to the petty-and-pseudo-bourgeois nationalists, as well as to the "vulgar" "Marxists" and the colonialists.

Did Marx hold that history began with the appearance of classes and class struggle? We've seen that he did not. This being so, how then did the issue arise? In *The Communist Manifesto*, one reads in the opening lines the broad claim that "The history of all hitherto existing society is the history of class struggles." It's this statement that serves all those who wanna claim that Marx(ism) "totalizes history," etc. It didn't seem to help that in a later edition of the *Manifesto*, Engels tried to clarify the line by saying: "That is, all **written** history. In 1847, the pre-history of society, the social organization existing previous to recorded history, was all but unknown..."[65] [my emphasis]

This is still Eurocentric, but note that it not only "leaves out of history" non-Europeans, but many European peoples as well. Whether Eurocentric or merely an "oversight," other language helps to slightly clarify the error, e.g., "the whole history of mankind (since the dissolution of primitive tribal society, holding land in common ownership) has been a history of class struggles, contests between exploiting and exploited, ruling and oppressed classes..."[66]

On the issue of the "stretching" of historical materialism (or, more properly, the materialist conception of history), Wyrick attempts to show a divergence between Marx and Fanon by first claiming that "history," for Marx, concerns "the material relationship of people to the means of production," and limits its application to 19th century European industrial capitalism. She then quotes Fanon (as if he's directly opposing Marx's premise), from (5.181): "The relation of man with matter, with the world outside, and with history are, in the colonial period, simply relations with food, and, by extension, with the ground on which it grows."[67]

i think We should immediately go to our copies of **Wretched** and examine the context within which Fanon's words were used. Let's start at (5.172), where he's discussing the "poverty and absurdity" of theories of colonialist scientists, and the important theoretical and practical questions that these theories raise for the decolonization process. It appears that the specific question under discussion is the "inherent criminality" of colonized peoples that is claimed by colonialism. Fanon wants to "break up" this idea, to further develop revolutionary and social consciousness, by "giving the explanation" for "criminality" of colonized peoples during the colonial period, i.e., before the war starts, and before the people begin the transformation of their social being.

Now, at (5.181), Fanon tells us that "since the beginning of the war, every thing has changed"—but, from what? to what? The remainder of (5.181) tells us the nature of things after the beginning of the war, while (5.182) tells us the nature of things before the beginning of the war:

> Under the colonial regime, anything may be done for a loaf of bread or a miserable sheep. **The relations of man with matter, with the world outside and with history are, in the**

> **colonial period, simply relations with food.** *For a colonized [person]... living does not mean embodying moral values or taking [one's] place in the coherent and fruitful development of the world...* (my emphasis)

Ordinarily, i'd say that We've seen enough to pull the cover off of Wyrick's true aim, and to show that, at least with her chosen example, Fanon does not reject the fundamental proposition of the materialist conception of history.

However, some people may question whether the "relations with food" and "the ground on which it grows," in an "underdeveloped" setting, may fundamentally differ from "material relationships of people to the means of production" in an industrial setting.

We've already addressed this question, in essence, as We went through Marx's idea of "history" as the activity of people in pursuit of their aims via the production of their means of subsistence—an alternate phrasing of the fundamental proposition of the materialist conception of history.

We've also addressed the question, in essence, as We covered Cabral's "stretching" on the question of the true and permanent motive force of history (or, social development).

However, a slightly more direct approach requires that We focus on the content and meaning of "means of production," and what constitutes a "material relationship" to them. That is, must there be an "industrial" or even a capitalist economic setting before people can have a "material relation" to the means of production? Does a relation to food and the ground/land on which it grows contradict or differ from a "material relation" to the means of production?

By "means of production" is meant the sum of the material elements of the productive forces, i.e., the "objects of labor" (upon which people work), and the "implements of labor" (the sum of tools, storage facilities, and land).

A "material" relation is, of course, a "physical" one, but it's also a social relation, reflecting the connection between the means of production on the part of both those who "own" or who have privately appropriated the social means of production, and those who have been deprived of ownership and are exploited. In other words, both those who are exploited, and the exploiters, have a "material" relation to the means of production.

i wonder if Fanon shared a similar understanding when, for example, he described independence as the condition for "truly liberated" people, i.e., people "who are truly masters of all the material means which make possible the radical transformation of society." (5.183)

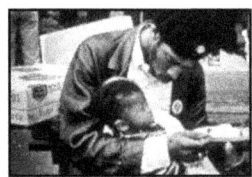

Next, as Wyrick claims to show us how and why "historical materialism" needs to be stretched, she claims that colonized peoples aren't alienated from "work," because they have no mass participation in an industrial economy—as if only through the exploitation of industrial labor does colonialism exercise its exploitation and dehumanization of colonized lands and peoples.

Wyrick's petty bourgeois interpretation of "Marxism" causes her to define alienation merely as the "separation and estrangement of a worker" from her or his "work." We understand alienation as a concept describing: both the process and the results of converting the practical and theoretical products of human activity, and of human properties and capabilities, into something independent of people and dominating over them; the transformation of some phenomena and relations into something different from what they are in themselves; the distortion in people's minds of their actual relations in life.[68] Alienation is the perversion not only of our relation to physical labor (narrowly defined), but also our relation to other people, to social institutions, and to nature and our own sense of "being"... "human"...

Capitalism (and its expression through imperialism and colonialism) is inherently alienating. What is colonialism if not alienating, dehumanizing? What is **Wretched**, if not an examination of the alienation of colonized people, and the effort to "dis-alienate" represented by the decolonization process? The loss of independence and control over their lives and the resources of their land alienates the colonized peoples. The decolonization process is the means used to regain or reconstitute the humanity of the colonized people, i.e., to reestablish their independence and sovereignty, their "natural" relation to each other and to nature.

Throughout **Wretched**, Fanon focuses upon the need for the development of the people's consciousness so that they can develop an understanding of the cause/sources of their alienation—to define their oppression as alienation—and to realize that just as it's caused by people and material relations (of production) it can be changed (eliminated) by the people themselves, and their creation of new material relations (of production, ownership, relation to means).

Moreover, the revolutionary consciousness that Fanon urges is one that understands that all of the colonized people are alienated, not just those engaged in industrial production or those occupying elitist positions. Thus, all of the people are obliged to develop revolutionary consciousness, become human again, and to reconnect their social reality/being on the base of material relationships; becoming, in the process, the collective masters of their society.

We now arrive at Wyrick's description of why and how our thinking on base and superstructure should be "stretched"—or, rather, her claims regarding Fanon's alleged position on the matter.

However, We may become a bit confused, because Wyrick: 1) rests her argument on a superficial and misleading definition of the categories, and, 2) she doesn't seem to know which of three "pivots" to make her stand on.

She begins with:

> Central to Marx's thought is the model of base (the material means of production, distribution, and exchange), and superstructure (the "cultural world" of ideas, such as art, religion, and law, which are determined by—not independent of—the base). In a capitalist society, the base depends on the unequal, dangerously unstable relationship between workers (the proletariat) and bosses (those who control capital); therefore, the job of the superstructure is to make the inequities of the base seem natural and good...[69]

Based on this definition, We probably need to discuss: 1) her narrow definition of base; 2) her narrow definition of superstructure; 3) her implication that the superstructure has no independence; 4) her attempt to restrict the application or relevance of the categories to capitalist/Western social settings, which coincides with her use of the term "model."

The base and superstructure are categories that characterize the basic structural elements of all social formations, and express the relation of being to thinking in the social realm. By underlying all ideas and institutions in the society, the base is the basis of all social life, i.e., not restricted to Wyrick's idea of "material."

The superstructure designates more than a narrowly conceived "cultural world," and ideas. It also designates institutions and organizations, the major one being the state. Despite Wyrick's assertion to the contrary, the superstructure does maintain a relative independence from the base—and it not only serves the base, but influences it. Finally, the elements of the superstructure are products and weapons of class struggle.

Wyrick presents the first of her "pivots" as follows: Fanon's ideas about base and superstructure resemble those of the French [Marxist] philosopher Louis Althusser...who refines the model in terms of power. For Althusser, "ideological state apparatuses" are elements of the superstructure—political parties, educational institutions, the media, literature—that "sell us" the status quo. In the process, they mask or mystify "repressive state apparatuses"— the police, law courts, the military—that impose the status quo by force. Fanon finds a similar distinction useful in analyzing the colonial situation.[70]

So, on one hand, Fanon's ideas on base and superstructure "resemble" those Marxist ideas of Althusser, i.e., he believes the repressive apparatus of the superstructure is operative in colonial situations.

We now go to her second "pivot":

> *Fanon doubts that Marx's base/superstructure model applies to the masses in colonized countries. He agrees that in capitalist societies, the superstructure generates "expressions of respect for the established order [that] serve to create around the exploited person an atmosphere of submission and of inhibition which lightens the task of policing considerably." In the colonies, however, "ideological state apparatuses" are eclipsed by "repressive state apparatuses." "Agents of government speak the language of pure force ... [They] do not lighten the oppression, nor seek to hide the domination" but maintain the status quo directly, "by means of rifle butts and napalm"* [**Wretched**, *(1.8)*] *To Fanon, colonial rule operates not through managing "consent" but through inflicting terror and despair.*[71]

If We take a look at paragraph (1.8) of **Wretched**, where Fanon draws the distinction between the role of the "repressive state apparatuses" in capitalist and colonized countries, even without our own critique of this paragraph and its context, We ask: Does it go to show, 1) an absence of base and superstructure in colonized countries; 2) Fanon's alleged divergence from Marx on the nature of base and superstructure; 3) that the "model" doesn't apply to colonized countries?

As i read it, whether the ideological or the repressive apparatuses are dominant in colonial countries, they are both elements of the superstructure. Maybe i'm just missing Wyrick's point…

However, as if she's not confident in the strength of these first two "pivots," Wyrick concludes with a third:

> *In fact, Fanon believes that colonialism causes the Marxist model of base and superstructure to collapse altogether because economic relationships are secondary to racial ones. That is, the Manichean thinking on which colonialism depends blots out other distinctions, hierarchies, and logical patterns. There is a superstructure in colonized countries, of course, but it operates upon the colonizers, convincing them that they're promoting universally wonderful values of civilization, enlightenment, redemption. It also operates upon the small percentage of the native population that's been "assimilated" into the colonial system. In order to promote the "genuine eradication of the superstructure built by … the bourgeois colonial environment"* [i must point out, here, that this quote of Fanon from (1.21) distorts by omission, and i'll return to it below] *Fanon turns his attention to the "native intellectuals" and the problem of national culture.*[72]

Where does Fanon say that economic relationships are secondary to "racial" ones? At (1.11)? No, i don't think so. At (1.12)? No, i still don't think so.

Where does Fanon say that he believes that no base and superstructure exists in colonized countries—other than that developed by colonialism?

The existence of Manichean thinking doesn't make economic relationships secondary to "racial" ones—it does exactly what it's supposed to do: It masks and mystifies the economic relationships; it blots out the "other distinctions, hierarchies, and logical patterns"—but it doesn't undermine their primacy. The Manichean thinking performs its role as a superstructural element by making "race" appear as external to and dominant over the economic motive of colonial relations. You'd think that anyone with a Ph.D. would be able to understand this. But then, as Fred Hampton used to say, We got people running around with degrees coming out the wahzoo, but they can't chew bubble gum and walk across the street at the same time. That is, they can't properly connect the stuff in their heads to the living reality around them.

Two other quick notes here: 1) Colonized societies clearly had their own base and superstructure prior to colonial subjugation, and these structural elements continue to maintain some independence and continue to develop even under colonial domination. In fact, during the decolonization struggle, "new" superstructural elements develop in direct opposition to the dominant superstructure of colonialism. 2) The superstructure imposed by colonialism does affect the majority of the colonized people, e.g., (5.182), (1.14), (1.16), and (1.59).*

---

* "The colonial world is a Manichean world. It is not enough for the settler to delimit physically, that is to say with the help of the army and the police force, the place of the native. As if to show the totalitarian character of colonial exploitation the settler paints the native as a sort of quintessence of evil. Native society is not simply described as a society lacking in values. It is not enough for the colonist to affirm that these values have disappeared from, or still better never existed in, the colonial world. The native is declared insensible to ethics; he represents not only the absense of values, but also the negation of values. He is, let us dare to admit, the enemy of values, and in this sense he is the absolute evil. He is the corrosive element, destroying all that comes near him; he is the deforming element, disfiguring all that has to do with beauty or morality; he is the depository of maleficent powers, the unconscious and irretrievable instrument of blind forces. Monsieur Meyer could thus state seriously in the French National Assembly that the Republic must not be prostituted by allowing the Algerian people to become part of it. All values, in fact, are irrevocably poisoned and diseased as soon as they are allowed in contact with the colonized race. The customs of the colonized people, their traditions, their myths—above all, their myths—are the very sign of that poverty of spirit and of their constitutional depravity..." (1.14)

5D. Fanon on "Race," Racism, Class, and the Struggle for Socialism: Meditations

It seems apparent that Wyrick has based her claims for the racialization of Fanon's thought on paragraphs (1.11) and (1.12). So, We should look fully at both of these, and then check them within the context of **Wretched** as a whole, i.e., look at all other references to the subjects of "race" and racism (and class and socialism), seeking a more complete and accurate picture of Fanon's views and his idea of "key category":

> *This world divided into compartments, this world cut in two, is inhabited by two different species. The originality of the colonial context is that economic reality, inequality, and the immense differences of ways of life, never come to mask the human realities. When you examine at close quarters the colonial context, it is evident that what parcels out the world is to begin with the fact of belonging to or not belonging to a given race, a given species. In the colonies the economic substructure is also a superstructure. The cause is the consequence: you are rich because you are white; you are white because you are rich. This is why Marxist analysis should always be slightly stretched every time we have to do with the colonial problem. (1.11)*

> *Everything up to and including the very nature of pre-capitalist society, so well explained by Marx, must here be thought out again. The serf is in essence different from the knight, but a reference to divine right is necessary to legitimize this statutory difference. In the colonies, the foreigner coming from another country imposed his rule by means of guns and machines. In defiance of his successful transplantation, in spite of his appropriation, the settler still remains a foreigner. It is neither the act of owning factories, nor estates, nor a bank balance which distinguishes the governing classes. The governing race is first and foremost those who come from elsewhere, those who are unlike the original inhabitants, "the others." (1.12)*

As We reflect upon (1.11), the first thing We should do is recall that Fanon opens the book on the theme of **"National liberation, national renaissance, the restoration of nationhood to the people."** (1.1) Nothing here implies that the colonized people are (to be) engaged in a "race struggle" or even a struggle for mere "racial equality."

If We can't sufficiently draw from the opening lines, then by the time We reach the fourth chapter We should be able to see that colonized people struggle to regain or to reestablish their sovereignty, through a struggle that "aims at a fundamentally different set of [material/social] relations between [people]," and which is to result in the *"disappearance"* of the colonized people—as a particular *"species."* (4A.19)

That is, the struggle seeks a "new humanity" that's to be represented by the liberated people—it "cannot do otherwise than define a new humanism both for itself and for others. It is prefigured in the objectives and methods of the conflict..." (4A.20) This is not a man holding "race" as the "key category" in colonial situations.

We should also read (1.11) within its proper context. That is, We should go back to (1.7), where Fanon tells us that We have to closely examine the "system of compartments" into which the colonial world has been divided. Paragraph (1.11) is part of that examination (and, so is 1.12).

Finally, We need to understand that We aren't examining mere structural relations, but the Manichean ideology that's characteristic of both the colonized and the colonizer, prior to and during, the decolonization process.

At (1.11), Fanon is speaking in the "voice" of those who are still locked within the constraints of color. The people who, at the beginning of the struggle, continue to believe that "race" parcels out the world, are not the people who later develop the consciousness and the practical means that secure their sovereignty and facilitate their transformation into "new people." For example, just take a quick look at (3.82), and relate the change undergone there in the people's consciousness to the "voice" in (1.11):

> *Taking these experiences as a starting-point, the functioning of the main laws of economics were explained to the people, with concrete examples. The accumulation of capital ceased to be a theory and became a very real and immediate mode of behavior. The people understood how that once a man was in trade, he could become rich and increase his turn-over. Then and then only did the peasants tell the tale of how the grocer gave them loans at exorbitant interest, and others recalled how he evicted them from their land, and how from owners they became laborers.* [Yaki: What's this—"peasants" who own/ed land?] *The more the people understand, the more watchful they become, and the more they come to realize that finally everything depends on them and their salvation lies in their own cohesion, in the true understanding of their interests and in knowing who are their enemies. The people came to understand that wealth is not the fruit of labor but the result of organized, protected robbery...* (3.82)

We can follow Fanon and trace the lines of this development, from the "colonial period" (i.e., prior to the beginning of the struggle) and through the "decolonization" period, during which the people maintain their adoption of the Manichean ideology:

> **The native replies to the living lie of the colonial situation by an equal falsehood.** (1.27)*

---

* "The problem of truth ought also to be considered. In every age, among the people, truth is the property of the national cause. No absolute verity, no discourse on the purity of the soul can shake this position. The native replies to the living lie of the colonial situation by an equal falsehood. His dealings with his fellow-nationals are open; they are strained and incomprehensible with regard to the settlers. Truth is that which hurries on the breakup of the colonialist regime; it is that which promotes the emergence of the nation; it is all that protects the natives and ruins the foreigners. In this colonialist context there is no truthful behavior: and the good is quite simply that which is evil for 'them'."

> Thus we see that the primary Manicheism which governed colonial society is preserved intact during the period of decolonization; that is to say that the settler never ceases to be the enemy, the opponent, the foe that must be overthrown. (1.28)
>
> It is in this manner of thinking that each of the protagonists begins the struggle. (1.89)
>
> To the saying "All natives are the same," the colonized person replies "All settlers are the same." (1.93)
>
> On the logical plane, the Manicheism of the settler produces a Manicheism of the native. To the theory of the "absolute evil of the native" the theory of the "absolute evil of the settler" replies. (1.94)

i think it's significant that at (1.28), Fanon doesn't paint the Manichean thinking with "racial" tones. But, since the thinking of the colonial system is also racialized, any racial thought held by the colonized people constitutes an "equal falsehood"!

When and how does the colonized people begin to abandon Manichean thinking?

> ...it is precisely at the moment he realises his humanity that he begins to sharpen the weapons with which he will secure its victory. (1.15)
>
> The well-known principle that all [people] are equal will be illustrated in the colonies from the moment that the [people claim] that [they are] the equal of the settler. One step more and [they are] ready to fight to be more than the settler... (1.17)
>
> Thus, the [colonized people] discover that [their lives]...breath... beating heart are the same as those of the settler. [They] find out that the settler's skin is not of any more value than [theirs]; and it must be said that this discovery shakes the world in a very necessary manner. All the new, revolutionary assurance of the [colonized people] stems from it... (1.18)

The people discover, after hard and costly experience, that they've suffered "a very great weakness" in the realm of knowledge, and that their consciousness has remained "rudimentary":

> ...all these reactions signified that to the dual world of the settler [they had] opposed [their] own duality. (2.61)

The recognition and reconstitution of the "humanity" of the people is the first step out of the Manichean constraint of color or "race," and dualism in general. This represents an example of the superstructure influencing the base, as ideas grasped by the masses become a "material force," leading to motion to change the system of property relations, i.e., to overthrow colonialism, regain national sovereignty, and begin to build socialism.

When the people begin to see themselves as "the same" as the settler, this allows them to begin to develop the struggle on the base of the truly "key category," e.g., to be "more than the settler" is to move beyond a biologically based identity and set of interests, and to begin the development of society on the basis of economic and political needs and interests. It's to understand that colonialism is fundamentally about the economic and political relations between those who are exploited, and those who do the exploiting— even though "race" or racism is a component tool used in the process.

All of this is a part of the "reality" that's later discovered and helps lead to the shaping of a plan for freedom. (1.43) The reality is that the struggle against racism is a necessary part of the struggle against colonialism, but, "the defeat of colonialism is the real object of the struggle..." (1.26)

Our examination of paragraph (1.11) and its context should close with some reflection on the closing paragraphs of **Wretched**'s second chapter, which in themselves should undermine any claim that Fanon saw "race" as the key category in colonial situations, or that he in any way characterized the decolonization process as a "race struggle."

We've already seen, at (2.61), Fanon raise the people's recognition of the "very great weakness" in their knowledge, and the "rudimentary" character of their consciousness. This "weakness" was also spoken to by Cabral, who again shows us the continuity between his thought and that of Fanon. Cabral developed this "seed" of Fanon's by elaborating upon the character of the "weakness" as one which failed to examine the class structure of the colonized society and the primacy of the economic base. Fanon writes:

> *Racial feeling, as opposed to racial prejudice, and that determination to fight for one's life which characterizes the native's reply to oppression are obviously good enough reasons for joining in the fight. But you do not carry on a war... in order to make racialism or hatred triumph. Racialism and hatred and resentment... cannot sustain a war of liberation... that intense emotion of the first few hours falls to pieces if it is left to feed on its own substance... hatred alone cannot draw up a program. You will only risk the defeat of your own ends if you depend on the enemy... to widen the gap, and to throw the whole of the people on the side of the rebellion...* (2.62)

Note the distinction between "racial feeling" and "racial prejudice." The use of the former term is a bit unlike its use at (3.23), where "race feeling in its most exacerbated form is triumphing," and becoming "racial prejudice." In this instance, "racial feeling" can, at one level, be compared to the kind of "national consciousness" spoken of in (3.2)—a kind of group or collective identity which hasn't yet reached its full potential. Or, it can be compared to "the hollow shell of nationality itself" spoken of at (3.26)—a necessary, but insufficient step in the process of becoming the new people. The war can't feed on the mere "substance" of "racial feeling"—much more than this is needed to develop a "program" i.e., one that will free the people politically and socially: "...There must be an economic program; there must also be a doctrine concerning the division of wealth, and social relations. In fact, there must be an idea of [humanity] and of the future of humanity..." (3.96)

Paragraph (2.63) further shows how reliance on mere "racial feeling" allows colonialism to later more easily disarm the people with "kindliness," and with reforms that "include" them into the colonial framework, through an assimilationist agenda focusing, ideologically, upon the masses, and programmatically on the "elite" and the creation of a "native middle class."*

At (2.64), genuine revolutionary leadership sees the need to reassess, and to politically educate the people, focusing on the underlying causes of colonialism, and the economic objectives and the protracted nature of the struggle.†

* "...The native is so starved for anything, anything at all that will turn him into a human being, any bone of humanity flung to him, that his hunger is incoercible, and these poor scraps of charity may, here or there, overwhelm him. His consciousness is so precarious and dim that it is affected by the slightest spark of kindliness... The native may at any moment let himself be disarmed by some concession or another."

† "...The struggle for national liberation does not consist in spanning the gap in one stride; the drama has to be played out in all its difficulty every day, and the sufferings engendered far outmeasure any endured during the colonial period. Down in the towns the settlers seem to have changed. Our people are happier; they are respected. Day after day goes by... They must not imagine that the end is already won. When the real objectives of the fight are shown to them, they must not think that they are impossible to attain. Once again, things must be explained to them; the people must see where they are going, and how they are going to get there. The war is not a single battle, but rather a series of local engagements; and to tell the truth, none of these are decisive."

Continuing to challenge the Manichean categorization of entire groups through a dualist lens (in this instance, those people living in the towns), Fanon urges insight that:

> ...certain fractions of the population have particular interests and that these do not always coincide with the national interests... The people will thus come to understand that national independence sheds light upon many facts which are sometimes divergent and antagonistic. Such a taking stock of the situation at this precise moment of the struggle is decisive, for it allows the people to pass from total, indiscriminating nationalism to social and economic awareness. The people who at the beginning of the struggle had adopted the primitive Manicheism of the settler—Blacks and Whites, Arabs and Christians—realize as they go along that it sometimes happens that you get Blacks who are whiter than the Whites and that the fact of having a national flag and the hope of an independent nation does not always tempt certain strata of the population to give up their interests or privileges... The militant who faces the colonialist war machine... realizes that while he is breaking down colonial oppression he is building up automatically yet another system of exploitation. This discovery is unpleasant, bitter and sickening: and yet everything seemed to be so simple before, the bad people were on one side, and the good on the other. The clear, unreal, idyllic light of the beginning is followed by a semi-darkness that bewilders the senses. The people find out that the iniquitous fact of exploitation can wear a black face or an Arab one, and they raise the cry of "Treason!"... But the treason is not national, it is social. The people must be taught to cry "Stop thief!"... (2.67)

In this first half of the paragraph, the focus is on the need of the people to pass from narrow nationalism (i.e., that which represents a "race") to social and economic awareness. Ask yourself this, tho: How, exactly, do you get "blacks" who are "whiter" than the "whites"? i mean, do the "blacks" change the color of their skins? If not, then being "white" refers to something other than skin color, doesn't it? Maybe it has something to do with the kinds of interests and privileges that certain strata of the population don't wanna give up. How did Fanon put it: "the iniquitous fact of exploitation can wear a 'black' face"... Let's continue with the paragraph:

> ...In their weary road towards rational knowledge the people must also give up their too-simple conception of their overlords. The species is breaking up under their very eyes. As they look around them, they notice that certain settlers do not join in the general guilty hysteria; there are differences in the same species. Such men, who before were included without distinction and indiscriminately in the monolithic mass of the foreigner's presence, actually go so far as to condemn the colonial war. The scandal explodes when the prototypes of this division of the species go over to the enemy, become Negroes or Arabs, and accept suffering, torture and death. (2.67)

Reflect on the meaning of the "too-simple conception of their overlords" that the people must give up, i.e., to consider them all in merely "racial" terms is surely at the heart of it—but it's more. Even when moving beyond "race" to the socio-economic and political, the people see "The species is breaking up under their very eyes," and We notice differences within the same "species." Just as earlier We had to reconfigure the images of "blacks" and "whites," now We have to figure out what it means when the settlers become "negroes or Arabs." The "differences" within the species—that is both "species," colonizer and colonizer—are marked by forms of thought and practice... "worldview"... "stand"... Thus, the people see that:

> The settler is not simply the man that must be killed. Many members of the mass of colonialists reveal themselves to be much, much nearer to the national struggle than certain sons [and daughters] of the nation. The barriers of blood and race-prejudice are broken down on both sides. In the same way, not every Negro or Moslem is issued automatically with a hallmark of

genuineness... Consciousness slowly dawns upon truths that are only partial, limited, and unstable. As we may surmise, all this is very difficult... (2.69)

Let's look a bit at a few key phrases in (1.11), starting with Fanon's use of the term "species." (And, note Wyrick's omission of the term in her quote of (1.11).)*

Unlike Fanon's use of the term "species" in the book's opening paragraph, he didn't accent it in (1.11), and he used the term "race" as if they were interchangeable. In the opening paragraph, there's no use of the word "race," and the "species" in question are characterized as "the colonizer" and the "colonized" i.e., "species" is used as a socio-political term, not a biological one, and refers to groups of individuals having common interests. However, the term can be used to refer to "racial" categories, but only within the Manichean framework.

Taking **Wretched** as a whole (e.g., his use of the term in (2.67)), i contend that Fanon uses not only the term "species," but also, at (1.11), the term "race" to refer to socio-political groups, and not biologically distinguishable groups.

(i think Sartre also uses the term "breed" in the sociological sense, at (P.22). There, with reference to the "coherent" process of struggle and the simultaneous creation of new people. Of particular interest there is his reference to the settlers as part of the dialectic: "...once the last settler [as 'species'] is killed, shipped home,

* "This world is divided into compartments, this world cut in two is inhabited by two different species. The originality of the colonial context is that economic reality, inequality and the immense difference of ways of life never come to mask the human realities. When you examine at close quarters the colonial context, it is evident that what parcels out the world is to begin with the fact of belonging to or not belonging to a given race, a given species. In the colonies the economic substructure is also a superstructure. The cause is the consequence; you are rich because you are white, you are white because you are rich. This is why Marxist analysis should always be slightly stretched every time we have to do with the colonial problem."

or assimilated, the minority breed disappears, to be replaced by socialism." The term "breed" ["species"] within the context of being "replaced by socialism" tells us We're talking about socio-political and economic structure, social relations and social being, not biology or genetics.)

Now, shift to the phrase: "The originality of the colonial context is that economic reality, inequality, and the immense difference of ways of life, never come to mask the human realities."

i recall the "originality" of the colonial situation first discussed at (1.2), where Fanon talks about the two "forces" being opposed to each other. There, the "originality" seemed to refer to "their *existence together*—that is to say, the exploitation of the native by the settler." (my emphasis) At bottom, the "originality" of the colonial setting is the economic contradiction between two socially heterogeneous groups, and the economic base is masked by "race."

The "human realities" are the results of the racialization of capitalist/colonialist oppression and exploitation, and all that colonialism's use of "race" brings to the setting through its employment of Manichean ideology and the "compartments" that divide the setting in all spheres. These "human realities" are never "masked" because "race" appears as external to the economic relations, and predominant, i.e., as "cause."

> *In the colonies the economic substructure is also a superstructure. The cause is the consequence: you are rich because you are white; you are white because you are rich.*

The base is also a superstructure because "race" makes the cause (economic relations) appear as a consequence of "whiteness," while being rich, or, the appropriation of the colony's wealth, appears as a consequence of this same "whiteness."

Fanon is here "stretching" the analysis, emphasizing the peculiar operation of base and superstructure under colonialism. As We've seen, the economic contradictions of the base manifest themselves on the level of the superstructure. In turn, the superstructure expresses and serves the base, and also influences the base. In this instance, the pattern of ownership and production relations of the base appear as "race relations" and manifest through the "human realities" of "racial discrimination" and "inequality" throughout the society—throughout all the superstructural phenomena—ideas, institutions, organizations, state apparatuses, etc. "Racism" is what's out front, working as a shadow. We're constantly screaming about the injustice of "racism" and the need to combat "racism," while neglecting the material reality that produces this shadow and which it serves and masks.

Let's leave (1.11) on this note: At (1.11), Fanon ain't saying that "race" is the key category in colonial situations. At most, he's saying that "race" is one of the keys to understanding how the economic base is masked, and that it's a component of colonialism. His point toward the need to "stretch" socialist analysis in this instance is so that We come to understand the "relation" of "race" to "class"… the role of "race" in colonial oppression and exploitation. It's on this basis that he points to the question of "legitimacy" in (1.12), i.e., how the superstructure performs the function of legitimizing colonialism with the use of "race." Again: there's really no "race structure," but a class structure that's been racialized…

With regard to (1.12): It's precisely because of the dialectical relation between the base and the superstructure in colonial settings (where the "idea" of "race" plays a key role), that Fanon says that We must "stretch Marxist analysis." At (1.12), he clearly states why. He draws up an image of "race" in colonial settings.

At (1.12), Fanon points out that a "reference to divine right is necessary to legitimize the statutory difference" between the serf and the knight. By "statutory" he refers us to the superstructure and its role in rationalizing not mere "difference," but the "economic reality," the "inequality" and the immense difference in ways of life that result from the oppressive and exploitative class positions of knight and serf—or, of colonized and or colonizer. "Divine right" is used to legitimize the oppression of the serf—what's used to legitimize the oppression of the colonized? What is it that "distinguishes the governing classes" in the colonial situation? "Race"? Well, yes—and no. On one hand, it's "first and foremost" the fact that the colonialists are "those who come from elsewhere." However, on the other hand, it is the fact that they "own" which, underneath the shadow of "race," does in fact distinguish those who rule from those who are subject to colonial exploitation. Yes, the colonialists used guns and machines—but why? For what purpose?

The fundamental difference between the situation of the serf and that of the colonized is that the former was exploited by a ruling class that wasn't "foreign"; the commonality between the serf and the colonized is that both were targets of a superstructural weapon used to make their oppression appear "normal" or "natural"…legitimized through "legal"/statutory means…or, ideas alleging biological difference.

Let's now return to consider Wyrick's distortion by omission that i spoke of above, as she quoted Fanon while claiming that he believed base and superstructure to "collapse altogether" in colonial situations. Wyrick's line in question is:

> …In order to promote the "genuine eradication of the superstructure built by… the bourgeois colonial environment" Fanon turns his attention to the "native intellectuals" and the problem of national culture. (Wyrick, p. 132)

What Fanon actually says is:

> In the colonial countries where a real struggle for freedom has taken place, where the blood of the people has flowed, and where the length of the period of armed warfare has favored the backward surge of intellectuals toward bases grounded in the people, we can observe a genuine eradication of the superstructure built by these intellectuals from the bourgeois colonialist environment. (1.21)

On one hand, the mere omission of the words "these intellectuals" changes Fanon's context and meaning, while also raising questions about Wyrick's aim and interests. On the other hand, We can see that the entire quoted line is taken out of context, and i'd say, deliberately so.

Even tho We can say, in the broad sense, that Fanon is talking about the destruction of the superstructure created by colonialism, that's really not the concern that he's voicing in this paragraph. As they say, the "subject" in this paragraph is "intellectuals"... the "backward surge" of colonized intellectuals, toward "bases grounded in the people." The subject is the "class suicide" of colonized intellectuals—and, the responsibility that they share in creating and reinforcing superstructural phenomena "native" to colonialism and the bourgeois world-view.

That is, We can read the paragraph to understand that it's not only the superstructural phenomena, but the colonized intellectuals, too, that are "from the bourgeois colonialist environment." Those intellectuals who, We must recall, masked the phenomenon of the mocking and vomiting up of Western values by the masses, and who "followed the colonialist with regard to the universal abstract," and is "permeated by colonialism and all its ways of thinking." (1.16–17)

It is the colonized intellectuals who "bring variants" to the petition of the people "that the last shall be first." (1.19–20) The context that Fanon sets between (1.16) and (1.20) is that within which We should read paragraph (1.21).*

The focus is upon the colonized intellectuals, within whom: "We find intact in them the manners and forms of thought picked up during their association with the colonialist bourgeoisie." (1.24)

* "...The colonialist bourgeoisie, in its narcissistic dialogue, expounded by the members of its universities, had in fact deeply implanted in the minds of the colonized intellectual that the essential qualities remain eternal in spite of all the blunders men may make: the essential values of the West, of course. The native intellectual accepted the cogency of these ideas, and deep down in his brain you could always find a vigilant sentinel ready to defend the Greco-Latin pedestal. Now it so happens that during the struggle for liberation, at the moment that the native intellectual comes into touch again with his people, this artificial sentinel is turned to dust. All the Mediterranean values— the triumph of the human individual, of clarity and of beauty—become lifeless, colourless knick-knacks. All those speeches seem like collections of dead words; those values which seemed to uplift the soul are revealed as worthless, simply because they have nothing to do with the concrete conflict in which the people is engaged."

> *In order to assimilate and to experience the oppressor's culture, the native has had to leave certain of his intellectual possessions in pawn. These pledges include his adoption of the forms of thought of the colonialist bourgeoisie… (1.25)*

Now, some of these intellectuals will commit "class suicide," but most of them will not, and they'll become the "spoilt children of yesterday's colonialism and of today's national governments," to "organize the loot of whatever national resources exist."

It's precisely the process of "class suicide" that Fanon refers to in (1.21) (and below) that stands as a condition for the "genuine eradication of the superstructure built by these intellectuals"! Therefore, We see some of the process of the eradication in (1.22), as "individualism is the first to disappear," and at (1.23), as they engage in people's democracy and "communal self-criticism."

Now, following Wyrick: When Fanon *"turns his attention to 'native intellectuals',"* it's for the explicit purpose of examining class structure and class struggle within the colonized nation. But, our focus will be on those references to "race" and its use by the bourgeois forces, since this example gives us evidence why Wyrick wants to promote the primacy of "race" over "class," while glossing over the responsibility of the colonized bourgeois forces in diverting the energies and confusing the minds of the people. **As Wyrick tries to hide this responsibility, Fanon exposes it.** The bourgeois forces wanna use "race"/ism for essentially the same reasons and in the same manner as the colonialists—to prevent the development of economic and political awareness among the masses, hinder the rise of revolutionary consciousness, and prevent the people from taking the path of socialism.

Let's venture into the third chapter of **Wretched** to see what We can see.

What is it—"unpreparedness," "laziness," "cowardice," and the "lack of practical links between them and the masses of the people" that leads to "tragic mishaps" in the course of struggle, caused by the actions or inactions of the colonized bourgeois forces? (3.1)*

> *National consciousness ... will be in any case only an empty shell, a crude and fragile travesty of what it might have been. The faults we find in it are quite sufficient explanation of the facility with which ... the nation is passed over for the race, and the tribe is preferred to the state ... [S]uch retrograde steps ... are the historical result of the incapacity of the national middle-class to rationalize popular action, that is to say their incapacity to see into the reasons for that action. (3.2)*

> *This traditional weakness ... is not solely the result of the mutilation of the colonized peoples by the colonial regime. It is also the result of the intellectual laziness of the national middle-class, of its spiritual penury, and of the profoundly cosmopolitan mold that its mind is set in. (3.3)*

* "History teaches us clearly that the battle against colonialism does not run straight away along the lines of nationalism. For a very long time the native devotes his energies to ending certain definite abuses: forced labour, corporate punishment, inequality of salaries, limitation of political rights, etc. This fight for democracy against the oppression of mankind will slowly leave the confusion of neo-liberal universalism to emerge, sometimes laboriously, as a claim to nationhood. It so happens that the unpreparedness of the educated classes, the lack of practical links between them and the mass of the people, their laziness, and, let it be said, their cowardice at the decisive moment of the struggle will give rise to tragic mishaps."

The nature of the colonized "middle-class" is bourgeois (3.5), and it's the tool of capitalism. (3.6) It has no progressive economic program and no idea as to how to form a "people's" state. (3.7) In fact, it simply refuses to "follow the path of revolution." (3.8)

> *Yet the national middle-class constantly demands the nationalization of the economy and of the trading sectors. This is because, from their point of view, nationalization does not mean placing the whole economy at the service of the nation*

and deciding to satisfy the needs of the nation. For them, nationalization does not mean governing the state with regard to the new social relations ... To them, nationalization quite simply means the transfer into native hands of those unfair advantages which are a legacy of the colonial period. (3.10)

...the native bourgeoisie which comes to power uses its class aggressiveness to corner the positions formerly kept for foreigners ... It waves aloft the notion of the nationalization and Africanization of the ruling classes. The fact is that such action will become more and more tinged by racism... (3.17)

The working-class of the towns, the masses of unemployed, the small artisans and craftsmen for their part line up behind this nationalist attitude; but in all justice let it be said, they only follow in the steps of their bourgeoisie. If the national bourgeoisie goes into competition with the Europeans, the artisans and craftsmen start a fight against non-national Africans ... From nationalism we have passed to ultra-nationalism, to chauvinism, and finally to racism. (3.18)

Summing up: We can read Chapter Three, in this instance, as an examination of the class use of "race" ... about the class struggle that must take place among the people if genuine national independence is to occur. i'd hope that We can read this chapter in particular with regard to our own struggle and the "lead" given us by the bourgeois forces in our midst, who also use "Africanization" as a cloak for their aim to dominate as a class, in alliance with their capitalist masters.

Fanon gives some advice on the means to be used to prevent neo-colonial situations:

...the bourgeoisie should not be allowed to find the conditions for its existence and its growth. In other words, the combined effort of the masses, led by a party, and of the intellectuals who are highly conscious and armed with revolutionary principles, ought to bar the way to this useless and harmful middle-class. (3.57)

Care should be taken to distinguish the "mass" of the intellectuals or the "class" of bourgeois and petty bourgeois forces, from those who have committed "class suicide." Not all intellectuals are "highly conscious," and not all petty bourgeois or pseudo-bourgeois forces are "armed with revolutionary principles." Most of all, in (3.57), Fanon is not saying that it's even the "revolutionary petty bourgeois/intellectuals" that "lead"—it's the "masses" that are to be "led by a party"—in principle, their party, which they combine with the efforts of those intellectuals that are highly conscious and armed with revolutionary principles—those who have "returned to the source" and have been "reborn"... Fanon says of the latter, at (3.63): "We must know how to use these [people] in the decisive battle," while "closing the road" to the bourgeois forces.

5E. Thoughts on The Deconstruction of "Race"

> *In the modern world, the race struggle has become part of the class struggle...*
>
> *It is only the ending of capitalism, colonialism, imperialism, and neo-colonialism, and the attainment of world communism that can provide the conditions under which the race question can finally be abolished and eliminated.*[73]

It seems right to close by planting seeds that should help to develop the process of the deconstruction of "race" as a concept, and the elimination of racism as a form of thought and practice.

Bouncing off of Nkrumah: The "race struggle" is the struggle to disauthenticate the concept of "race," upon which the practice of racism (as a tool of capitalism) stands. However, We must perceive and manage this process as one component of the larger battle to overthrow capitalism and to build socialism.

That is, the "race struggle" is part of the struggle between oppressed and oppressing classes (and/or nation-classes), because racism disguises the material reality upon which capitalist exploitation is based, and promotes the view that the "tool" (racism) is the "cause."

My position has been that Fanon regarded "race" and racism as significant obstacles in the path of true freedom—that he saw "race" as a shadow that derived its "substance" from the stability and operation of the base. As the base was attacked—as the people waged the national-class struggle, on the political and economic fronts—the base lost stability, and the shadow began to fade and lose its ability to confuse and divert energies.

The third chapter of **Wretched** provides the best example, as We see the racialized thought and practice of the bourgeois forces uprooted as a result of the people's effort to politically overthrow and negate the power of the bourgeois forces. It's through this process that the people assume control over all the material means required to build and safeguard their new social order. Thus, We're provided with the guides to our own action in developing the primary components of our process of deconstruction of "race" and racism.

That is, the process is part of the national-class struggle—a struggle that unfolds in all social spheres, and which has three major forms: ideological, political, and economic. The national-class struggle is the motive force for social development, in this case meaning it aims to change the relations of production and the pattern of ownership of the means of production, which in turn becomes the condition for corresponding changes in the superstructure, i.e., to free the process of development of the productive forces (people) and usher the creation of the all-round environment in which "race" as a concept is eliminated, and the thought and practice of racism is uprooted.

What did i just say? The battle against racism must be waged, but fighting that battle in isolation from the other forms of national-class struggle will be insufficient. Fighting racism alone won't end racism, anymore than directing blows at a shadow will eliminate that shadow. However, this is not to say that the battle against racism is not necessary. The deconstruction of the concept "race" and the battle against racist thought and practice are pivotal to the revolutionary process. Pro-capitalist and anti-socialist forces have historically relied on the shadow of "race," racial thought and practice, to undermine class/national revolutionary struggle. The very idea of "race" has to be sufficiently dismantled so that people can more easily overcome its appeal.

Mao Tse-Tung

For example, if "racial" identity is a form of collective mental illness, then We need to engage whatever psychological means necessary to effect a cure. If racism is a "bad idea," then We need to focus attention on the source of origin and the means of its reproduction, so that We can change it with a "correct" idea:

> *Where do correct ideas come from? Do they drop from the skies? No. Are they innate in the mind? No. They come from social practice, and from it alone; they come from three kinds of social practice, the struggle for production, the class struggle, and scientific experiment. It is man's social being that determines his thinking. Once the correct ideas characteristic of the advanced class are grasped by the masses, these ideas turn into a material force which changes society and changes the world...*[74]

In short, We gotta engage the battle on the ideological front, using whatever superstructural elements necessary and applicable. But We also have to combine the efforts on the ideological front with efforts on the political (which is also superstructural) and economic fronts, in a comprehensive campaign to change people, society, and the world.

> ...That racism is an ideology and not a scientific theory should be obvious to most people today. Virtually all attempts at scientific classification of races and racial characteristics have ended in failure. This is because "race" is not a concept that arose from scientific investigation; rather, it developed historically among whites as a social idea to "explain" the inferior status assigned to nonwhites. Thus, when we discuss racism we are dealing with a set of social ideas that reflect established social relations. If we want to know how these social relations originally came to be established, we must look beyond the ideology. Once racism began developing as an ideology, however, there was no lack of scientific "experts" who sought to lay upon it the mantle of scientific objectivity.[75]

> ...[M]any scholars have abandoned the use of the concept of "race" as a way of categorizing peoples. Skin color and other physical features do not reveal much about the genetic makeup of an individual or group. Two individuals with the same skin color and hair texture may be more genetically different from one another than they are from two persons with another pigmentation. For this reason, scholars have concluded that African, and other peoples as well, are so internally different that the old way of classifying people according to physical appearance or "race" is no longer useful.[76]

Part of the battle on the ideological front involves, as Allen implies, pulling the pseudo-scientific veneer off of the concept "race" and the ideology of racism. However, as We read Allen's words, We also see another aspect of the ideological battle: the elimination of racial language (which involves calling it to question whenever and wherever We come across it), and the need to develop and promote language that truly reflects the reality of capitalist hegemony and exploitation, and the revolutionary interests and vision of the people.

Pulling off the pseudo-scientific veneer goes to the heart of "race" being a social construction, i.e., that it was not scientifically derived, and is a fictitious categorization of peoples, having no existence—no "reality"—apart from the subjective interpretations of perceived distinctions.

Not only must We expose "race" as an imagined categorization; We must also promote the genuine scientific knowledge on the origin and diversity of the single human species. That is, for example, that human skin color and other physical and physiological differences between groups of people are results of adaptations to environment (amount of sunlight, in the case of skin color) and socio-economic factors, as migrations from an African center resulted in a number of isolated populations existing in a variety of climatic and environmental conditions. (Note the work of Dr. Rebecca Cohn, showing that the "first Eve"—a woman in Africa living over 150,000 years ago—is the genetic mother of all humans.)

> *Slavery is nearly as old as human civilization itself, but when the Henrietta Marie [earliest slave ship ever recovered] first landed in Barbados on July 9, 1698, with 250 Africans aboard, the construct of "race" was hardly formulated. The African slave trade was sustained by profit-hungry elites of all kinds: Christians, Muslims, Jewish, Europeans, Arab, African and American. Yet the distinctive feature of New World slavery was its "racial" character. After a few decades of trans-racial slavery—in which whites, blacks, and reds were owned by whites—the ancient form of subjugation became an exclusively black and white affair. This racialization of American slavery was rooted in economic calculation and psychological anxieties that targeted black bodies...*

> *In fact, the human family was carved into modern "racial" pigeonholes—white, black, red, brown, yellow—in order to control, confine, discipline and dishonor Africans. Racialized persons and racist practices were systematized and canonized*

> *principally owing to the financial interests and psychic needs that sustained the slave trade and New World slavery…*[77]

Take Allen and West together on the theme of racial language: With Allen, even while telling us that "race" is an unscientific, social construction, he reinforces the "reality" of "race" by continuing the convenient use of phrases such as "classification of races" (where he could have said "of peoples AS 'races'"), and "racial characteristics," "whites" and "nonwhites" (rather than naming specific people(s), e.g., Spanish, Ashanti, etc.).

With West, he tells us that the construct of "race" was hardly formulated in 1698, yet he, too, reinforces its "reality" through the same persistent use of, first, the phrase "trans-racial" slavery, and then using the invented categories "whites, blacks, and reds"… and "exclusively black and white affair"… "black bodies"…

Remaining embedded in racialized thought is largely the result of failing to follow the logic of one's analysis. That is, if you analyze the historical situation and see that "race" is a fabrication, have the courage and political/revolutionary morality to follow the logic of that analysis and became consistent in your use of language, theory, and political practice. If i truly believe that "race" is a fiction, i can't reasonably string together words like "Virtually all attempts at scientific classification of RACES and RACIAL characteristics have ended in failure." Why, of course they have! Therefore, the sentence should read, say, "Virtually all attempts to classify the various human groups as RACES and to term their physical differences as RACIAL, have ended in failure."

Rather than say, "After a few decades of trans-RACIAL slavery—in which WHITES, BLACKS, and REDS were owned by WHITES—this ancient form of subjugation became an exclusively BLACK and WHITE affair," why not say something like "…decades of 'New World Slavery' in which peoples of Europe, Africa, and the native inhabitants of the 'New World' were colonized by peoples of

Europe" and it became "exclusively a European and an African...a Euro-American and a New Afrikan...affair"?

Making the effort to use more appropriate language forces us to engage in the creation of a more accurate picture of historical and contemporary reality, while also giving shape to the new vision and the articulation of the revolutionary interests of the people. The struggle to uproot old/bad bourgeois ideas promotes new socialist/humanist ones in the process.

Recall: As **Wretched** opens, Fanon tells us that decolonization "influences individuals and modifies them fundamentally," and that it's "introduced by new [people], and with it a new language and a new humanity." (1.3)

The deconstruction of "race" as a concept and the struggle against racism on the political front starts by understanding "politics" as everything related to our lives, and not just those things related to the electoral arena. More precisely, We can define politics as a concentrated expression of economics, concerned with the acquisition, retention and use of state power, which is used to realize revolutionary interests of society. Politically, the deconstruction of "race" attacks the cause, and seeks to prevent the use of "race" to disguise it.

For example: The struggle against "racial profiling" ain't a mere struggle against racism, but one against 1) colonial aggression, and 2) capitalist exploitation under the guise of "racial discrimination." In such instances where We combat "racial profiling," slogans should always be raised that target the capitalist body which projects the racial shadow.

Economic struggle against racist practice and the deconstruction of "race" must also be connected to the battle against the body and not be confused and diverted by the shadow. For example, "racial" discrimination in housing, wages and employment, health care, etc., should all be placed within the context of national-class oppression and exploitation—as "inequalities" expressing and reinforcing economic exploitation and political domination of oppressed nationalities and classes... to sustain capitalism... as fundamental expressions of capitalism and not mere racism, perceived as external to capitalism.

Bottom line: Anyone claiming to attack racism while claiming that racism is the only thing wrong with this system, is either terribly confused or an outright enemy of the people and their interests. If We truly wanna get rid of racism, We have to overthrow capitalism... first.

The new language developed on the ideological front is used in the political and economic fields to name the enemy and define the reality... to identify the interests and goals of the people. The language of the bourgeois forces sees classes and nations as "races" and seeks to confine our struggle within "racial" boundaries, e.g., for a kind of "racial equality" within the capitalist order. That We haven't made more "racial progress"—for the masses/people as a whole—is no wonder...

End of PART THREE

Notes to Part Three

1. Amilcar Cabral, "Connecting the Struggles," *Return to the Source*, Monthly Review Press, 1973, p. 77.

2. Deborah Wyrick, *Fanon for Beginners*, Writers and Readers Publishing, Inc., 1998.

3. Stokely Carmichael, "Black Power and Racism," 7-28-66; speech printed by SNCC.

4. Stokely Carmichael, "Power and Racism," *New York Review of Books*, 9-22-66.

5. Amilcar Cabral, "The Weapon of Theory," *Revolution in Guinea: Selected Texts*, Monthly Review Press, 1969, p. 110.

6. Ibid., pps. 93–96.

7. Julius K. Nyerere, *Ujamaa: Essays On Socialism*, London: Oxford University Press, 1968, pps. 38–39.

8. Robin Williams, Jr., "Prejudice and Society," *The American Negro Reference Book*, ed. John P. Davis, NY: Prentice-Hall, 1966, p. 72.

9. Kwame Nkrumah, *Class Struggle in Africa*, NY: International Publishers, 1970, p. 29.

10. Wyrick, op. cit., p. 41.

11. Frantz Fanon, *Black Skin, White Masks*, NY: Grove Press, 1967.

12. Wyrick, op. cit., p. 24.

13. Abby Ferber, *White Man Falling: Race, Gender, and White Supremacy*, Rowman and Littlefield, 1998.

14. Paul Gilroy, quoted in "Taking Black Studies to the Streets," Jeff Sharlet, *The Chronicle of Higher Education*, 5-19-2000.

15. Wyrick, op. cit., p. 34.

16. Ibid., p. 54; Fanon, op. cit., p. 88.

17. Wyrick, Ibid., p. 39.

18. Ibid., p. 40.

19. Ibid.

20. Ibid.; Fanon, op. cit., p. 137.

21. Wyrick, Ibid., p. 41.

22. Ibid., p. 35.

23. *Black Dialogues*, N.P., pps. 479–482.

24. Wyrick, op. cit., p. 124.

25. For those who may still think of racism only within the "black/white" binary, here's food for thought: "…Racism, I maintain, was not simply a convention for ordering the relation of European to non-European peoples, but has its genesis in the 'internal' relation of European peoples…" Cedric J. Robinson, *Black Marxism: The Making of the Black Radical Tradition*, London: Zed Press, 1983, p. 2.

26. Wyrick, op. cit., p. 100.

27. Ibid., p. 62.

28. Ibid., Glossary.

29. Robert L. Allen, *Black Awakening in Capitalist America: An Analytic History*, NY: Doubleday, 1970, p. 265.

30. *Black Dialogues*, N.P., p. 330; from LeRoi Jones, "'Black' Is A Country," *Home: Social Essays*, NY: William Morrow, 1966, pps. 82–86.

31. Wyrick, op. cit., p. 37.

32. Leith Mullings, quoted in Jeff Sharlet, op. cit.

33. Wyrick, op. cit., p. 123.

34. Ibid., p. 123.

35. Walter Rodney, "Marx and the Liberation of Africa," a paper delivered at Queen's College, NY, 1975; published as "Marxism and African Liberation" in *Yes! To Marxism*, by the People's Progressive Party, Guyana, 1985, pps. 15–16.

36. Ibid., p. 15.

37. Kwame Nkrumah, "African Socialism Revisited," in *Revolutionary Path*, International Publishers, pps. 438–439.

38. Huey P. Newton, *In Search of Common Ground*, NY: W. W. Norton, 1973, p. 27.

39. Rodney, op. cit., pps. 4–5.

40. Ibid., p. 7.

41. Ibid., pps. 11–12.

42. Wyrick, op. cit., p. 124.

43. Ibid., p. 124.

44. Ibid., p. 127.

45. Ibid., p. 125.

46. Karl Marx, *The 18th Brumaire of Louis Bonaparte*, in *Selected Works of Karl Marx and Frederick Engels, Vol. I*, Moscow: Progress Publishers, 1969.

47. Karl Marx, *The Holy Family*, in *Essential Writings*, ed. David Caute, NY: Collier Books, 1967.

48. Wyrick, op. cit., p. 129.

49. Amilcar Cabral, "The Weapon of Theory," op. cit., p. 93.

50. Ibid., pps. 93–94.

51. Ibid., p. 95.

52. Ibid.

53. Ibid., p. 96.

54. Ibid., pps. 96–97.

55. Ibid., p. 98.

56. [Editors: Yaki apparently made a typing error and skipped this source in his list.]

57 Ibid., p. 102.

58. Ibid., p. 103.

59. Ibid., p. 107.

60. Ibid., pps. 96–97.

61. V.I. Lenin, "Our Program," *Collected Works, Vol. 2*, Moscow: Progress Publishers, p. 21.

62. Karl Marx, *The Holy Family*, op. cit., p. 50.

63. Karl Marx, *The German Ideology, Selected Works*, op. cit., p. 20.

64. V.I. Lenin, op. cit.

65. Karl Marx and Frederick Engels, *The Communist Manifesto*, 50th Anniversary Edition, Introduction by Robin D. G. Kelly, Chgo: Charles Kerr Publishing, 1998, p. 12.

66. Ibid., pps. 7–8.

67. Wyrick, op. cit., p. 127.

68. *Dictionary of Philosophy*, ed. Ivan T. Frolov, International Publishers, 1984, p. 14.

69. Wyrick, op. cit., p. 130. We should let Marx and Engels speak for themselves on the questions of the relative autonomy of the superstructure, and on the matter of all superstructural phenomena being reducible to material/economic causes:

> *In the social production of their life, men enter into definite relations that are indispensable and independent of their will,*

relations of production which correspond to a definite stage of development of their material productive forces. The sum total of these relations of production constitutes the economic structure of society, the real foundation, on which rises a legal and political superstructure and to which correspond definite forms of social consciousness. The mode of production of material life conditions *the social, political and intellectual life processes in general. It is not the consciousness of men that determines their being, but, on the contrary, their social being that determines their consciousness.* [my emphasis—Yaki] (Marx, Preface to A Contribution to the Critique Of Political Economy, in Selected Works Vol. 1.)

Engels addressed the questions in at least two instances:

Political, juridical, philosophical, religious, literary, artistic, etc., development is based on economic development. But all these react upon one another and also upon the economic base. It is not that the economic situation is cause, solely active, while everything else is only passive effect. There is, rather, interaction on the basis of economic necessity, which ultimately always asserts itself. (Engels to W. Borgius, 1894, in *Selected Works*, Vol. 3, p. 502.)

Engels held that he and Marx were themselves "partly to blame for the fact that the younger people sometimes lay more stress on the economic side than is due to it," and further explained:

According to the materialist conception of history, the ultimately determining element in history is the production and reproduction of real life. More than this neither Marx nor I have ever asserted. Hence, if somebody twists this into saying that the economic element is the only determining one, he transforms that proposition into a meaningless, abstract, senseless phrase. There is an interaction of all these elements which, amid all the endless hosts of accidents (that is, of things and events whose inner interconnection is so remote or so impossible of proof that we can regard it as non-existent, as negligible) the economic movement finally asserts itself as necessary. (Engels to Block, Marx and

Engels: Selected Correspondence, Moscow: Progress Publishers, 1965, pps. 417–148.)

70. Wyrick, op. cit., p. 130.

71. Ibid., p. 131.

72. Ibid., p. 132.

73. Kwame Nkrumah, *Class Struggle in Africa*, op. cit., p. 29.

74. Mao Tse-Tung, "Where Do Correct Ideas Come From?," *Five Essays On Philosophy*, Peking: Foreign Languages Press, 1977, p. 155.

75. Robert L. Allen with Pamela P. Allen, *Reluctant Reformers: Racism and Social Movements in the United States*, NY: Anchor Press, 1975, p. 6.

76. Colin A. Palmer, "The First Passage," in *To Make Our World Anew*, eds. Robin D. G. Kelly and Earl Lewis, NY: Oxford University Press, 2000, p. 4.

77. Cornel West, "The Ignoble Paradox of Modernity," *The Cornel West Reader*, Basic Civitas Books, 1999, pps. 51–52.

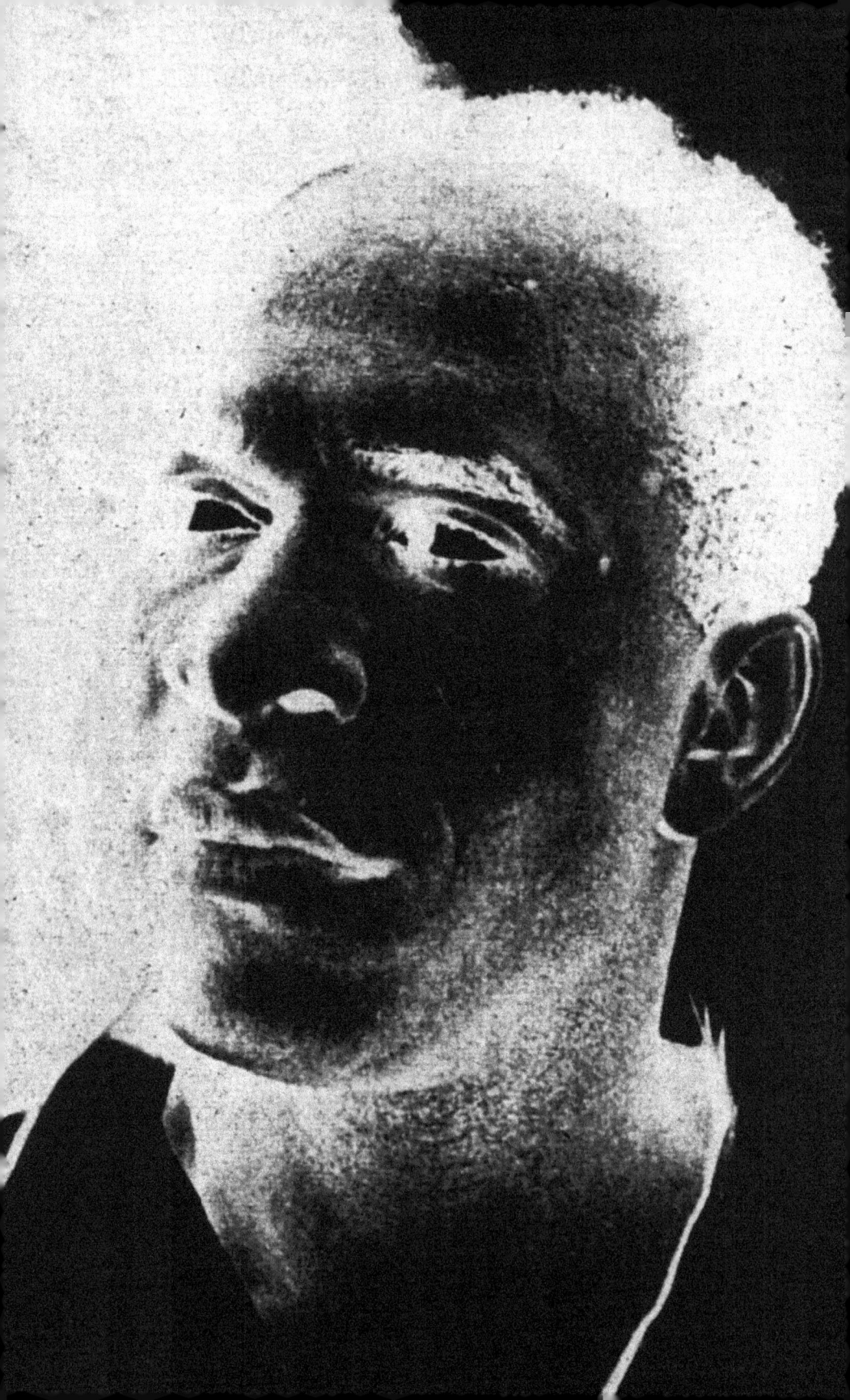

A REMINDER...

Yaki finished Parts One, Two, and Three of Meditations, but Part Four was never completed. Part Four starts out as a rough first draft, where trial wordings are mixed with notes to himself to add this or say that. Often such notes to himself are marked by special brackets: {{like this}}. Soon enough, it is mostly notes and possible quotes to be used. The chapter is choppy, fragmentary, but still roughly completes an arc. The projected parts Five and Six that Yaki came to think were necessary, never, as far as the editors know, saw paper or were even in outline form. His cancer came on too rapidly and lethally for that. We will have to work without these.

PART FOUR

ON THE "RESTORATION OF NATIONHOOD," THE CONSTITUTION OF REVOLUTIONARY (NATIONALIST) CONSCIOUSNESS, AND THE SOCIALIST/HUMANIST OBJECTIVE

CONTENTS

6. Point of Departure (Or, In Case You Missed It)

6A. The Nation, the (People's) State, and National Culture
  1. The "Nation" Is
  2. The Nation and the (People's) State—
     According to Fanon
  3. Culture: National and Revolutionary

6B. The Misadventures of National and Class Consciousness
  1. National Consciousness:
     Bourgeois and Revolutionary Nationalism
  2. Class Consciousness:
     Bourgeois and "Proletarian"/Socialist

6C. The Taking on of "New Skin" ... and, Reparations
  1. "New Skin" and Socialist Humanism
  2. AFTERWORD:
     Reparations, Self-Reliance, and "De-Linking"

Note: to the best of the editors' knowledge sections 6B and 6C were never begun.

6. Point of Departure
(Or, In Case You Missed It)

> *There are two kinds of nationalism: revolutionary nationalism, and reactionary nationalism. Revolutionary nationalism is first dependent upon a people's revolution, with the end goal being the people in power. Therefore, to be a revolutionary nationalist you would by necessity have to be a socialist. If you are a reactionary nationalist, you are not a socialist, and your goal is the oppression of the people.*
>
> Huey P. Newton

> *The fundamental contradiction in the process of development of a thing, and the essence of the process determined by this fundamental contradiction, will not disappear until the process is completed; but in a lengthy process, the conditions usually differ at each stage. The reason is that, although the nature of the fundamental contradiction in the process of development of a thing and the essence of the process remain unchanged, the fundamental contradiction becomes more and more intensified as it passes from one stage to another in the lengthy process. In addition, among the numerous major and minor contradictions which are determined or influenced by the fundamental contradiction, some become intensified, some are temporarily or partially resolved or mitigated, and some new ones emerge; hence, the process is marked by stages. If people do not pay attention to the stages in the process of development of a thing, they cannot deal with its contradictions properly.*
>
> Mao Tse-Tung

In **Part Three**, i wrote:

> We need to critically study everything ever written on the origin of the word and concept "nation," and on the evolution of "nationalism." While engaged in this study, We must avoid the quagmire of both bourgeois and doctrinaire or vulgar "Marxist" interpretations...
>
> Like "race" and "class," the word and concept "nation" has also been socially constructed by peoples as they've made their own history—one defined from the perspective of their own needs and interests...
>
> ..."nations" existed in the world prior to their appearance in Europe. We must come to distinguish "modern" from "pre-modern," capitalist from pre-capitalist, nations—sovereign from oppressed, nations. And, just as there is pro-capitalist bourgeois nationalism, there is also pro-socialist revolutionary nationalism, whereby peoples shape a new nationality "in the implacable struggle which opposes socialism to capitalism." (1.79)

We need to discuss what the/a "nation" is, so that We get a better understanding of what We fight for, and how to conduct the fight... This discussion is especially necessary for those who: 1) think that they can fight for socialism without engaging national realities, and those who 2) think that the/a nation is the same as "the race" or, that "black" liberation and national liberation are the same...

We need to discuss Fanon's idea of the nation (and those ideas of the nation held by the radical or rev. wings of the bourgeois-nationalist forces—see **WE**, 2.39) even if to simply understand his use throughout **Wretched** of such terms as "national", "national character" (3.6–7), "nationalism" (_____), national consciousness (_____), and "nationality" (_____), so that We come to understand that he (and why he) makes a fundamental distinction between bourgeois/reactionary nationalism, and revolutionary/

socialist nationalism...Fanon distinguishes (bourgeois) nationalism from "national consciousness" (____), while also showing that nationalism and national consciousness are both necessary, but that neither, alone, is sufficient to acquire genuine liberation/social revolution, and that (bourgeois) nationalism can lead the people up blind alleys. No matter the contemporary terms: we are still engaged in a fight over the fate of "nations"... a fight to build new "nations" and new types of "nations"...*

{ use graph to distinguish new section }

As with **Part Three**, i feel the need to open with a reminder: These meditations are not merely about the thought of Fanon, as it's particularly expressed in ***Wretched.*** These reflections also address those of us who are concerned about where WE are, how We got here, and WHY We got here, as We did. These reflections are also about where We must go, and what We must begin to do if We hope to get there.

These meditations are made with the hope that by "accident" and by design, they will become part of the process of winning the war now being fought within what's now known as the U.S., and throughout the world, to end all forms of the oppression and exploitation of peoples, and to build socialism.

These reflections are offered to inspire critical thought, and to engender revolutionary (i.e., socialist) practice. It's my hope that they will be useful to YOU, no matter who you are, and no matter the front that you struggle on, or the issue(s) around which you base your activity and your thought.

* "So we can observe the process whereby the rupture occurs between the illegal and legal tendencies in the party. The illegal minority is made to feel that they are undesirables and are shunned by the people that matter. The legal members of their party come to their aid with great precaution, but already there is a rift between the two tendencies. The illegalists, therefore, will get in touch with the intellectual elements whose attitude they were able to understand a few years back; and an underground party, an off-shoot of the legal party, will be the result of this meeting. But the repression of these wayward elements intensifies as the legal party draws nearer to colonialism and attempts to modify it 'from the inside'. The illegal minority thus finds itself in a historical blind alley.

"Boycotted by the towns, these men first settle in the outskirts of the suburbs. But the police network traps them and forces them to leave the towns for good, and to quit the scenes of political action. They fall back towards the countryside and the mountains, towards the peasant people. From the beginning, the peasantry closes in around them, and protects them from being pursued by the police. The militant nationalist who decides to throw in his lot with the country people instead of playing at hide-and-seek with the police in urban centres will lose nothing. The peasant's cloak will wrap him around with a gentleness and a firmness that he never suspected. These men, who are in fact exiled to the backwoods, who are cut off from the urban background against which they had defined their ideas of the nation and of the political fight, these men have in fact become 'Maquisards' [guerrillas—editors]. Since they are obliged to move about the whole time in order to escape from the police, often at night so as to not attract attention, they will have good reason to wander through their country and to get to know it. The cafes are forgotten; so are the arguments about the next elections or the spitefulness of some policeman or other. Their ears hear the true voice of the country, and their eyes take in the great and infinite poverty of their people. They realise the precious time that has been wasted in useless commentaries upon the colonial regime. They finally come to understand that the changeover will not be a reform, nor a bettering of things. They come to understand, with a sort of bewilderment that will from henceforth never quite leave them, that political action in the towns will always be powerless to modify or overthrow the colonial regime.

"These men get used to talking to the peasants. They discover that the mass of the country people have never ceased to think of the problem of their liberation except in terms of violence, in terms of taking back the land from the foreigners, in terms of national struggle, and of armed insurrection. It is all very simple..." (2.38–40)

i'm gonna talk about the "nation" here, but probably not as you might expect. i'm gonna use words that you're familiar with, but they'll be given a twist... invested with slightly new meanings. i'm gonna give some initial shape to what for most of us will be a new concept of "nation," while also pointing toward new paths and motions for REVOLUTIONARY nationalist (i.e., socialist) thought and practice. i must say that i feel, these days, confident that these seeds will inspire greater imagination and initiative within those of us who truly want to Serve the People, and to help clear the way for a better world—if not for ourselves, then surely for those who come behind us.

Why talk about the "nation"?

Because it's real! Nations are real. It amazes me how easily those who rant and rave against all talk of nations and nationalism (revolutionary) manage to overlook the fact that they are, in some sense, "nationalists" themselves. By that i mean that they are "nationalists" because they seek a new unity, grounded in shared interests. The "nation" is—before and after all else—a "new unity"... Let me repeat that: The "nation"... a "nation"... is (before and after everything else one might say about it), a "New Unity."

(Similarly, i'm gonna talk about the "state"—but again, with a twist... new meanings. i/We stand against any apparatus that would stand separate from and above the people, and used to suppress the people's unhindered exercise of their social (very broadly speaking) powers. Maybe We'll come up with a new name for the apparatus that We need, but need one, We do. We need a people's, socialist, state apparatus, not a bourgeois, capitalist, authoritarian, state apparatus.)

Now, why talk about Fanon's ideas about the "nation"? Why do so while meditating on **Wretched?**

Surely, not many people would open their comment on **Wretched** by saying that it's about "revolutionary nationalism," or, that it's about the pitfalls of narrow, "cultural nationalism" (these days i think analogous terms may be certain forms of "post-modernism," "post-structuralism," or maybe even "post-colonialism").

> **Need to insert remarks on why "read" is in quotes, i.e., refer to post-structuralist interpretations, esp. in lit., etc.

In our "reading" of **Wretched**, the first time around, most of us didn't get it. (Isn't there a line in Spike Lee's *Bamboozled*, where a would-be radical says: "You better be glad that i ain't read **Wretched** yet!"? What does that really mean? What can We draw from it—after We get all between and underneath it?)

(Maybe We could begin by saying: There are those among us who ARE glad that so few of us have "read" **Wretched**. Even a mere "reading" will produce a significant change in your thought and behavior. There are those among us who are euphoric because so few of us have STUDIED **Wretched**, and thus have not obtained from it that which would inspire new forms of thought and practice, aided by the insight and guidance provided to us throughout its pages… that would enable us to see through most or all, hopefully, of the b.s. that's passing as "progressive" thought these days…)

(It occurred to me, as i reflected upon that line ["You better be glad that i ain't read *Wretched* yet!"] that pseudo-bourgeois and petty-bourgeois forces IN OUR MIDST, tremble in fear at the thought of untold millions even merely "reading" **Wretched**, because these millions would discover that the book is an indictment of the intellectual production/practice of so many who now feign as "public intellectuals," "leaders," and "spokespersons.")

(i mean: **Wretched** is about how "the people as a whole" {**explain what this means**} must LEAD and conduct the struggle to build A NEW TYPE OF NATION, AND, A NEW TYPE OF STATE—a "people's state" We may call it. The book warns us not to let the bourgeois forces take power DURING and AFTER the struggle to liberate/build the nation, and acquire a "formal" independence.)

(Check it: You think Fanon was addressing himself only to the peoples on the Afrikan continent—peoples everywhere, **outside** the U.S.? The truth is, tho, he was also addressing himself TO YOU, too, as you struggled, here, against both the external imperialist power (the U.S. government and capitalist state), and against the internal bourgeois forces of your/our own oppressed nation—forces aligned with the imperialist power, and who sought to become the "new ruling class" within the post-neo-colonialist apparatus that was emerging even as early as the late 1960s.)

(The whole "post-modern"/"post-structural" movement among the bourgeois forces was meant to prevent "the people as a whole" from developing and pursuing REVOLUTIONARY, SOCIALIST, AND ANTI-CAPITALIST objectives. That crowd of (bourgeois) nationalists that came to adopt the line that "nationalism is dead" {THIS, TOO, MUST BE EXPLAINED}—they did so only to prevent YOU from adopting REVOLUTIONARY nationalism. When they began to push the line on "the need to recognize the 'diversity' within the African-American community"—that was designed to get you to accept the existence and the so-called "leadership" of the bourgeois forces as legitimate. So, i say again: We all missed it, and because We did, We don't truly know where We are, nor do We know how We got here, and why.)

(How many times must it be repeated? The last truly revolutionary thrust was exhausted in the late 1960s and early 1970s. The rev. failed; the rev. was defeated. There has been no revolutionary MOVEMENT within the U.S. for nearly thirty-five [35] years! The bourgeois forces of the oppressed and oppressor nations are "in power and secure," as George (Jackson) would say.)

(You've been bamboozled. You've been hood-winked. You've got so-called spokespersons who speak only for themselves, talking over, under, and all around you, but addressing themselves to their masters (tho they like to think of themselves as "partners" in the process). You've got so-called leaders who are in fact MIS-leading you, dulling your senses rather than helping to awaken you, to inspire and to assist you in the attack upon the contemporary manifestations of the forms of your oppression and exploitation.)

This is nothing but capitalism and imperialism, re-formed. You've even got so-called heroes that are nothing more than criminals (e.g., Michael Jordan, who robs you every time you buy a pair of "his" shoes, while he also signs off on the exploitation of the people who make the shoes). We won't get there until we can see that michael jordan and those like him are criminals… they're partners in the exploitation of peoples here and abroad… they're criminals… and so are you…

So again: In our mere "reading" of **Wretched**, the time around, most of us didn't get it. The problem, now, is that We think that We did, even when there's so much proof that We didn't—a proof that's so pervasive that it's smothering us, blinding us, and making us deaf and dumb...

Go check it out: Fanon opens the book by talking, rather straightforwardly, about "the restoration of nationhood to the people"! In the final paragraph of the body of the book, he ends with a reminder that it's a REVOLUTIONARY nationalism that must be sought:

> INDEPENDENCE *is not a word which can be used as an exorcism, but an indispensable* CONDITION FOR *the existence of men and women who are truly liberated. In other words, who are truly* MASTERS OF ALL THE MATERIAL MEANS *which make possible the radical transformation of society.* (5.182; my emphasis)

And what else did he say?

> ...*The living expression of the nation is the moving consciousness of the whole of the people; it is the coherent, enlightened action of men and women ... The national government, if it wants to be national [i.e., revolutionary] ought to govern by the people and for the people, for the outcasts and by the outcasts...* (3.96)

We need to STUDY and to discuss Fanon's ideas about the "nation" and (revolutionary) nationalism, because he had things to say which remain relevant to us, to the issues that We confront, and to the objectives that We pursue. Fanon and **Wretched** are relevant to your concerns over your next paycheck, or lack thereof; relevant to your concerns over your health care, or lack thereof, and to every other concrete issue that touches your life. Fanon said things in the book about the NARROW nationalists that can help you to change the political relations in your neighborhood, where today the petty-bourgeois politicians and business people are calling shots that are not in your interests… i only hope that i can string together the words that will make all of this, and more, clear to you—clear enough that you begin to think differently and to act differently… to think differently about your self, your so-called "leaders," and about YOUR ability to become a leader, i.e., a fully responsible citizen of your nation—no matter what it's called…

How does the song go—*"It's winter in America, and no one knows what to save"*? Well, it's still "winter"—inside U.S. borders and throughout the world—and too few of us seem to know what to "save," i.e., what to fight for, and We have no sense of how to conduct the fight under present conditions. {e.g., We got gadgets and We think we got more $$, etc., and that "things are better" but we ain't looking at the whole picture, and we ain't making a comparative analysis… the master still lives in the big house and we still live in shacks, but both the big house and the shacks are simply "more modern," and the wealth that's been stolen from people throughout the world has "trickled down" a bit to even the slaves… and our problem is that we need to develop an awareness and a conscience about this…}

It's frighteningly common to hear people exclaim their confusion while often justifying their lack of greater initiative by pointing to the bewilderment and lack of political activity that surrounds them.

People admit their confusion, yet don't know why they are confused. They profess their ignorance even as they "read" profusely the media-favored intellectuals. It would seem that there'd be less confusion if the authors We're reading were really doing what We assume they are to do…

We need REVOLUTIONARY orientation, but few, if any, of the favored authors are real revolutionaries. Who among them stand to the left of Fanon? People today remain confused because, in large part, those they read have led them astray, led them up blind alleys. Few of these authors even invoke Fanon's name and work, or critique it in any depth and breadth—because it ain't easy to assimilate Fanon (and **Wretched**) into the bourgeois ambit, or to turn Fanon into a friend or mouthpiece of the bourgeois forces!

We became confused, in part, because even "back in the day" We didn't know what to fight for. Some of us, at one point or another, thought that the fight was for "civil rights," and when We were told that the "civil rights movement" had run its course, We believed that the "real fight" was over—yet We weren't quite comfortable with that lack of freedom that we knew/know still exists. The struggle has always been about/for more than mere "civil rights," and that movement simply marks one STAGE (see Mao quote, above) in the long process of resolving the fundamental contradiction between ourselves and capitalist America (imperialism).

Some of us thought that We were fighting for a "black power," which was to manifest itself through electoral participation within the boundaries of bourgeois hegemony. We thought "black power" would take the form of vaguely defined "community control" or "equality" or "parity" or "pluralism"—also to be exercised within the bounds of capitalist hegemony. So, when we were told that the "black power movement," too, had "matured" and turned "green," We again coudn't understand why We didn't feel like "full citizens," sharing and exercising real power in U.S. society.

Then too, many of us thought that we were fighting for a "black" skin liberation, and as we continue THAT struggle today, we can't understand why the goal—why even the struggle itself—remains so elusive and amorphous, and why it's so hard to "unite" the people around the slogans that are based on a narrow nationalism…

As the 1960s came to a close, we entered the first few years of the 1970s becoming more and more frustrated and disoriented, as the revolutionary thrust was defeated through a combination of the weakness of the revolutionary forces, the struggle for power and "leadership" over the people that was waged by the internal bourgeois forces, and the external attack by the oppressive state. We lost our momentum; the continuity was broken, and the revolutionary forces lost or abandoned their ties to the people. A "low tide" was the result. So then—so now—the question is: What to do, "after the revolution has failed"?

> *After revolution has failed, all questions must center on HOW a new revolutionary consciousness can be mobilized around the new set of class antagonisms that have been created by the authoritarian reign of terror. At which level of social, political and economic life should we begin our new attack?*
>
> George Jackson

There has to be a raising of questions, and a search for answers and for new inspiration and guidance. Although too many of us think otherwise, part of the reason for the lack of greater REVOLUTIONARY momentum at the present time is that We haven't raised enough questions, or, We've been raising the wrong questions. We haven't sufficiently uncovered the lessons to be drawn from previous experience, and not brought that knowledge to bear upon the present... and the problems that we confront as we head into the future...

Relatedly, We've failed to maintain our grasp upon, and failed to continue to develop, the tools that we were beginning to use during the revolutionary thrust that failed—thinking that our path had been wrong, rather than our way of walking it. We felt that we had to abandon "old" sources of insight and guidance... to abandon "old" schools of thought. We were told that we had to become "post-moderns" or "post-structuralists," and we didn't know (and still don't) the inherent dangers of these, with their bourgeois orientations. We accepted the lies (even as We told ourselves that we didn't) that "history" had come to an end, that the struggle for socialism was dead, and that revolutionary movements would never rise again. (Of course, there WILL be a "next wave," but the question is: Will it be determined by spontaneity, or by consciousness?) The new theoretical and ideological offensives launched by the capitalist state, and carried out by its intellectual agents and the petty-bourgeois forces in our midst, contributed to our "forgetting" what we were—what we are—fighting for.

We fight, today, for the same things that we fought for as Fanon wrote *The Wretched of the Earth*. We engage the same foes that we engaged then, too. Despite what our enemies have told us, and despite what many of us now believe, we haven't yet reached the end of the social-collective-subject.

The contradiction between capitalism and socialism is still fundamental in all national societies. The contradiction between imperialism (capitalism as a world-dominating system) and REVOLUTIONARY nationalism (i.e., national revolutions that aim to de-link from the world-dominating capitalist system, and to build socialist societies), is still fundamental in the world. This is why you need to be reminded... it's what you need to be reminded of.

We're still engaged in the same process—it's simply reached a different stage, and we witness and experience changed forms of the major and minor contradictions that are determined and influenced by the fundamental contradiction. In fact, the fundamental contradiction, itself, appears to be "new" only because of the changes undergone as it passed from its previous stage to its present one, while its essence has remained the same.

i opened with words from Huey and Mao…

Huey's words are used to set the foundation for the theme which argues that Fanon is the prototypical "revolutionary nationalist," and that **Wretched** is the manifesto that helped to shape our still-developing understanding of REVOLUTIONARY nationalism.

It was part of Huey's genius that allowed him to make the distinction between REVOLUTIONARY nationalism, and bourgeois nationalism (after "reading" **Wretched**?)—a distinction uncommonly made at the time, and still seldom made, e.g., by those who condemn all nationalism as reactionary, or, those who perceive all nationalism as revolutionary. {work in the quotes by bobby seale and eldridge}

Although we may re-articulate some of the concepts shaping it, or identify it with the use of other terms, revolutionary nationalism remains the objective for most of the world's peoples. (For emphasis: Revolutionary nationalism is where the nation [a new unity among a politically organized group of people] carries out a national(ist) revolution—against capitalism, and to build socialism. Revolutionary nationalism is not only, tho, anti-capitalist; it's also anti-patriarchal, and it abhors all forms of gender oppression.)

In **Wretched**, Fanon took aim at the fundamental contradiction in the world, that between imperialist oppression and the struggle for national liberation. Put another way: Fanon took aim at the contradiction between capitalism and the struggle for the development of socialist societies.

Wretched is about the struggle to shape new, socialist nations—to shape a new type of nationalism in the still-bourgeois dominated era. **Wretched** links "culture" to the process of "making history" AS new, socialist nations. It links "national consciousness" to socialist consciousness, via the revolutionary character of national(ist) struggles in the era dominated by imperialism.

At (P.6), Sartre echoes Fanon: "…In order to triumph, the national revolution must be socialist: if its career is cut short, if the native bourgeoisie takes over power, the new state, in spite of its formal sovereignty, remains in the hands of the imperialists..." Later, Sartre reminds us that Fanon had urged the peoples of Africa, Asia and Latin America, to "achieve revolutionary socialism all together, everywhere, or else one by one We will be defeated by our former masters." (Yeah, clearly, We need a new International for the 21st century, and beyond.)

"National liberation" means: that peoples struggle (for the independence) to choose the content and direction of their socio-economic lives, i.e., to choose to move along the capitalist, or the socialist, path. The struggle for socialism can only occur within boundaries marking out (new, people's, democratic) nations, and states.

Put another way: Everything is connected, and everything is about making a choice between capitalism and socialism. At this point, even the world-wide struggle to arrest and eliminate the AIDS epidemic is linked to the struggle against capitalism, and the struggle for socialism. "Environmental justice" is unthinkable outside the context of a struggle to build socialist societies, worldwide. Whatever the issue, whatever the struggle, it's linked to the choice between capitalism or socialism.

No surprise, then, that oppressed peoples the world over took so fervently to **Wretched** and, like those of us within U.S. borders in the late 1960s (e.g., the Black Panther Party), everyone understood that one of Fanon's prime targets was the pseudo- and-petty-bourgeois forces in our midst. No surprise, either, that **Wretched** remains so relevant to the combat of the contemporary forms of "post-colonial" oppression (i.e., neo-colonialism and post-neocolonialism).

If i had the time or the inclination, i could argue that Lenin could also stand as an example of a revolutionary nationalist. Similar arguments could be made with regard to Mao, Ho Chi Minh, Fidel, and a number of others who aren't normally considered in that light.

As i reflect on it a bit, maybe i'd best cast Lenin as one who planted the theoretical seeds of revolutionary nationalism, e.g.:

> ...imperialism means that capital has outgrown the framework of national states; it means that national oppression has been extended and heightened on a new historical foundation... we must link the revolutionary struggle for socialism with a revolutionary program on the national question...
> "The Rev. Prol. and the Right of Nations to Self-D"

Note well: Lenin didn't say that national states (i.e., nations or nationalism) were no longer relevant; he didn't say that national oppression (i.e., nationalism) had to be SUBORDINATED to the struggle for socialism. He said that the oppression of nations—in the era of imperialism—had been "extended and heightened" on a foundation that increased its relevance and importance to the struggle for socialism. He said that the struggles for national liberation (revolution) and socialism, had now to be "linked"—as also says Fanon.

As also said Mao, when he posed that anti-colonial struggles were "applied internationalism," and that, therefore, there was no contradiction (antagonistic) between "patriotism" (nationalism) and communism:

> ...In the era of imperialism, all anti-colonial wars are revolutions against international capital, and they are part of the proletarian/socialist world revolution.
> Mao Tse-Tung

We should also recall the flak that Ho Chi Minh caught (especially from so-called orthodox Marxists or doctrinaire communists) as he was labeled a "nationalist"—folks couldn't understand how he could be a REVOLUTIONARY nationalist, and, a communist... These were—are—people who understood/understand neither revolutionary nationalism, nor communism...

i used words from Mao, as i opened, to remind us that **Wretched** repeatedly warns us to pay attention to the stages in the process of the development of the struggle to carry out the socialist revolution in nations dominated by capitalist-imperialism. **Wretched** foretold the consequences that would result if the revolution failed, i.e., should the people not block the rise to power of the bourgeois nationalist forces (i.e., the rise to power of the "new black middle class" in the U.S., after our revolutionary thrust failed—same book, different page; and in 2003, different terms used to describe—or mask—the same process).

Wretched continues to offer us insight and guidance—if We open ourselves to it—as we enter the middle of the first decade of the new century. It offers us perception, and direction, as we engage the forces of "globalization" (it's still imperialism, in a new form, at a new stage), which wages war upon the people of Iraq, threatens the people of Iran and North Korea, assists in the genocide of the Palestinian people, and ravages the lands and peoples of Afrika, Asia, and Latin America.

Wretched remains relevant to our search for POLITICAL identity, ideological purpose, and revolutionary direction—as we continue the necessary debates and struggles over philosophical stands and theoretical formulations... issues of "race" and class, nationalism and anti-authoritarianism, communism and capitalism. **Wretched** remains relevant and useful as we struggle to develop the theory and practice that will help to mobilize the majority of the people(s) in opposition to those who now rule. It remains relevant to our effort to construct new forms of inter-national solidarity against rapacious (international) capital, and to build free, socialist societies. Nations.

6A. The Nation, the (People's) State, and National Culture

1. The "Nation" Is
2. The Nation and the (People's) State—According to Fanon
3. Culture: National and Revolutionary

6A.1 The "Nation" Is
Thinking of how to open this section, the following seems a good enough hook:

> *Europeans often forget that colonial peoples, too, are nations.*
> V.I. Lenin, *A Caricature of Marxism and Imperialist Economism*

We all think that We know what a "nation" is. However, some of us have "forgotten," while others have never known. In either case, it boils down to allowing those who oppose our interests, to tell us what to think, rather than aiding us in the process of learning how to think.

As i look back, now, i'm amazed to see how quickly and uncritically i accepted (or rejected) various definitions of "nation" (and "nationalism"). i'm amazed at my failure to undertake an examination of the particular contexts (e.g., political, historical) out of which various definitions of "nation" arose. i'm amazed at my failure to seek to uncover the true purposes that those definitions were meant to serve.

(At some point in the near future—after i complete several unfinished projects—i would like to take on a rather broad study and critique of "nation" and "nationalism," focusing on the predominant bourgeois-Eurocentric orientation that now passes as the only true, full, and legitimate point of view. i'd also, of course, pick up and develop, as best i could, some or all of the ideas contained throughout MEDITATIONS relative to our revolutionary future. This can't be the time. i can, tho, try to point the way. i can plant a few seeds. i think that i can provide a foundation for the understanding of "nation" that i think We need to develop.)

> ...the nation clearly appears in (1) complete tributary societies (China, Egypt) where the tribute was centralized by the state, and the tributary class was a state class, in contrast to incomplete tributary societies (like European feudal societies) where tribute collection was not centralized, and (2) capitalism, where the competition among capitals (with the resulting equalization of profits) and the mobility of labor are controlled by the state through legislation, the monetary system, and state economic policy... The European situation—the absence of nations during the feudal era, the concurrent birth of the nation and capitalism—accounts for the West-centered distortion of the concept of nation. This distortion appears not only in the works of Stalin, but also in those of Marx, Engels, and Lenin...
>
> Class and Nation: Historically and in the Current Crisis
> Samir Amin, Monthly Review Press, NY, 1980, p. 20

Why do We need a new understanding of "nation" (and "nationalism")?

We can start, on the low end, with this example: Lenin also sometimes "forgot" that colonized peoples were nations, and at other times he "remembered." Whether he "forgot" or "remembered" depended, i think, on his interests at the particular time that he found himself having to address the "national question," "the self-determination of nations," or related issues.

i hesitate to say that Stalin "forgot" what the nation was, because: As he developed that oft-quoted, so-called definition of "nation," he was guided by the interests of the "USSR" (i.e., the Russian empire). Yeah, Stalin's definition of "nation" was/is not truly objective or scientific. It was, rather, designed to help hold together the empire... to help develop a policy on the "nationalities" (i.e., nations) that would prevent them from seeking national independence, and from possibly pursuing political and economic interests that could have become antagonistic to those of Russia.

Now, moving a bit toward the high end... We need a new understanding of... a new and better grasp of... a new image concept of "nation" (and "nationalism") because We have chosen—and We can choose—our (new) nationality, and "the content of its character"! Right on!

Moreover, We need to shape a new concept of "nation" (and "nationalism") to help us to understand what i mean when i say that everyone is a "nationalist" of one sort or another. The only question is: What kind of nationalist are you (e.g., bourgeois, or revolutionary; in the "closet" or genuinely ignorant of the significance of your daily practice and choices)? What goals do you pursue? Where do your loyalties lie? What kind of nation do you want to live in—capitalist, or socialist?

i know there are those ("black" and "white"—see "Note #1") who'll quickly object to my characterization here. Stop and think a bit on the many ways that your thought and practice so often contradicts what may come out of your mouth about your not being a "nationalist"... Think about it the next time you talk about "our government" or "our country" or "bring our boys/troops home." An "American nationalist" is what far too many of you are, and color or "race" has nothing to do with it... If you're here and calling yourself an "American"—"Black American" or "white American" or "African-American"—what are you doing if not proclaiming your nationality?!?

Now, if you were an American *revolutionary* nationalist, We'd be on the same page. Most of you are American *bourgeois* nationalists. You support—even in your inaction—capitalism and its rape and plunder. Revolutionary nationalism—even the American kind—would make you one engaged in struggle against capitalism, and for socialism. That would be *real* "anti-imperialism"... real revolution...

Far too many people still see everything in racialized terms // [as We'll see, again, Fanon's idea of the nation and revolutionary nationalism was not racially based... tho the nation is a new unity... and because of the racialized character of much of contemporary national liberation/social revolutionary struggles, it must be said that the new unity is not racial. It's not about uniting only with those who look like you, but it's a matter of uniting with those who think like you and who want what you want... who're willing to put their lives on the line while fighting to realize the new world...] // while our enemies are wiping out "population groups" and destroying the planet, in the name of profit (yeah, they want power, too, but only to help them acquire the profit).

Deep reflection on Fanon's thought, as particularly expressed in **Wretched**, has helped me to see that i can't limit my responsibility to, say, five of the states within present U.S. borders. The Nation is all of us; it's wherever We are. And, our new concept of the nation (and nationalism) must be linked to the re-shaping of our ideas about the world. The world is and must be understood as our "village"... We need a "world-nation"... a new unity on an inter-nation(al) scale...

Most of the commonly propagated and accepted defs of nation either omit or only superficially tell you what "nation" is, but say more about the kinds of "clothes" it wears. Most of us accept these "politically loaded" defs without questioning the particular interests, biases, or ideo-theoretical handicaps of those who put them forward.

Shared by these defs is their placing of Europe, and the rise of capitalism (in Europe) at their center. They hold that "nation" didn't exist until it appeared in Europe, 16th–18th century, depending upon who's making the def/who you read. (Some of the more "objective" writers will, as We'll see below, almost in passing point up a distinction between "modern" nations and "pre-modern" nations, and point up the "modern" and "pre-modern" uses of the very term "nation," i.e., they will say that "nations" did in fact exist outside of europe and prior to the rise of capitalism, but that these were "primitive" nations, etc....) This line that no nations existed until they appeared in Europe, with the concurrent rise of capitalism, has a correlative line which holds that non-european peoples did not have or make history until they were dragged into history (european/western/world) upon being "discovered" or colonized or otherwise conquered and exploited...

i don't care who you are, you probably have a need to re-examine your present idea of the "nation." It's probably been influenced by some dictionary or encyclopedia which has served to confuse and mislead you. Let's check this composite dictionary/encyclopedia def. of nation that i've drawn up and see what We find:

> *Nation: 1) from the Latin "natio"=birth; fr. "natus," the p.p. of "nasci"=to be born; akin to the Latin "gignere"=to beget; 2) a politically organized nationality/group; a community of people/a people having a common origin, tradition, language, customs, historic continuity, and social collective consciousness, possessing a*

common and defined independent territory; 3) modern meaning: a group of people who have a sovereign government/state.

In a def. such as this, i think that the first and most important thing to reflect upon is the matter of "birth," i.e., the bringing together of two (or more) heretofore separate entities, which then assume a new form. This is "the nation"... at its core, its essence... a new unity. It's from this new unity that there arises the (new) nations' "common origin, tradition, language, customs, historic community, and social collective consciousness"...

[**It's said that "nation" means—or, that a "nation" is—a birth, or, a new birth. i prefer to call it a unity, or, a new unity.]

The "nation" means—the nation is—a new unity.

A birth, or, a new birth, is a result of combining distinct elements into a (new) whole. Unity, or a new unity, is a combination of elements (in this case, individuals and groups/peoples) that come to form a complex and systematic whole—a oneness in purpose, and action.

A nation is a new group unity and a new group identity. This new identity of the new group suppresses or supersedes previous separate identities that were based on locality, lineage, physical characteristics, etc. The nation is all-inclusive—it's the people as a whole, in their collective, socio-political capacity. The nation is the new unity of previously separate groups, which now shares a common cause, a collective consciousness, and seeks to share collective mastery/responsibility for their social order... (see 3.96)

—shared culture; individuals & groups profess loyalty to the nation/new unified collective, w/ its new morality, values, goals...

Now, also pay attention to the way in which the "modern meaning" of "nation"… how what a "nation" is… is contingent upon its having sovereign government and/or state apparatus. Which is to say, for example, that if today you're an independent nation, but you lose your independence tomorrow, then you thereby also lose your right to claim existence as a "nation." And, you become—what? A "colonized people"? An "enslaved people"? A "tribe" or "federation of tribes"? "Negroes"? "Black people"?…

Now, let's check out a *Dictionary of Philosophy*, which was produced in Russia/the USSR, re: "nation" and "nationality":

> "*Nation*": *A historically formed community of people which succeeds nationality. The nation is distinguished first of all by common material conditions of life: common territory and economic life; common language and certain traits of [common] national character manifested in the [unified] national peculiarity of its culture. The nation… comes into being with the appearance and development of the capitalist formation. Liquidation of the feudal disunity, the consolidation of economic ties between regions within a country, the merging of local markets into a [unified] national market, served as the economic basis for the formation of nations…*[2]

> "*Nationality*": *One of the forms of community of people, which follows historically the clan and tribal community; it is formed in the period of the consolidation and merging of separate tribes, of the replacement of the relations inherent in primitive-communal society by those of private ownership and of the emergence and development of classes. The formation of Nationality is characterized by the change-over from blood relationship to territorial community, from a variety of tribal languages to a common language with a number of local dialects still in use. Each Nationality receives a collective name and accumulates elements of common culture. Nationalities existed both under slavery (the Egyptian, Grecian nationalities, and others) and feudalism (the*

> Old Russian, French nationalities, and others). The nation, a new historical form of the community of people, comes into being on the basis of developing capitalist relations. Since under capitalism pre-capitalist relations still remain along with the capitalist ones, not all nationalities grow into nations. As a rule, the consolidation of nationalities and their growth into nations are hindered in the dependent countries oppressed by the monopoly capital of the imperialist countries...[3]

i must admit: When i first read the *DOP* def of "nation" some years ago, it didn't occur to me that i should have raised my first question as soon as i finished the first sentence. How can you have a "nationality" before you have a "nation"? Maybe i'm just slow... However, it really seems that the elements used in the *DOP* def of "nation" are, essentially... fundamentally... the same as those they use to describe the process of the formation of "nationalities"...

Now, when the *DOP* def of nation claims that it/they arose with the appearance of "the capitalist formation," it appears that they only describe European social formations—this peculiarly european factor appearing again in the *DOP* def of nationality as it claims that some of them don't develop into nations "in the dependent countries oppressed by the monopoly capital of the imperialist countries..." [a little "a posteriori"?]

What really ticks me off about the *DOP* def of nationality, etc., (or, et al.) is their projection of that tired periodization of modes of production, perpetuating and claiming, in the process, that Egypt was not only not a nation (and/or an empire) but that it was characterized as a formation of the "slave mode," meaning, among other things, that it wasn't as developed and civilized as those states of the "feudal mode" like the old russian and the french, i.e., the europeans...

Now, let's check out Ernest Gellner, who for many bourgeois scholars is like the godfather of the theoretical development of nationalism... Speaking to the question "what is a/the nation," Gellner holds:

> *1. Two men are of the same nation if and only if they share the same culture, where culture... means a system of ideas and signs and associations and ways of behaving and communicating.*
>
> *2. Two men are of the same nation if and only if they recognize each other as belonging to the same nation... [N]ations are the artifacts [products] of men's convictions and loyalties and solidarities. A mere category of persons (say, occupants of a given territory, or speakers of a given language, for example) becomes a nation if and when the members of the category firmly recognize certain mutual rights and duties to each other in virtue of their shared membership of it. It is their recognition of each other as fellows of this kind which turns them into a nation, and not the other shared attributes, whatever they might be, which separate that category from non members. (p.7, Gellner...) (from here, he conditions this def on "culture," p. 11)*

- he claims neither of two above are adequate because they are hooked/dependent/contigent upon "culture" and what it does...
- his def of "culture" is hinged on his def of literacy, i.e., the written word/script, which must be "unversalized" and "standardized" and incorporate "the people as a whole"—thus he claims "nations" can only exist in "industrial" (i.e., cap.) societies
- see notes, pps. 3A–4; p. 11;

***Miroslav Hrock, SON, holds nations are older than Gellner's "modernist" account allows... he also holds:
- nations are large groups of people, integrated by a combination of eco, pol, hist., religious, cul and geo. relationships, and by a subjective perception of a collective consciousness

of belonging together; a conception of equality of all members of the group as a civil society. And no matter what term people used to describe themselves/others, if they had these, the term's equivalent is that which is now called "nation." see pps. 93–94

***O'Leary, *SON*, note 109, p. 88: "...nations are authentically felt expressions of collective identity."

[Here Yaki paraphrases and in part quotes from the Hrock paper, "Real and Constructed: The Nature of the Nation," as well as Brendan O'Leary's "Ernest Gellner's diagnoses of nationalism: a critical overview, or, what is living and what is dead in Ernest Gellner's philosophy of nationalism" in John A. Hall's anthology, *The State of the Nation: Ernest Gellner and the Theory of Nationalism*—Editors]

CLOSE THE SECTION...
with quote from Stokely, and say:

What i've been implying here is not necessarily that the nation is what i say it is, but that may in fact be so. Why is my voice less authoritative than Stalin's or Lenin's, or the guys that wrote the *DOP*, or Gellner or the folks that put the *Webster's* or the *Compton encyclopedia* together?

The aim has been to lay the ground for an exam. of Fanon's idea of the nation, etc....

And, to lay some ground for our possibly recognizing each other as members of the same nation, no matter color, but conviction...

> "When I use a word," Humpty Dumpty said in a rather scornful tone, "I mean just what I choose it to mean, neither more nor less." "The question is," said Alice, "whether you can make

> words mean so many different things." "The question is," said
> Humpty Dumpty, "who is to be master." That is all. That is all.
> Understand that ... the first need of a free people is to define their
> own terms.
>
> > Stokely Carmichael, on Lewis Carroll, 1967, quoted in:
> > *New Day In Babylon: The Black Power Movement and American
> > Culture, 1965–1975* William L. Van Deburg,
> > u of chgo press, chgo., 1992, p. 11

6A.2 The Nation and the (People's) State—According to Fanon

Fanon knew that nations were a reality in the world prior to their appearance in Europe. He understood that nations existed on the Afrikan continent prior to their disruption by colonialism. Fanon understood the difference between the qualitative character of the "old" pre-colonial nations, and the nations that began their development in the course of anti-colonial struggle. The "old" nations never ceased to exist, tho their development was arrested. The old nations were, in some cases, "absorbed" into larger units, as a manifestation of the new unity that all nations are. The old nations were transformed. For Fanon, the new nations were expressed by new collective consciousness, new sets of social relations. The new nations were all-inclusive, and no longer based on racialism, "tribalism" or regionalism.

For Fanon, the new nations were bounded by common cause; they were shaped by common destiny—e.g., a destiny to "skip the bourgeois phase" of national existence (3.58; 3.61), and move straight ahead to socialism:

> Of course we know that the capitalist regime, in so far as it is a way of life, cannot leave us free to perform our work at home, nor our duty in the world. Capitalist exploitation and cartels and

monopolies are the enemies of under-developed countries. On the other hand, the choice of a socialist regime, a regime which is completely oriented towards the people as a whole, and based on the principle that [people are] the most precious of all possessions, will allow us to go forward more quickly and more harmoniously, and thus make impossible that caricature of society where all economic and political power is held in the hands of a few who regard the nation as a whole with scorn and contempt. (1A.6)

Fanon understood that the (new) nations struggled to regain the <u>recognition of</u> their sovereignty—and, that the newly exercised sovereignty would have to have characteristics suited to the new era and its demands. The very term "sovereignty" had now come to mean that the whole people would now exercise collective responsibility over all of the nation's affairs—that the new "state apparatus" would truly be of, by, and for the people, and not exist separate from them, nor standing above them.

National liberation, national renaissance, the restoration of nationhood to the people, commonwealth: whatever may be the headings used or the formulas introduced, decolonization is always a violent phenomenon. At whatever level we study it... decolonization is quite simply the replacing of a certain "species" of men by another "species" of men. Without any period of transition, there is a total, complete and absolute substitution. It is true that we could equally well stress the rise of a new nation, the setting up of a new State... But we have precisely chosen to speak of that kind of tabula rasa which characterizes at the outset all decolonization. Its unusual importance is that it constitutes, from the very first day, the minimum demands of the colonized. To tell the truth [though] the proof of success lies in a whole social structure being changed from the bottom up... (1.1)

i had to read the entire book several times before i realized that the title of the first chapter (Concerning Violence) tends to mislead. We aren't accustomed to thinking of "violence" as anything other than armed forms of struggle, so We get side-tracked by the "always a violent phenomenon" line.

> *Check it out: Here We are reading a chapter on "violence"— which most of us think of only in terms of arms or physical force—but how much does Fanon actually talk of arms or physical force? You might expect every page to contain some mention of guns, knives, armed encampments, guerrillas training in the forests, nightly raids on the farms of settlers, attacks on local police stations or military outposts—but how much of this is actually there, in this first chapter on "violence"? Not much, you say?* **Well, why do you think that is?...**
> Meditations. Part Two, p. 186

> *In most cases, colonial violence in armed/physical forms is preceded by unarmed and nonphysical forms of aggression, in the guise of traders, academics, missionaries—who seek not only to lay hold of the land and labor of the peoples, but also to lay hold of their minds, their customs, and their languages. These <u>violent</u> actions serve to suppress, distort, injure, frustrate, infringe, profane, and unduly alter the targeted peoples and their social orders, and cripple the people's ability to resist and to regain their independence!*
> Meditations. Part Two, p. 199

Yeah... Fanon is talking about "violence" in Ch. 1, but We need to re-focus: He's not (simply) talking about "picking up the gun"—he's talking about a kind of "violence" that requires that you <u>change your mind</u>. He's talking about an "atmosphere" of "violence" that should come to prevail within oppressed communities, such that "individualism is the first to disappear." Do you recall <u>that</u> line? (1.22)

> *Individual experience, because it is national and because it is a link in the chain of national existence, ceases to be individual... (3.94)**

It's about the little "i" and the big "We"; it's not "me" and "mine," but "us" and "ours"...

> *The violence which has ruled over the ordering of the colonial world, which has ceaselessly drummed the rhythm for the destruction of native social forms and broken up without reserve the systems of reference of the economy, the customs of dress and external life, that same violence will be claimed and taken over by the native at the moment when, deciding to embody history in his [or her] own person, [he or she] surges into the forbidden quarters... (1.13)*

Prior to the experience of writing these reflections, i would read that passage and focus only on the line "surges into the forbidden quarters." My focus was on the narrow forms of violence... i was wrapped up in my own "riot stage." (Aside from not being able to understand "violence" from a revolutionary standpoint, i was clearly unable to grasp what it means to "embody history"—a subject We'll have to take up below.)

The "restoration" of nationhood to the people requires a revolutionary violence, a total contestation of colonial and bourgeois hegemony {{define}}, by which means the people free the process of development of their social productive forces; they renew, and reshape, their "social forms" and the "systems of reference" of their economy. The nation is: the restoration of "the ways of life and of thought" of the people. (1.16)*

In Ch. 1, Fanon talks about the need for oppressed peoples to mock and to vomit up Western (i.e., bourgeois/capitalist) values—do you recall <u>that</u> line? (1.16) Re-read the chapter, only now focus on the words that call for fundamental change of the entire system of social relations—to change "a whole social structure"—not, tho, "from the bottom up," but rather, from vertical to horizontal…

We read Ch. 1 and get thrown off track as Fanon makes his points about the people's state of mind "at the outset," when they wrongly think, for example, that changing things "from the bottom up" (or, that merely replacing the foreigner) is <u>the</u> objective

---

* "As soon as the native begins to pull on his moorings, and to cause anxiety to the settler, he is handed over to well-meaning souls who in cultural congresses point out to him the specificity and wealth of Western values. But every time Western values are mentioned they produce in the native a sort of stiffening or muscular lockjaw. During the period of decolonization, the native's reason is appealed to. He is offered definite values, he is told frequently that decolonization need not mean regression, and that he must put his trust in qualities which are well-tried, solid, and highly esteemed. But it so happens that when the native hears a speech about Western culture he pulls out his knife—or at least he makes sure it is within reach. The violence with which the supremacy of white values is affirmed and the aggressiveness which has permeated the victory of these values over the ways of life and thought of the native mean that, in revenge, the native laughs in mockery when Western values are mentioned in front of him. In the colonial context the settler only ends his work of breaking in the native when the latter admits loudly and intelligibly the supremacy of the white man's values. In the period of decolonization, the colonized masses mock at these very values, insult them, and vomit them up."

of the struggle; or, that there will not and need not be a "period of transition." Such thinking was corrected only after years of sacrifice and struggle, e.g.:

> ...all now are seen, in the light of experience, to be symptoms of a very great weakness. While [the people] thought that [they] could pass without transition from the status of a colonized person to that of a self-governing citizen of an independent nation, while [they] grasped at the mirage of [their] muscles' own immediacy, [they] made no real progress along the road to knowledge. [Their] consciousness remained rudimentary... (2.61)

> ...The struggle for national liberation does not consist in spanning the gap at one stride... (2.64)

> ...The objectives of the struggle ought not to be chosen without discrimination, as they were in the first days of the struggle... (2.65)

Throughout Ch. 1, Fanon talks about the nation—what it is, and what it ought to become. He talks about how the struggle to liberate and to <u>develop</u> the nation should be conducted, so that the nation-becoming will have a chance to realize its full potential, and avoid the pitfalls of spontaneity, narrow/bourgeois nationalism, and to escape the reactionary rule of the nation's own bourgeois forces.

In the Preface to **Wretched**, Sartre echoes Fanon, as he characterizes anti-colonial (anti-capitalist) violence as "man recreating himself" (that is, as peoples recreating themselves...as nations transforming themselves). The people come to feel a national soil underfoot; their revolutionary consciousness broadens and deepens; they come to see that <u>they are the nation</u>—that the nation is "one with [their] liberty." (P.21)

Read Ch. 1 and begin to find out what the nation is/should be—according to Fanon. The nation should influence individuals, and modify them, fundamentally—transforming "spectators" into "privileged actors" in the daily drama of national life. (1.3) The nation is where "the interests of one will be the interests of all" (1.22), and where "all resources should be pooled." (1.26) The "violence" that Fanon discusses is of a kind that "introduces into each [person's] consciousness the ideas of a common cause, of a national destiny, and of a collective history." (1.97)

> ...*The living expression of the nation is the moving consciousness of the whole of the people; it is the coherent, enlightened action of men and women...* (3.96)

The nation is, according to Fanon, a new unity—at its best, it's a new revolutionary/socialist unity; at its worst, if it's formed under the leadership of bourgeois forces, it becomes a new unity that rests on a narrow, "racial" base. (1.19)

{{see attached re: UNITY, esp. ch. 2—see (1.98), re: preliminary to unification of the people//caids & chiefs...}}

As the people strive to create a revolutionary unity for themselves, their efforts are opposed, first, by the colonialists/capitalists of the oppressor nation(s), and then by the puppet and neo-colonialist bourgeois forces of the nation-becoming. The people's unity, and the people's interests, stand in opposition to the interests of <u>all</u> exploitative forces, particularly those who "have come to power in the name of a narrow nationalism, and representing a race..." (3.33) Representing a "race" is not the same as representing revolutionary/socialist interests...

> *The peoples of Africa have... decided, in the name of the whole continent, to weigh in strongly against the colonial regime. Now the nationalist bourgeoisies, who in region after region hasten to make their own fortunes and to set up a national system of*

> *exploitation*, do their utmost to put obstacles in the path of this "Utopia." *The national bourgeoisies, who are quite clear as to what their objectives are, have decided to bar the way to that unity… This is why we must understand that African unity can only be achieved through the upward thrust of the people, and under the leadership of the people—that is to say, in defiance of the interests of the bourgeoisie.* (3.36)

Too bad not enough of us—here, or on the African continent—understood the full import of these words in the 1960s and 1970s. If We had, Africa could have been spared much political turmoil and economic and social devastation. And, it's still hard for us to see that <u>most</u> of what passes as "black leadership" these days is actually the post-neocolonial rule of collaborationist bourgeois forces…

Fanon understood that oppressed nations have existed as sovereign entities prior to colonial domination (as when he speaks of the struggle as one to "re-establish the sovereignty of the nation." (4A.19)) However, he also believed that the sovereignty of the people was not an end, but a means—a condition for the free operation of the social development. Once independent of foreign control, the people must widen and deepen their revolutionary consciousness, and pursue the nation's development along socialist lines.

While there is a relation between what's called the "vitality" of a nation {{explain this, i.e., that some people claim lack of sovereignty alone means end of national reality}} and its sovereign existence, the lack of sovereignty doesn't of itself lead to the erosion of national reality. Rather, it's the violence of colonialism that undermines national reality, as colonial violence is exerted in all spheres of the people's lives. [see (4A.1, 2, & 6), and the discussions of culture, below.] Consequently, the national reality can be reinvigorated prior to any declaration of "formal" independence, by the people's conscious action, in all spheres of social life, and in opposition to the negative external influences of colonialism...

Under his discussion of the phase during which spontaneity reigns, Fanon describes for us part of the process through which the people begins to "will itself to sovereignty":

> *This people that has lost its birthright, that is used to living in the narrow circle of feuds and rivalries, will now proceed in an atmosphere of solemnity to cleanse and purify the face of the nation as it appears in the various localities. In a veritable collective ecstasy, families which have always been traditional enemies decide to rub out old scores and to forgive and forget. There are numerous reconciliations. Long-buried but unforgettable hatreds are brought to light once more, so that they may more surely be rooted out. The taking on of nationhood involves a growth of awareness. The national unity is first the unity of a group, the disappearance of old quarrels, and the final liquidation of unspoken grievances... In undertaking this onward march, the people legislates, finds itself, and wills itself to sovereignty... The circle of the nation widens, and fresh ambushes to entrap the enemy hail the entry of new tribes upon the scene. Each village finds that it is itself both an absolute agent of revolution, and also a link in the chain of action. Solidarity between tribes and villages—national solidarity—is in the first place expressed by the increasing blows struck at the enemy...* (2.53)

Reflect: "...the face of the nation as it appears in the various localities." That's a single face, not the several faces of the localities—the national identity supersedes the local identities; it's not about "East Coast" and "West Coast," "North Side" or "South Side"... it's no longer about "tribes"...

Reflect: "...the taking on of nationhood involves a growth of awareness. The national unity is first the unity of a group..." Awareness. So-called "large" nations don't fall from the sky. At its simplest: "Nation" is the unity of two or more "groups," whether you're talking several thousand years ago on the African or Asian continents, several hundred years ago on the European or North American continents, or, in the 21st century on the North American continent...

> ...the settlement was begun on the very first day of the war, and it will be ended not because there are no more enemies left to kill, but quite simply because the enemy, for various reasons, will come to realize that his interest lies in ending the struggle and in recognizing the sovereignty of the colonized people... (2.65)

How is this so? i.e., how was the settlement begun on the first day of the war??!! And, in what way does the enemy "recognize" the sovereignty of the colonized people?

The very existence of a state of war implies the existence of a sovereign people—a people rejecting foreign incursion and undue influence; a people asserting its own supreme power over its social order...

The enemy comes to <u>acknowledge</u> this sovereignty...

> ...The African peoples were quick to realize that dignity and sovereignty were exact equivalents, and in fact, a free people living in dignity is a sovereign people... (3.90)

REWORK: {{We're gonna have to deal again with Fanon's ideas on the nation, as We cover issues of "culture," "history," and nationalism, below. However, before We discuss Fanon's views on the State, and close out this section, i wanna reflect on several other passages and subjects...

> ...the reconstruction of the nation continues within the framework of cut-throat competition between capitalism and socialism. (1.76)

> ...all those bands armed with cutlasses or axes find their nationality in the implacable struggle which opposes socialism and capitalism. (1.79)

Altho We touched this a bit in one or two places above, it won't hurt to take another look. Based on the lines from the two paras. just quoted, We can even make the point from within two contexts:

1) As oppressed peoples struggle to regain national independence, their new nationality is informed by the demands of the fundamental contradiction in the world, particularly as this contradiction is manifested upon their internal, national reality. The new nation can't take a "third way," because there is none. The new nation must choose between the capitalist way (which means continued inequalities, oppression and exploitation, at home and abroad) or it must choose the socialist way. That is, <u>revolutionary</u> nationalists must make this choice... 2) If you don't wanna claim nationalism of any sort, it remains a fact that whoever and wherever you are, you must make the choice between capitalism and socialism. Thre's no "third way" for you, either. Nor is there any chance or likelihood of merely reforming capitalism so that it harmonizes with the vision of the truly just society that you (may) envision...

> In certain circumstances, the party political machine may remain intact. But as a result of the colonialist repression and of the spontaneous reaction of the people, the parties find themselves out-distanced by their militants. The violence of the masses is vigorously pitted against the military forces of the occupying power, and the situation deteriorates and comes to a head. Those leaders who are free remain, therefore, on the touchline [the sideline boundary marking the field of play in rugby or English football—editors]. They have suddenly become useless, with their bureaucracy and their reasonable demands; yet we see them, far removed from events, attempting the crowning imposture—that of

> *"speaking in the name of the silenced nation."* As a general rule, colonialism welcomes this god-send with open arms, transforms these *"blind mouths"* into spokesmen, and in two minutes endows them with independence, on condition that they restore order. (1.70)

While mindful of the context, my reflection centered on the matter of bourgeois forces and their imposture of speaking in the name of "the silenced nation." If the people were silent—pre-or-post-"independence"—then it wasn't solely a result of the pressures of colonialism. It was also a result of the "failures" of the bourgeois nationalist forces, who never made the serious attempt to help the people to find and use their own voice, to exercise their role as leader of the nation's struggle...

As Fanon closes out the first chapter, he reminds us that through their active participation in the struggle to re-build the nation, the people have the opportunity to regain their self-respect, and their sense of responsibility for the entire social order, and that,

> ...*Even if the armed struggle has been symbolic and the nation is demobilized through a rapid movement of decolonization, the people have the time to see that the liberation has been the business of each and all, and that the leader has no special merit*... When the people have taken violent part in the national liberation, they will allow no one to set themselves up as "liberators." They show themselves to be jealous of the results of their action, and take good care not to place their future, their destiny, or the fate of their country, in the hands of a living god. Yesterday, they were completely irresponsible; today, they mean to understand everything, and make all decisions... (1.99)

i used the above paragraph in **Part Two** (*Meditations*, p. 214), and referred to it as the ideal outcome of that stage of the struggle that ends with the formal establishment of the independence of the nation from foreign control. However, that ideal won't be realized if there's no genuine <u>people's war</u>, and if formal independence is achieved by a quick neo-colonial solution devised by colonialism and its agents inside the nation, who come to head the new state. We have to keep in mind that **Wretched** is about what the people <u>need to do</u> in order to win real independence AND to pursue a self-determined, socialist development.

Reflect, now, on the way Fanon closes the first chapter, and, on the way that he opens the second chapter. There's a "difference of rhythm" between the people and the leaders of the bourgeois nationalist party... a difference of "rhythm" between the people and the "intellectual elite engaged in trade"... a difference of "rhythm" between the people and all of those who constitute the "bourgeois fraction of the nation," which includes "feudal lords," "tribal chieftains, leaders of confraternities and traditional authorities." (2.1; 2.7)

Reflect, too: What's the title of the book?! **The Wretched of the Earth!** THE BOOK IS ABOUT HOW THE "WRETCHED" can <u>transform themselves</u> into the ENLIGHTENED and the SELF-GOVERNING!! If you don't take anything else away with your reading of this book, you must take this.

> ...The more the people understand, the more watchful they become, and the more they come to realize that, finally, everything depends on them, and their salvation lies in their own cohesion, in the true understanding of their interests, and, in knowing who are their enemies... (3.82)

Everything depends on the people, themselves.

The salvation of the people lies in their cohesion.

The people must have a true understanding of their interests.

The people must know who their enemies are—internal enemies, and external enemies.

{{THIS is "class consciousness"! It's what, for now, We can call a true "proletarian" or revolutionary consciousness—as opposed to a bourgeois (nationalist) consciousness...}}

> ...consciousness of themselves... the masses are equal to the problems that confront them... experience proves that the important thing is... that the whole people plan and decide, even if it takes them twice or three times as long. The fact is that the time taken up by explaining, the time "lost" in treating the [person] as a human being, will be caught up in the execution of the plan. People must know where they are going, and why... the future remains a closed book so long as the consciousness of the people remains imperfect, elementary, and cloudy... The awakening of the whole people will not come about all at once; the people's work in the building of the nation will not immediately take on its full dimensions: first, because the means of communication and transmission are only beginning to be developed; secondly, because the yardstick of time must no longer be that of the moment... but must become that of the rest of the world and lastly, because the spirit of discouragement which has been deeply rooted in people's minds by colonial domination is still very near the surface... Public business ought to be the business of the public... (3.85)

{{FINISH RE: "P.E." see pps. 20, A & B:

> ...the need for effort to be well-informed, for work which is enlightened and freed from its historic intellectual darkness. To hold a responsible position... is to know that in the end everything depends on the education of the masses, on the raising of the level of thought, and on what we are too quick to call "political teaching." (3:88)

> In fact, we often believe, with criminal superficiality, that to educate the masses politically is to deliver a long political

> *harangue from time to time ... political education means opening their minds, awakening them, and allowing the birth of their intelligence ... To educate the masses politically* [means to try] *relentlessly and passionately, to teach the masses that everything depends on them; that if we stagnate it is their responsibility, and that if we go forward it is due to them, too; that there is no such thing as a demiurge, that there is no famous man who will take the responsibility for everything, but that the demiurge is the people themsselves and the magic hands are finally only the hands of the people...* (3.89)
>
> *...To educate the masses politically is to make the totality of the nation a reality to each citizen. It is to make the history of the nation part of the personal experience of each of its citizens...* (3.93)}}

CONCLUDE SECTION re: "People's Democracy"...

Such P.E. is necessary as part of the "New Politics" ("national, revolutionary, and social" (2.70)) that are required as part of the process of "intensifying the struggle and of preparing the people to undertake the governing of their country clearly and lucidly..." (2.57) HOW??? SEE: (2.67); (3.57); (3.62); (3.63), and then follow with:

> *All this taking stock of the situation, this enlightening of consciousness and this advance in the knowledge of the history of societies are only possible within the framework of an organization, and inside the structure of a people. Such an organization is set afoot by the use of rev. elements coming from the towns at the beginning of the rising, together with those rebels who go down into the country as the fight goes on. It is this core which constitutes the embryonic pol. org. of the rebellion. But on the other hand the peasants, who are all the time adding to their knowledge in*

the light of experience, will come to show themselves capable of directing the people's struggle... (2.67)

...The living party, which ought to make possible the free exchange of ideas which have been elaborated according to the real needs of the masses of the people... helps the people to set out its demands, to become more aware of its needs and better able to establish its power... (3.48)

...In under-developed countries, the bourgeoisie should not be allowed to find the conditions necessary for its existence and its growth. In other words, the combined effort of the masses, led by a party, and of intellectuals who are highly conscious and armed with rev. principles, ought to bar the way to this useless and harmful middle-class. (3.57)

...Many intellectuals, for example, condemn this regime based on the domination of a few... There are certain members of the elite, intellectuals and civil servants, who are sincere, who feel the necessity for a planned economy, the out-lawing of profiteers, and the strict prohibition of attempts at mystification. In addition, such men fight in a certain measure for the mass participation of the people in the ordering of public affairs. (3.62)

...there almost always exists a small number of honest intellectuals... We must know how to use these men... (3.63)

...The party is not a tool in the hands of the government. Quite on the contrary, the party is a tool in the hands of the people; it is they who decide on the policy that the government carries out... For the people, the party is not an authority, but an organism through which they as the people exercise their authority and express their will... (3.73–74)

It's the people who must lead themselves and control all social affairs...

...the setting up of a new State, its diplomatic relations, and its economic and political trends... (1.1)

Fanon didn't seem to doubt the need for the new nation to have a state apparatus. The only question(s) for Fanon: In whose hands would the new state apparatus rest? In whose interests would the new state apparatus operate? Would it be a people's state, i.e., revolutionary, democratic, and socialist, or would it be a neo-colonial, "fascist" and bourgeois state? {{(i know some folks out there question my use of the term "fascist" but this, too, needs re-examining, because... Fanon uses the term at_____, and it really means a petty-bourgeois ruled apparatus and form of social hegemony...)}}

Some of us, like Fanon, don't question the need for a NEW TYPE OF STATE, while others hold opposing views. Others wisely debate the issue, and seek new ways to define "state," moving away from the rigid, doctrinaire positions of both the old left and of the right. The "state" doesn't have to be whatever it was; it doesn't have to be whatever it is—it can be whatever the people choose to make it.

The state, according to Fanon, was an instrument that the people needed (to control) in order to protect themselves and the goals of the revolution. (Don't we all wish that everyone would "just get along"—but it don't work like that in the real world.) The people need to protect their interests against those whose "objective is not the radical overthrowing of the system" (1.46) and who "avoid the actual overthrowing of the [present, bourgeois] state…" (1.61) There are those among us who claim credentials as "radicals," but who want to reform capitalism, and not overthrow it. At bottom, they, too, still prefer the "tribe" as opposed to a new type of people's democratic state (and nation). There are those among us who claim to be "radicals," and they use the language of radicals. But, their practice shows that they don't even attempt genuine "class suicide," i.e., to repudiate their own nature "in so far as it is bourgeois" (3.5), and to put themselves to school with the people. (3.6)

It's not really a stretch of contexts to say that such "radicals" even these days "mobilize the people with slogans of independence, and for the rest leave it to future events. When such parties are questioned on the economic program of the State that they are clamoring for, or on the nature of the regime which they propose to install, they are incapable of replying…" (3.7) The bottom line being, tho, that pre-and-post-"independence," such forces refuse "to follow the path of revolution." (3.8)

> *Seen through its eyes, its mission has nothing to do with the nation; it consists, prosaically, of being the transmission line between the nation and a capitalism, rampant though camouflaged, which today puts on the mask of neo-colonialism… (3.12)*

***We have to go back to the question We raised about what **Wretched** is really about, i.e., how to transform the "wretched" into the enlightened and the responsible, the self-governed. What We should be able to glean from **Wretched**'s pages are the stages of the process, and the general procedures to be adapted by the people in the process of struggle, that allow them to: 1) combat their internal and external enemies; 2) begin to build, even prior to formal independence, the apparatus/institutions that will serve their interests in the creation of a new social order that guarantees to all citizens the freedom to develop as all-round human beings…the freedom from exploitation and discrimination—and alienation—in all forms…

You should be able to glean these, IF, that is, you're serious about challenging the oppressive state for the power that should be in the hands of the people…

Surely, Fanon discusses "the foreigner" in **Wretched**'s pages; he rails against colonialism as the primary EXTERNAL obstacle in the path of the people's liberation and development. But don't fail to notice the time he spends to detail the thought and practice of the bourgeois forces that constitute the people's primary INTERNAL ENEMY. Fanon notes their thought and practice prior to the beginning of the struggle…during the struggle…and their actual and potential thought and practice after formal independence is declared—for what usually turns out to be a neo-colonial client state of imperialism. Fanon wants us to avoid having to go through that stage:

> …*Closing the road to the national bourgeoisie is, certainly, the means whereby the vicissitudes of newfound independence may be avoided, and with them the decline of morals, the installing of corruption within the country, economic regression, and the immediate disaster of an anti-democratic regime depending on force and intimidation. But it is also the only means towards progress.* (3.63)

Like the new (type of) nation, the new (type of) people's… democratic… state, begins to take shape in the course of the struggle to topple the oppressive power.

Key: Remember, you're not dealing with some doctrinaire concept of "coercive power"—but also with a new, revolutionary/socialist <u>morality</u>...

Take your stand with Fanon: The people need a (new type of) state—it's only a question of what kind of state it will be... and in whose hands it will be... The character of the state ultimately depends on—will be determined by—the character of the people in whose hands the state rests. There's no such thing as the state being "inherently authoritarian" for instance—unless people are inherently authoritarian and there's no way to change this. The (new) state will be whatever the people make of it—or allow others to make of it... if it's truly theirs and if they begin to build it now... a building that begins with the discussion and dissemination of the vision, the reasons why we need it and the discussion of the kind of state it ought to be and what it ought to do and not do...

> ...In the colonial situation, culture, which is doubly deprived of the support of the nation and of the State, falls away and dies. The conditions for its existence is therefore national liberation and the renaissance of the State. (4A.16)

> ...A nation which is born of the people's concerted action and which embodies the real aspirations of the people while changing the State, cannot exist save in the expression of exceptionally rich forms of culture. (4A.20)

***see (3.68–69) for poss. use prior to (4A.16 & 20)

NEXT:

6A.3 CULTURE: NATIONAL AND REVOLUTIONARY

(FIND and place Mao quote)

** Chapter 4: Is about NATIONAL culture, especially regarding the "blind alley" "African"/"negro" culture and the need to emphasize NATIONAL culture and NATIONAL consciousness, as the people make the shape of the struggle against colonialism along revolutionary and not bourgeois or "fascist" lines…

** Chapter 4A: Is about the relation between the NATION and "culture"—it complements Ch. 4, but emphasizes the dependence of "culture" upon the…

> We must rid ourselves of the habit, now that we are in the thick of the fight, of minimizing the action of our fathers or of feigning incomprehension when considering their silence and passivity. They fought as well as they could, with the arms that they possessed then, and if the echoes of their struggle have not resounded in the international arena, we must realize that the reason for this silence lies less in their lack of heroism than in the fundamentally different international situation of our time. It needed more than one native to say "We've had enough"; more than one peasant rising crushed, more than one demonstration put down before we could today hold our own, certain in our victory. As for us who have decided to break the back of colonialism, our historic mission is to sanction all revolts, all desperate actions, all those abortive attempts drowned in rivers of blood. (4.3)
>
> In this chapter we shall analyze the problem, which is felt to be fundamental, of the legitimacy of the claims of a nation. It must be recognized that the political party which mobilizes the people hardly touches on this problem of legitimacy. The political parties

> start with living reality and it is in the name of this reality, in the name of the stark facts which weigh down the present and the future of men and women, that they fix their line of action. The political party may well speak in moving terms of the nation, but what it is concerned with is that the people who are listening understand the need to take part in the fight if, quite simply, they wish to continue to exist. (4.4)

See: (4.10)

Does the first paragraph seem a bit out of place, to you? Does it seem out of place in relation to the second paragraph, or to the theme of the entire chapter?

O.K., now, read the first paragraph again—what's that paragraph saying? What's its relation to the second paragraph—or, put another way, what's its relation to the chapter as a whole... what's its relation to the book, as a whole? Well, maybe it's a bit unfair of me to ask these questions... especially if you haven't read the entire chapter or if you've failed, for some strange reason, to grasp the relation between, say, "negritude" and "afrocentricity" (at least in its most rightward expressions). Am i moving too fast?

i had originally intended to begin reflections on Chs. 4 and 4A by starting with some comment on para. (4.4). The first paragraph has always seemed, to me, to be out of place. Even Fanon seems, at first glance, to actually begin addressing the theme of the chapter(s) with the second paragraph, and not the first...

> {{why does fanon begin the chapter with what can be termed an apology to the poets of negritude? why not simply quote Toure and open with the second para.? Clearly, there's a reason, or, he had a reason for wanting to say what he did. Is that reason worth a comment here????}}

However, i think that he may have placed the first para. there as his way of letting everyone know that although he would come down heavily upon the heads of "the poets of negritude" (a circle that he had once been identified with), he was not minimizing their progressive action.

The fact is, tho, that i don't think that many folks have placed the first para. within the proper context. The first line of the para. is probably the most often quoted line from the book, yet few of those who use it bother to quote the remaining lines—the lines that actually express the thought that, i think, Fanon intended to convey. Let's check it out again, but this time, pay more attention to everything other than the first sentence...

i think that Fanon wanted to tell us not to minimize the PROGRESSIVE action/contributions of those that pushed the negative aspects of "negritude." And, it's particularly good advice, for us, since We're now faced with the task of analyzing and critiquing the contemporary forms of "negritude"-like concepts and movements within our own environment... So, We should let our words and actions in this regard be influenced by the guidance provided by Fanon, and Mao...

> *This historical necessity in which the men of African culture find themselves to racialize their claims and to speak more of African culture than of national culture will tend to lead them up a blind alley... (4.18)*

Chapters 4 and 4A may or may not read rather straightforwardly, depending upon how clear your head is; upon the kinds of connections you can make between there and here... between the past and the present. Moreover, it depends upon whether or not you can find and explore the nuances and subtleties, or, the "swerves" that fill Fanon's discussion of culture and history, of negritude (which, these days, We may tend to identify as "Afrocentricity," esp. its rightist tendency, and sometimes going under the labels of "cultural studies"), and of "niggerhood... as a type of relationship"...

The above passage from (4.18) captures the message in Ch. 4: Fanon encourages a NATIONAL culture, as opposed to both a racialized or a continental, "African culture"—and We need to ask why... We need to "interrogate" the matter, as they say these days... In Ch. 4A, Fanon suggests that a national culture can truly exist and develop only if the people are free... only if the nation is liberated and taking the socialist road...

As i read these chapters, i found it necessary to also raise and reflect upon the following questions (among others, of course), and always looking for connections between our past and present, as well as trying to more fully grasp Fanon's thought:

+ what is "culture"?
+ what is NATIONAL culture?
+ why does Fanon take a stand opposed to "black" culture and "black republics"? (esp. see (4.44) and Note 1 re: Senghor)
+ what's the relation between "culture" and "history"?

Now, don't think that the answers to some or all of these questions are or will become as easy as it may at first appear. Going to a dictionary or some other reference source may help a wee bit, but it won't suffice. i mean, there's a reason that We have to ask these questions—anew. We need a new take. We need some re-orientation. In many cases, depending upon *Webster*, et. al., is part of our problem, i.e., that's why We're stuck and confused...

Fanon opens directly on theme (after the "preface" of 4.1) by saying that the chapter examines the fundamental problem of "the legitimacy of the claims of a nation." (4.4; also see 4.10) Now, what exactly does he mean?*

Don't take it for granted that the nation exists, because the "problem" is that the national reality has been—for the people—called into question. Fanon means, here, that the people must be made aware of the nation's existence. He means that We need to point out the boundaries of the nation's culture; that We must trace the development of the nation's history—a history... and a culture—that existed prior to any contact with the colonizing forces...

We've previously discussed the line which holds that no nation existed (in Africa, or elsewhere), prior to those nations formed in Europe (when they were formed depends upon who you read—some say as early as the 16th century, while most say the 18th century). This line is a variation of, or, runs parallel to, the line holding that non-european, colonized peoples had no "history" prior to their being colonized and "brought into history." The fact is, however, that if peoples had (have) a culture (that's distinct from that of the colonizer), then they also had (have) a history that's developed independently of colonial intervention. If they had (have) a culture, and a history, then they had (have) a national reality.

* "...It must be recognized that the political party which mobilizes these people hardly touches on this problem of legitimacy. The political parties start from living reality and it is in the name of this reality, in the name of the stark facts which weigh down the present and the future of men and women, that they fix their line of action. The political party may well speak in moving terms of the nation, but what it is concerned with is that the people who are listening understand the need to take part in the fight if, quite simply, they wish to continue to exist.

"Today we know that in the first phase of the national struggle colonialism tries to disarm national demands by putting forward economic doctrines. As soon as the first demands are set out, colonialism pretends to consider them, recognizing with ostentatious humility that the territory is suffering from serious under-development which necessitates a great economic and social effort. And, it so happens, that certain spectacular measures (centres of work for the unemployed which are opened here and there, for example) delay the crystallisation of national consciousness for a few years. But, sooner or later, colonialism sees that it is not within its powers to put into practice a project of economic and social reforms which will satisfy the aspirations of the colonized people. Even where food supplies are concerned, colonialism gives proof of its inherent incapability..." (4.4–5)

So, We're back to the purpose of this chapter, i.e., analyzing why and how the legitimacy of the nation must be established...

In the first place, at (4.5), Fanon tells us that "in the first phase of the national struggle, colonialism tries to disarm NATIONAL demands," and to "delay the crystallization of NATIONAL consciousness." (my emphasis)

Keep in mind: "National" means "of the whole" people; one, out of many. Other identities (e.g., lineage, language or dialect, geographical, religious, etc.) are to be superseded by the NEW UNITY, i.e., the national identity. The nation now stands opposed to the enemy, as embodied by colonialism and capitalism... bourgeois culture... and by the philosophy and values that uphold them. The new unity is embodied by the people's shared interest in building a humanistic/socialist society. Colonialism's efforts to disarm (and delay) the development of the (new) national consciousness can be traced to its point of intervention:

> ...*Perhaps we have not sufficiently demonstrated that colonialism is not simply content to impose its rule upon the present and the future of a dominated country. Colonialism is not satisfied merely with holding a people in its grip and emptying [its] brain of all form and content... it turns to the past of the oppressed people, and distorts, disfigures, and destroys it. This work of devaluing* PRE-COLONIAL HISTORY *takes on a dialectical significance today.* (4.9) (my emphasis)

Now, let's be clear on this point: The devaluing of the people's HISTORY is the devaluing of the nation's reality! You may need to repeat this to yourself several times, in several different ways, because the import can easily escape you. We so often talk about "the distortions of our history" or the "omissions" in the story presented in the schools that We and our children attend, etc. Do you now fully realize what's happening when this process unfolds? Do you have a better sense now of why it's so hard to generate discussion of the past and present NATIONAL reality? (It may help you a bit if you jump, right now, and read the first two paragraphs of chapter 4A!)*

Now, above, We've seen Fanon talk about colonialism's devaluation of the people's HISTORY, and this is within the context of what the people need to do to recover that value ... to overcome the self-doubt that hinders forward motion. Below, he again links "history" to "culture":

> *When we consider the effort made to carry out the CULTURAL ESTRANGEMENT so characteristic of the colonial epoch, we realize that nothing has been left to chance, and that the total result looked for by colonial domination was indeed to convince the [people] that colonialism came to lighten their darkness. The effort consciously sought by colonialism was to drive into the [people] ... the idea that if the settlers were to leave, they would at once fall back into barbarism, degradation, and bestiality. (4.10) (my emphasis)*

Thus, "...The claim to a national culture in the past does not only rehabilitate that nation and serve as a justification for the

---

* "Colonialism, because it is total and tends to over-simplify, very soon manages to disrupt in spectacular fashion the cultural life of a conquered people. This cultural obliteration is made possible by the negation of national reality, by new legal relations introduced by the occupying power, by the banishment of the natives and their customs to outlying districts by colonial society, by expropriation, and by the systematic enslaving of men and women.

"Three years ago at our first congress I showed that, in the colonial situation, dynamism is replaced fairly quickly by a substantification of the attitudes of the colonial power. The area of culture is then marked off by fences and signposts. These are in fact so many defense mechanisms of the most elementary type, comparable for more than one good reason to the simple instinct for preservation. The interest of this period for us is that the oppressor does not manage to convince himself of the objective non-existence of the oppressed nation and its culture. Every effort is made to bring the colonized person to admit the inferiority of his culture which has been transformed into instinctive patterns of behavior, to recognize the unreality of his 'nation', and, in the last extreme, the confused and imperfect character of his own biological structure." (4A.1–2)

hope of a future national culture," but it also serves to help change the self-image of the people, and to inspire that people to struggle to liberate the nation and to take the lead in shaping its socialist future. (4.9)

Moreover, the efforts of the intellectuals—IN THIS REGARD—are "a necessity in any coherent program." (4.12)

i can't help but make an aside, tho it's not really an aside...

To me, there's a similarity between... a parallel between the line that Fanon says is used by the foreigner to frighten the people into submission to colonialism by claiming they'll fall back into an alleged barbarism... and the line that they use on us today when We righteously shout the need to abandon capitalism and to struggle for and to build socialism. What do they use to frighten us with? They say that We'll starve under a socialist system; that We won't have (bourgeois) democracy under socialism—when all the time, the people are starving under capitalism. We lack adequate food for both body and spirit; We lack genuine (people's) democracy at this very moment... lack it to the extent that We don't even know that there are forms of democracy other than and superior to the bourgeois democracy that tramples us...

So... where were We?...

Yeah... It is necessary for the intellectuals—the "cultured individuals"—to point up the legitimacy of—the reality of—the nation, the nation's culture, and the nation's history, esp. w/ re to the pre-colonial development. However, this action clearly doesn't prevent these—or, some of these—individuals from entering the "blind alley" that Fanon spoke to us about as We opened these reflections... How does that happen?... "practice without theory is blind..."

Well, Fanon begins to explain it to us by showing, at (4.7), where the "cultured individuals"/intellectuals make their appearance, mark out a special battlefield, whereupon they make "the demand for a national culture, and the affirmation of the existence of such a culture." While the "politicians" [the "rev. nats."?] inside the nationalist parties take their stand upon "living reality" and their desire that the people "take part in the fight" (4.4) the "cultured individuals" ("cultural nats"?) take their stand in the field of history. (4.7)

(It may be of interest to note that the distinction drawn by Fanon between the "politicians" and the "cultured individuals" is a likely basis for the drawing of distinctions between "rev. nats" and "cultural nats" among bloods here, in the 1960s and 70s. At that time, We made a rather superficial distinction if only because "standing in living reality" can represent a reactionary, bourgeois world view, and those working in the field of history, or culture, can represent rev. interests of the people...)

Note that Fanon says that colonialism reacts only slightly to the aggressive response of the colonized intellectuals—in part because "the ideas developed" by them are also "widely professed by specialists in the mother country," who, on their part, have "rehabilitated the African, Mexican, and Peruvian civilizations..."

...knowledge re: pre-colonial greatness has little immediate relevance to the present oppression of the masses, and the search for precolonial culture is undertaken by the intellectuals because of their anxiety re western culture. The truth is, however, NATIONAL reality, and NATIONAL consciousness of the people...

** Check out the first two paragraphs of Chapter 4. Go ahead. check 'em out. (4.3):

> *Each generation must, out of relative obscurity, discover its mission, fulfill it, or betray it. In under-developed countries the preceding generations have both resisted the work of erosion carried on by colonialism and also helped on the maturing of the struggles of today. We must rid ourselves of the habit, now that we are in the thick of the fight, of minimizing the action of our fathers or of feigning incomprehension when considering their silence and passivity. They fought as well as they could, with the arms that they possessed then; and if the echoes of their struggle have not resounded in the international arena, we must realize that the reason for this silence lies less in their lack of heroism than in the fundamentally different international situation of our time. It needed more than one native to say "We've had enough"; more than one peasant rising crushed, more than one demonstration put down before we could today hold our own, certain in our victory. As for us who have decided to break the back of colonialism, our historic mission is to sanction all revolts, all desperate actions, all those abortive attempts drowned in rivers of blood.*

EDITORS' NOTE: HERE THE ROUGH FIRST DRAFT AND NOTES TO HIMSELF FOR PART 4 END, ALTHOUGH YAKI'S WORK WAS FAR FROM FINISHED. IN HIS CONVERSATIONS HE WOULD MENTION SEEING THE NEED FOR A FUTURE PARTS 5 AND 6 TO APPLY FANON'S VISION EVEN FURTHER, NOW THAT A "POST-CIVIL RIGHTS" NEOCOLONIAL U.S. EMPIRE HAD EMERGED. BUT YAKI'S LIFE WAS CUT OFF TOO SOON. OTHERS WILL HAVE TO CARRY ON THE FIRE HE CAREFULLY FED.

Since 1998 Kersplebedeb has been an important source of radical literature and agit prop materials.

The project has a non-exclusive focus on anti-patriarchal and anti-imperialist politics, framed within an anticapitalist perspective. A special priority is given to writings regarding armed struggle in the metropole, and the continuing struggles of political prisoners and prisoners of war.

The Kersplebedeb website provides downloadable activist artwork, as well as historical and contemporary writings by revolutionary thinkers from the anarchist and communist traditions.

Kersplebedeb can be contacted at:

> Kersplebedeb
> CP 63560
> CCCP Van Horne
> Montreal, Quebec
> Canada
> H3W 3H8
>
> email: info@kersplebedeb.com
> web: www.kersplebedeb.com
>   www.leftwingbooks.net

Kersplebedeb

Your online source of ideas to change the world...

www.leftwingbooks.net

leftwingbooks.net

www.ingramcontent.com/pod-product-compliance
Lightning Source LLC
Chambersburg PA
CBHW031312160426
43196CB00007B/496